P9-DHS-417

FROM Gutenberg TO OPENTYPE

FROM Gutenberg TO OPENTYPE

AN ILLUSTRATED HISTORY OF TYPE
FROM THE EARLIEST LETTERFORMS
TO THE LATEST DIGITAL FONTS

ROBIN DODD

HARTLEY & MARKS PUBLISHERS

VANCOUVER · DUBLIN · AMSTERDAM

Contents

First published in North America by
Hartley & Marks Publishers Inc.

3661 West Broadway
Vancouver, BC V6R 2B8
Canada

Copyright © 2006 The Ilex Press Limited

This book was conceived by
ILEX, Cambridge, England

Library-of-Congress control number 2006921981

ISBN 0–88179–210–1

All rights reserved. No part of this publication may be
reproduced or used in any form, or by any means—graphic,
electronic, or mechanical, including photocopying, recording,
or information storage-and-retrieval systems—without the
prior permission of the publisher.

Printed and bound in China

Introduction

It's often said that the printed book is endangered by the computer, and yet both are products of the creative imagination. The advent of the printing press made possible the spreading of knowledge, debate, thoughts and ideas, and this provided the learning that eventually inspired the computer. Today the personal computer is used in the conception and production of the modern book.

Traditional skills in modern hands
A demonstration of the traditional craft of punchcutting at the punchcutter bench at the Imprimerie Nationale de France, *in the* Cabinet de Poincons.

The term "printing press" belies the true originality of the printing revolution. It is movable types and the process of their manufacture that are the root of the invention of printing. These cast metal letters that could be used again and again were the basis of Johannes Gutenberg's eventual breakthrough—the "soldiers of lead that have conquered the world," as they have been called.

The computer has changed the printing industry, just as it has many other industries. Professional designers and the general public now have, literally at their fingertips, hundreds of typefaces available. For the professional graphic designer, the computer brings under his or her control the minutiae of typesetting and print production that were once craft skills acquired by years of training. The general personal computer user has at their disposal an array of letterforms that were previously the arcane province of the printer. What was once looked at but rarely seen, has become a subject of interest. Typographers and printers have always been occupied by the merits of this or that typeface, but now the writer of a "thank you" letter, who once took up a fountain pen, can now sit at a keyboard and scroll through a collection of fonts, choosing one at random with no knowledge of its origins.

The first printers
During the late 15th century, printing from movable type spread fast. The demand for books was fired by the spread of learning and books became desirable as status symbols. In this woodcut the printer's colophon can be seen to the right, on the upright timber of the printing press.

Among the thousands of digital fonts now available are the classic typefaces from over 500 years of printing, some of which have been in existence since long before reading was a basic requirement of everyday life. These were innovations in their time, setting standards and styles. Each has a story, and each fulfilled a role that it continues to do today. This book endeavors to tell the fascinating story of those typefaces, the context within which they have contributed to the world of printed communication, and their continuing contribution to type design.

The heart of the story lies with the punchcutter seated at his work bench. The great punchcutters, with simple, unremarkable tools, with the skill of their hands and the conviction of their eye by the tightening of a curve or the thinning of a serif, were able to transform a commonplace letterform into a character of unique personality.

At first, typefaces were cast from a mold that was fitted with a matrix, so that when the molten metal was poured into the mold, the reversed, indented letterform of the matrix dictated the type's shape. A matrix is a die of a single type, and a punch is required to make it. The punchcutter starts with a small bar of steel. It is his task to cut a punch from the steel for

Interior of 16th-century printer's workshop
The engraving shows the rigorous activity of the various trades involved in publishing a book. To the right, two compositors are setting type as they sit at the type cases. In the background are readers checking proofs, as supplied by the two presses in the central background. On the left, an edition is being produced by the two press hands, and in the foreground are the printed sheets and blank sheets awaiting print.

each character of a font—capitals, lower case, figures, and punctuation. If a character includes an enclosed space, like "O," "B," or "a," in one technique of punchcutting, a counterpunch is required. This is cut to the shape of the enclosed space and driven into the letter punch. The punchcutter cuts using gravers and files, and he checks his work with gauges. Then, passing the punch over a lighted candle to coat it with soot, he presses it onto paper, to ensure uniformity with the style of the other characters. When complete, the set of punches is hardened. Any number of matrices could be made by the process of a "strike," when a punch was driven into a small bar of copper. These were then trimmed ready to fit into the mold.

Johannes Gutenberg's most original invention was his adjustable mold, which would fit to the character widths of different type sizes. With the matrix fitted, a small amount of molten metal was poured quickly into the mold, and within seconds a piece of type could be removed. This was then dressed, tidied up, and prepared for use. This procedure was continuously modified and refined for over 400 years, until the late 19th century when the American typefounder Linn Boyd Benton invented another way to cut matrices, when he introduced his punchcutting machine. The skills of type design then moved from the punchcutter-designer to the draftsman-designer, where they remain today.

Casting types
A 16th-century foundry worker sits on a bench close to the furnace, in which the metal alloy is heating. He holds the mold in his left hand, while pouring molten metal from a ladle into it. A basket by his feet contains the cast types waiting to be passed to the finishers.

Typefaces are voices that impose a visual tone. Their form affects the message in ways that are not always clear. No typeface is truly neutral. In spite of the changes in technology and the method of generating types for printing and the web, the classic typefaces are still working and still held in high regard by contemporary designers.

Among the typefaces cut by Francesco Griffo for Aldus Manutius in the closing years of the 15th century was the typeface that was a model for the 20th-century Bembo design, revived as hot metal type and then in digital form. It has worked harder in more recent times than it ever did for its original

masters. Griffo created generously proportioned, clear-cut letterforms that provide comfortable legibility, a quality that is still much appreciated today. Likewise, at the end of the 18th century, the hours that Giambattista Bodoni spent perfecting his highly refined types resulted in a letterform that conveys an aristocratic elegance that is still appreciated as a masterpiece of style to this day.

These are just two of the typefaces that have achieved the status of high art. Like great music and great literature, they still fulfil a practical need and provide aesthetic satisfaction after generations of use.

Inking the forme
Two men operate this press below. While one positions the sheet to be printed, and removes it afterward (as here), his colleague on the right uses two barons (leather pads) to ink the pages of type before a new impression is taken (pulled). In the background, two compositors are busy setting type from two type cases, one above the other. The upper case contained the capitals and the lower case contained the more frequently used small letters, or "lowercase" letters.

Operating a wooden printing press
Using his left hand, the pressman winds the page of type across the bed of the press to position it under the platen. By pulling on the handle in his right hand, the pressman causes the platen to press the paper head onto the inked type, receiving an impression. This work required physical strength. You can see the pressman has his foot on the base of the press to obtain more leverage. On the right, the compositor sits at the type case with a compositor's stick in his left hand as he assembles a line of type.

1 Before Printing

The alphabet we use today in America and Western Europe is derived from the Roman inscriptional letterforms of the first century AD. One of the finest examples of these letterforms is cut into the plinth at the base of Trajan's Column in the Forum in Rome, which was erected around AD 114 as a monument to the exploits of Roman emperor and soldier Marcus Traianus.

ABCDEF GHIL MNO PQ
ABCDEFGHIKLMNOPQ

Trajan's Column
Above shows a second-century Memorial to the Roman Emperor Traianus. Pen-written square capitals were used for a variety of documents, both formal and informal. A full-size replica can be seen in the Victoria and Albert Museum, London.

The Romans adapted their alphabet from the Greek system of writing, and the Greeks had modified the Phoenician system by adding letters to represent the vowels. Trajan's Column inscription contains most of the letters of the alphabet we use, but the early Roman alphabet did not contain the letters "J," "U," or "W." The letter J was not introduced until the 17th century, because it was not previously differentiated from the letter "I."

These chisel-cut letters are known as quadrata or, more commonly, square capitals. The technical term for these letterforms is majuscules. These capitals were used to express authority, as they do today, and their form contains the structural proportions that still inform the basic proportions of our current lettering and typefaces. Look at the full forms of "O" and "D," and the narrower forms of "E" and "S." Such forms represent classical proportions, geometric relationships of form established by ancient Greek and Roman cultures, which have become ingrained in our letterforms and have been returned to time and again for inspiration through history. They are examples of the origins of the European cultural aesthetic.

These letters would have been carefully drawn out and then cut into the stone, and therefore represent permanence and formality. This is in contrast to the handwritten form, which can be formal but also informal, created in a more immediate way on wax or papyrus, and that is of course less permanent.

An important feature of Roman letterforms is the serifs, the small cross-lines that complete the end of a stroke. Their existence has been the subject of academic study, as their presence does not have a bearing on the letters' meaning since the letters function perfectly well without them. Father Edward Catich's explanation has general acceptance, which is that serifs are formed as a

Square capitals
These are the origin of our present-day alphabet. Note how the serifs, which are not crucial to the identity of the letterform, seem to derive from the nature of the broad pen or brush.

R S T V X

R S T V X

result of the scribe drawing out the letters with a brush as the panel was planned, before the mason finally cut them into the stone. This would explain the bracket-like shapes formed in the example above.

While square capitals were for monumental inscriptions, there was also an informal handwritten version of the capitals for ordinary occasions. This form is known as rustic. These more condensed forms appeared during the second to fourth centuries AD. Although there are examples of carved rustics, it was a form used largely for the recording of more ephemeral information—everyday documents such as contracts, bills of sale, legal, and domestic letters. Literary manuscripts were also written in rustics, for example Virgil's Aeneid.

UNCIAL EVOLVES

During the fourth century, rustic capitals were modified to a more rounded form, adapted to the convenience of writing with a pen. A form known as the uncial (from the Latin for "inch") gained success over the rustic because it was easier to read. The handwritten form using a broad pen created a broad, vertical stroke that contrasted with the thin, horizontal stroke as the pen was moved across, up and down, and up and round. Further changes came about over time as the hand and pen dictated the form more distinctly. A preference for curves brought about the more economic half-uncial, creating the minuscule form. From this development, one can see the first signs of what is, in typographic terms, the lowercase letterform.

The uncial form
Many years of use and the increasing importance of writing caused modification of the square capitals, so that by the fourth century a more cursive form evolved. This later became known as the uncial. Note the circular form of the "e," heralding the development of the lowercase letterform.

A B C
e F G
η I L
N O
P q R

Regional hands
By the seventh century, a regional style of half-uncials had emerged. Below is a page from the famous Book of Kells *kept in Trinity College, Dublin, that exemplifies the Insular (Anglo-Irish) hand.*

THE HALF-UNCIAL

The half-uncial flourished throughout Europe because of its use in mostly religious works. It developed regional or national styles, each with distinct characteristics that made it possible to identify its place of origin: the Merovingian style referred to France, the Beneventian to Italy, the Visigothic to Spain, and the Insular to Ireland and England. One of the greatest achievements of the art of the scribes and illuminators of the period is the *Book of Kells*, a beautiful product of an Irish monastery, which contains a Latin version of the Gospels and dates from approximately 800 AD.

CHARLEMAGNE

The Holy Roman Emperor Charlemagne (742–814) had united most of Western Europe by 804. He intended to consolidate the Christian faith by reforms that included the establishment of a system of education, and the patronage of the arts and literature. He was concerned at the diversity of written hands throughout his Empire, and as part of his reforms he commissioned Alcuin of York to set up a new scriptorium at the Royal court in Aachen, now in Germany, where he was to create a script to become a new standard for manuscript writing throughout the Empire. It was based on the Insular half-uncial and the Merovingian hand. The new script has become known as the Carolingian script. It was a ninth-century attempt to improve communication by the introduction of standardization.

1340 French manuscript illustration
A scribe seated at his writing desk with his tools. The exemplar from which he is making a copy is open on the stand before him.

a b c d e f z g h i k l m n o p q r s t u x y z

The half-uncial
During the sixth century, the half-uncial was established as a forerunner of the present lower case. Note the triangular form of the "a" has modified into a continuous circular form. The tail of the "G" has also lengthened considerably.

THE MONASTERIAL AGE

From the fall of Rome in the fifth century through to the 12th century, monasteries and other establishments related to the church had a monopoly on book production, and were therefore able to control the content and circulation of manuscripts. For many centuries, manuscripts were the only written medium for recording and conveying ideas. The place where the manuscripts were copied was called a scriptorium and most scriptoria were attached to a church or a monastery. The work of the scribe was to copy religious manuscripts, Bibles, and books of prayer. Most original exemplar manuscripts were owned by the libraries of the church, or by nobles, and were loaned out to the scriptoria for copying. People employed as stationers were responsible for recording the loans of the exemplar manuscripts and checking that they had been copied correctly.

The Luttrell Psalter
In this Psalter, the text demonstrates the strong, vertical strokes of a broad pen and was completed separately to the illumination, despite the integrated appearance. The Psalter was commissioned by the English Lord Geoffrey Luttrell c.1320.

The eighth-century hand
To the left is an example of a text from Alcuin of York's Acts of Council of Ephesus from the Tours school and Abbey in France, where Alcuin of York was latterly Abbot. Note the use of initial Letters in this decorative uncial-formed alphabet as used for manuscript missals.

SECULAR SCRIPTORIA

From the end of the 12th century, the church monopoly was challenged as universities established their own scriptoria. Although the monasteries continued to produce manuscripts for their own devotional needs, the establishment of the new universities, and the development of learning among the laity, created a new kind of reader.

After the monasterial age, the secular age brought only small technical changes. The major innovation was the introduction of paper. Traditionally, books and other manuscripts were written on parchment, which was expensive and depended on an adequate supply of animal skins. The universities' growing demand for books made the expanding manufacture of paper an alternative to be encouraged, especially as the students required a less elaborate product.

REGIONAL SCRIPTS

During the centuries following the introduction of the Carolingian script, the influence of Charlemagne's revisions began to fade and regional writing styles slowly began to reappear. In northern Europe there gradually emerged the group of heavy, solid, manuscript hands called Gothic or blackletter. Textura was one of this group, and by the early 15th century, with minor variants, it was a standard script in German-speaking regions for formal book work. It was on the Textura letterform that Johannes Gutenberg based his first type designs. "Gothic" was the disparaging term used by the Renaissance humanists of Italy, who had, through the church bureaucracy, reintroduced a form of Carolingian script considered to best reflect the values of humanist philosophy.

Illuminated initial letter
To the right is an illumination from the 14th century. Within the letter, a monk is shown writing a manuscript of romances.

THE BIRTH OF PRINTING

The production of books written and illustrated by hand was a highly organized, but slow and labor-intensive process. By the 15th century, the demand for books was increasing. Printing from a raised surface had been known for many years, but only from woodcut blocks, not individual letters. At markets and fairs it was possible to buy block books—booklets printed from woodcuts, with pictures of religious events illustrating a short, handcut text. Making prints from a raised and inked surface (letterpress printing) is the oldest method of printing, and it maintained supremacy over other methods of printing well into the 20th century.

Many technological advances depend on the coming together of a number of new developments. In the case of printing, it was paper that played the key role. Compared to parchment, paper offered a suitably manageable and more economical material for printing.

Papermaking was a craft that originated in China, and is believed to have been the discovery of Tsai Lun, who was responsible for establishing the royal workshops in AD 104. The first papermill in Europe was established in Catalonia (now in Spain) in 1238, followed by mills in Fabriano in Italy in 1276, and in Nuremberg in Germany in 1389. Papermaking required specific conditions to operate effectively. The mills needed to be near water for power and for processing; and they also needed to be near a sustainable supply of rags, which were then the basic ingredient of paper, so the mills had to be close to large population centers.

Chinese papermaking
A Chinese drawing depicting two papermakers preparing paper. The wet sheets of pulp were smoothed onto screens to dry out.

乾 焙 火 透

European papermaking
A worker dips his mold into a vat of paper pulp, while the apprentice carries away a pile of ready sheets. In the background, the blades of the watermill that drive the pulping hammers can be seen through the open window.

2 The Renaissance

The Renaissance was a vigorous period of cultural and economic change that began in the 14th century and continued into the 16th century, bringing to a close to the Middle Ages, and representing a definable step toward the modern world.

Renaissance art
The Rout of San Romano (c.1439) by Paulo Ucello (above). The artist employs one-point perspective, expressed in the foreshortening of figures and the broken lances strewn on the ground.

The Middle Ages had seen the collapse of the Roman Empire and the consolidation of Christianity throughout Europe, with the construction of the great cathedrals, such as those of Chartres, Notre-Dame, Canterbury, and Cologne. By the 15th century, feudalism, previously the dominant social and economic structure, was beginning to give way to a monetary economy.

The main thrust of the Renaissance was the rediscovery and admiration of the ancient pre-Christian cultures of Greece and Rome, and a new belief in the value of those artifacts and manuscripts that had survived into the 14th and 15th centuries. The ancient civilizations offered knowledge of every aspect of human endeavor: art, literature, architecture, engineering, philosophy, medicine, science, and government. The integration of Greek and Roman knowledge and wisdom with Christian morality brought about the concept of humanism.

The humanist ideals were individualism, originality, and a general proficiency that was the basis of Renaissance education. This was expressed in the importance attached to the visual arts; these were patronized by the church, rich merchants, and dignitaries, so that they developed from workshop-based artisan activity to the heights of creative skill and imagination. This is exemplified in the achievements of artists such as Michelangelo Buonarotti (1475–1564), Leonardo da Vinci (1452–1519), and Raphael (1483–1520).

A germinal figure in the cultivation of humanist learning was Leon Battista Alberti (1404–1472), papal secretary, architect, and artist. His 1435 text *Della Pittura* ("On Painting") is still in print today. He designed a number of buildings in Florence and Mantua, Italy, inspired by his study of the ten books of treatises on architecture by the first-century Roman architect and engineer Vitruvius. It was from these texts that Leonardo da Vinci made his famous drawing *The Proportions of Man*.

DRIVING FORCES

At the same time, the developing international trade in goods and services created an increasing number of successful merchants, whose power and economic importance brought about the institution of banking. Although officially forbidden by the church, the growing desire by the wealthy and powerful to make use of credit to maintain their power, and to possess and consume goods, was supported by an increasing reliance on loans with interest or concessions.

It was in the climate created by the two driving forces of commerce and passion for knowledge that the invention of printing from movable type was to grow so quickly. Even though printing could provide classical and religious texts for an increasing audience at a more acceptable cost compared with handwritten manuscripts, printers and publishers needed considerable financial support as printing a book was an expensive undertaking.

There were other endeavors during the Renaissance that required substantial financial support. There were many courageous expeditions of discovery, such as the four sea journeys to the New World of the Americas undertaken by the Italian explorer Christopher Columbus (1451–1506) in 1492, 1493, 1498, and 1502, and the 1521 voyage round the tip of South America to the Pacific and the Philippines made by the Portuguese sailor Ferdinand Magellan (1480–1521).

Leonardo's notebooks
Leonardo da Vinci represents the Renaissance man as being someone with a vigorous interest in all things. Beginning in 1508, he kept notebooks, writing notes and treatises in them, and making drawings on many subjects, from the mechanics of war to anatomy. As he was left-handed, he wrote using "mirror writing" from right to left.

Albrecht Dürer
Born in Nuremberg, Germany, Dürer (1471–1528) was a leading member of the Northern Renaissance, and a brilliant draftsman and master of woodcut and engraving. His engraving Melencolia *(left) is filled with symbols of mathematics and alchemy.*

JOHANNES GUTENBERG *& Movable Type*

Johannes Gutenberg
This steel engraving is a popular imagined portrait of Gutenberg, no genuine likeness is known to exist.

The 42-line Bible
Gutenberg's masterpiece was completed c.1450. The design consisted of two 42-line columns per page. Also known as the Mazarin Bible, and printed as two volumes, it contains some 1,200 pages. About 180 copies were produced, of which 48 are known to have survived to the present day.

There is still some controversy surrounding the origin of the invention of printing from movable types in Europe. However, it is generally accepted that Johannes Gutenberg (also known as Johannes Gensfleisch), in the years between 1440 and 1450, produced the first-known book to be printed in this way.

It is sometimes claimed that Laurents Coster of Haarlem had discovered a method of printing prior to Gutenberg, and that Gutenberg had contact with Coster and either stole or developed his ideas. However, what little evidence there is implies that Gutenberg preceded Coster.

Little is known about Gutenberg. He was born in the German town of Mainz, capital of the Rhineland Palatinate, in about 1394, he lived for some time in Strasbourg, and died in Mainz in 1468. What we do know about him is derived largely from the court records in Mainz, at the time a city of 6,000 inhabitants.

It is likely that Gutenberg employed a number of people to help him with the development of his printing invention. This possibly led to the financial problems that he experienced during the years of his research and development. The court records refer to a legal dispute over a loan of 800 guilders. The loan for "work on the books," was made by Johannes Fust, a lawyer. A further loan of 800 guilders was made, which also named Fust as a partner. It appears that in 1455, Fust decided to take over Gutenberg's invention rather than accept the return of his investment, which would suggest that Gutenberg was enjoying success with his innovation. Fust continued printing in partnership with Peter Schoeffer, originally Gutenberg's foreman. Schoeffer had a good knowledge of the printing process, and later married Fust's daughter. After the loss of his types and presses, little more is known of Gutenberg, except that after 1460 he is believed to have given up printing. However, this may not have been the case, since it is recorded that he received a pension from the Archbishop of Mainz until his death.

Gutenberg's achievement was to invent a system of mass production, enabling books to be produced in greater numbers and more economically. His invention played a fundamental role in the development of the modern world, and

was the single most important factor in the spread of knowledge and the move toward universal literacy in the West. As with most significant inventions, there was a generally perceived need for improvements on current methods, no doubt recognized by many others as well as Gutenberg.

At this time all skills, trades, and professions were guarded jealously by their practitioners, so it is not surprising that there was so much secrecy surrounding Gutenberg's experiments. For centuries a training in printing, as in many other trades, had to be bought through apprenticeship if you were not lucky enough to be born into the family of a printer.

THE ADJUSTABLE MOLD

The brilliance of Gutenberg's invention was in adapting several existing technologies to make them suitable for his own requirements, and, possibly, in using earlier ideas by others such as Coster. Gutenberg's innovations included the modification of the screw press, originally used to crush fruit, and the adaptation of the techniques of punchcutting, brass mold-making and metal-casting, which were already familiar to silversmiths and engravers. Gutenberg's key innovation was the adjustable mold. This was a mechanism of two fitting parts that could be adjusted to fit the matrix of each letter width to be cast, overcoming the problem of the necessity of a mold for each letter. Gutenberg also manufactured a thick, oil-based ink that could achieve a quality of black similar to that of the scribes' inks. His experiments resulted in the inclusion of antimony as part of the metal alloy (mostly lead with some tin) that produced a sharp letter cast from the mold without shrinkage as the metal cooled.

Rotunda
This printed page uses one of the main forms of blackletter, or Gothic Letter, also known as round text.

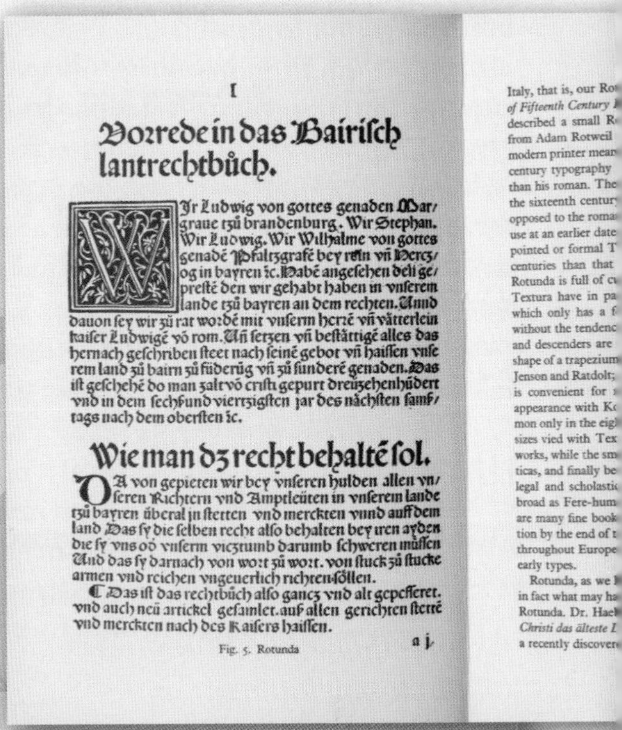

I

Vorrede in das Bairisch lantrechtbůch.

Wir Ludwig von gottes genaden Margraue tzů brandenburg. Wir Stephan. Wir Ludwig. Wir Wilhalme von gottes genadē Pfaltzgrafē bey rein vñ Hertzog in bayren ꝛc. Habē angesehen deli gepreſtē den wir gehabt haben in vnſerem lande tzů bayren an dem rechten. Unnd dauon ſey wir zů rat wordē mit vnſerm herrē vñ vätterlein kaiſer Ludwigē vō rom. Vñ ſetzen vñ beſtättigē alles das hernach geſchriben ſteet nach ſeinē gebot vñ haiſſen vnſerem land zů bairn zů fůderūg vñ zů ſunderē genaden. Das iſt geſchehē do man zalt vō criſti gepurt dreützehenhůdert vnd in dem ſechßund viertzigſten jar des nächſten ſamſtags nach dem oberſten ꝛc.

Wie man dz recht behaltē ſol.

Da von gepieten wir bey vnſeren hulden allen vnſeren Richtern vnd Amptleüten in vnſerem lande tzů bayren überal jn ſtetten vnd merckten vnnd auff dem land Das ſy die ſelben recht alſo behalten bey iren ayden die ſy vns od vnſerm viczumb darumb ſchweren müſſen Und das ſy darnach von wort zů wort. von ſtuck zů ſtucke armen vnd reichen vngeuerlich richten ſöllen.

¶ Das iſt das rechtbůch alſo gancz vnd alt gepeſſeret. vnd auch neü artickel geſamlet. auß allen gerichten ſtettē vnd merckten nach des Kaiſers haiſſen.

Fig. 5. Rotunda

a j.

Bastarda
One of the four main groups that cover vernacular blackletter texts, an example of Bastarda is shown below.

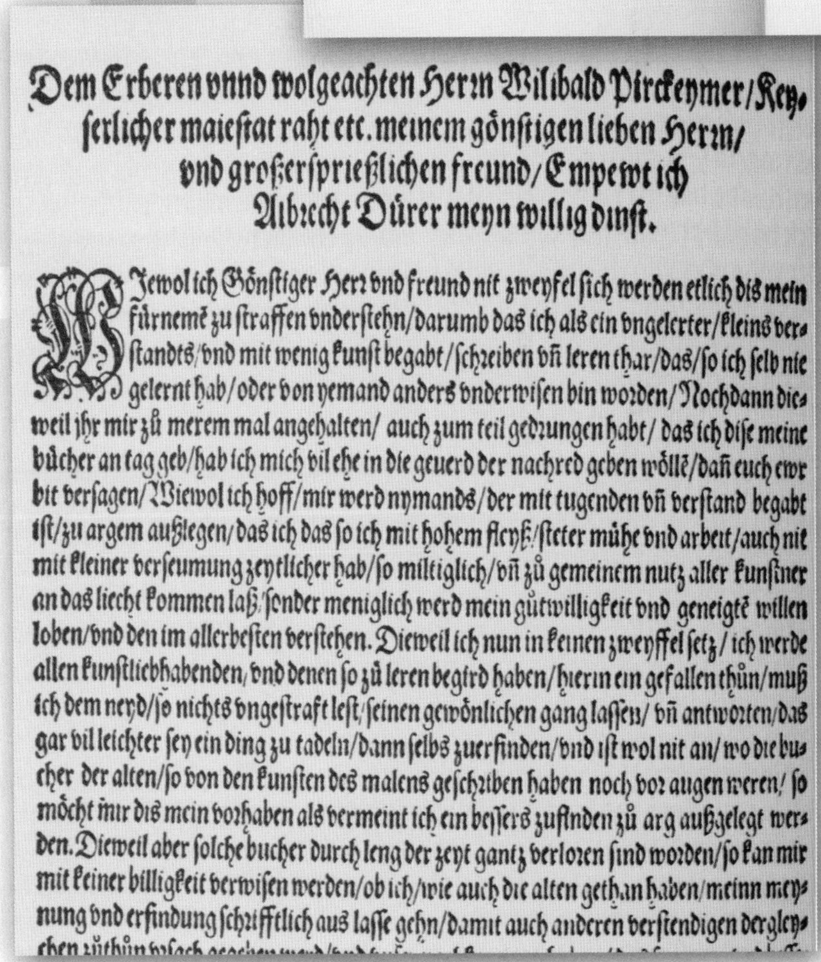

Dem Erberen vnnd wolgeachten Herrn Wilibald Pirckeymer/Keyſerlicher maieſtat raht etc. meinem gönſtigen lieben Herrn/ vnd groſzerſprieſzlichen freund/Empewt ich Albrecht Dürer meyn willig dinſt.

Wiewol ich Gönſtiger Herr vnd freund nit zweyfel ſich werden etlich dis mein fürnemē zu ſtraffen vnderſtehn/darumb das ich als ein vngelerter/kleins verſtandts/vnd mit wenig kunſt begabt/ſchreiben vñ leren thar/das/ſo ich ſelb nie gelernt hab/oder von yemand anders vnderwiſen bin worden/Nochdann dieweil jhr mir zů merem mal angehalten/ auch zum teil gedrungen habt/ das ich diſe meine bůcher an tag geb/hab ich mich vil ehe in die geuerd der nachred geben wöllē/dañ euch ewr bit verſagen/Wiewol ich hoff/mir werd nymands/der mit tugenden vñ verſtand begabt iſt/zu argem außlegen/das ich das ſo ich mit hohem fleyß/ſteter mühe vnd arbeit/auch nit mit kleiner verſeumung zeytlicher hab/ſo miltiglich/vñ zů gemeinem nutz aller kunſtner an das liecht kommen laß/ſonder meniglich werd mein gůtwilligkeit vnd geneigtē willen loben/vnd den im allerbeſten verſtehen. Dieweil ich nun in keinen zweyffel ſetz/ ich werde allen kunſtliebhabenden/vnd denen ſo zů leren begird haben/hierin ein gefallen thůn/muß ich dem neyd/ſo nichts vngeſtraft leſt/ſeinen gewönlichen gang laſſen/ vñ antworten/das gar vil leichter ſey ein ding zu tadeln/dann ſelbs zuerfinden/vnd iſt wol nit an/ wo die bucher der alten/ſo von den kunſten des malens geſchriben haben noch vor augen weren/ ſo möcht mir dis mein vorhaben als vermeint ich ein beſſers zufinden zů arg außgelegt werden. Dieweil aber ſolche bucher durch leng der zeyt gantz verloren ſind worden/ſo kan mir mit keiner billigkeit verwiſen werden/ob ich/wie auch die alten gethan haben/meinn meynung vnd erfindung ſchrifftlich aus laſſe gehn/damit auch anderen verſtendigen dergleychen

agit. ut huana diuinis tribuat auctoritate: cu pocius humanis diuina de-
buerint. Que nunc sane omittamus, ne nihil apud istos agamus. et i infinitu
materia pcedat. Ea igr queramus testimonia. q̄bus illi possint aut credere:
aut certe non repugnare. Sibillas plurimi et maximi auctores tradiderut
grecoy: Aristoricus: et Appollodorus: Erithreus: nostroy Varro et Fenestella. Hi omes pcipuam et nobilem preter ceteras. Erithream fuisse co-
memorat. Appollodorus q̄dē ut de ciui ac populari sua gloriae. Fenestella
uero etiā legatos Erithreos a senatu eē missos refert. ut huius Sibille car-
mina Roma deportarenē. et ea consules Curio et Octauianus i capitolio
quod tuc erat curante Quinto Catulo restitutu: poneda curarē. Apud hac
de sumo & conditore reru deo huiusmoi uersus reperiutur. Αφθαρτος
κτιστης αιωνιος αιθερα μαιων τοις ακακοις ακακον προ-
φερων πολυ μειζομα μισθον τοις δε κακοις αδικοις τε
χολον και θυμον ετειρων. id est icorruptibilis et conditor eternus
in aere habitans. bonis bonu pferens. iustis multo maiore mercedem. in-
iustis aut & malis iram et furorem excitans. Rursus alio loco enumerans.

Sweynheim and Pannartz
Two printers working in Subiaco, Italy, in about 1465, cut a typeface for an edition of Cicero (above) that was a lighter, fuller form than that of Textura.

Typographically, Gutenberg's greatest achievement was the *42-line Bible*, completed in about 1455, which imitated the style of the handwritten book to a remarkable degree. His typeface was based on Textura, the formal script of northern Germany. Research suggests that to imitate the inconsistencies and abbreviations that appear in a handwritten manuscript, Gutenberg must have cast at least 300 characters in order to provide slight variations of letterform throughout the text.

EARLY PUBLICATIONS

There are four main groups of blackletter: Texturas, Gotico-antiquas or Fere-humanisticas, Rotunda or round text, and Bastards (vernacular types).

The partnership of Fust and Schoeffer published several books using Gutenberg's types, including the *Mainz Psalter* (1457), a beautiful book with red and blue initial letters tha t can claim to be the first example of color printing, and a *48-line Bible* (1462) bearing the date of publication and their colophon.

That same year, as the result of a political power struggle, Mainz was subjected to considerable violence and destruction. The resulting desolation and evictions helped to hasten the spread of printing across Europe, as printers became itinerant and were forced to look for new markets. Many ambitious printers would have looked to Italy, the center of the new cultural force that was spreading

Trade secrets
Early printers, like all tradesmen of the time, jealously guarded their craft secrets and practices. This did not, however, stop them from being the subject of artists' engravings.

ipfum eorum regem in omnibus corporeis elementis: Nam fi animę ut btā fit corpus eft omne fugiendum: fugiant dii eoℛ de globis fyderum: fugiat Iuppiter de cęlo & terra: aut fi non poffunt miferi iudicentur. Sed neutrum ifti uoluut:qui neque a corporibus feparationé audent dare diis fuis: ne illis mortales colere uideantur: nec beatitudinis priuationem:ne infelices eos cē fateantur. Non ergo ad beatitudinem cófequendam omía fugienda funt corpora: fed corruptibilia: grauia:moribunda:non qualia fecit primis homíbus bonitas dei:fed qualia effe compulit peccati poena.

S Ed neceffe eft inquiunt: ut terrena corpora naturale pondus uel i terra teneat:uel cogat ad terram: & ideo in caelo effe non poffunt. Primi quidem illi homiés in terra erant nemorofa atque fructuofa: quae paradifi nomen obtinuit.Sed quia & ad hoc refpondendú eft:uel propter chrifti corpus cum quo afcendit in caelum:uel propter fanctorum qualia in refurrectione futura funt: intueantur paulo attentius pondera ipá terrena. Si enim ars humana efficit: ut ex metallis quę in aquis pofita continuo fubmergunt:quibufdam

across Europe—and in particular Venice, hub of international trade, and Rome, the home of the Pope and the center of Western Christianity. For Venice, the invention of printing became yet another opportunity for trade and greater wealth. For the church, mass-produced books that spread ideas not in line with Rome's policies eventually became a grave challenge to its authority.

FROM GOTHIC TO ROMAN

The early years of printing, from Gutenberg's *42-line Bible* up to the 1500s, are referred to as the Incunabula Period. In Britain, printing was first introduced by William Caxton (1421–1491). Caxton occupied the post of Governor of English Wool Merchants in Bruges, Belgium. He studied the craft of printing in Cologne, Germany in 1471–1472. He printed his first books in English in Bruges in 1475: *The Recuyell of Historyes of Troye* and *The Game and the Playe of the Cheese* [chess]. The types he used for these were supplied by Johann Veldener, his typographic mentor.

In 1476, Caxton returned to England to set up a printing press at the Abbey Precinct, Westminster, "by the sign of the Red Pale." His first book printed in England was *The Dictes and Sayings of the Philosophers* (1477). When he died in 1491, having published some 73 books in English, his assistant Wynkyn de Worde took over the running of the press.

The typeface of early northern European printing was the established Gothic blackletter. This was not acceptable to humanist southern Europe, because it was considered representative of the Gothic Middle Ages. The script used by the Italian scribes in the latter half of the 15th century was the Chancery script, a standard hand favored by the scribes of the Vatican chancery. It carried the influence of classical Rome, and was a revival of the Carolingian script-style, but

The da Spira Roman
In Venice, Italy, the brothers Johannes & Wendelin Da Spira cut a type (above) that was strongly influenced by the humanist hand, itself a rejection of the Gothic form of northern Europe.

lighter, more cursive, and fully formed. It still influences modern handwriting. The fuller form of the script was an expression of the aesthetic philosophy of the humanist Italian Renaissance.

The first printers hoping to be successful in Italy had to take account of the new aesthetic. Conrad Sweynheim of Mainz and his partner Arnold Pannartz, printing at Subiaco near Rome in 1465, produced a type that was a lighter calligraphic form than Textura. It showed the influence of humanist script, and demonstrates the first move toward the "White Letter," the lighter, fuller "roman" letterform, although still retaining signs of the Gothic pen.

Five years later, in Venice, two brothers, Johannes and Wendelin da Spira, cut a type that was closer in style to a roman letterform—a 14-point type recognized as an advance on the type designs of Sweynheim and Pannartz. However, it was another newcomer to Italy, Nicholas Jenson (1420–1480), a Frenchman who settled in Venice in 1468, who was responsible for cutting the first outstanding version of the roman typeface. Cut

A plate from Moxon's Mechanical Exercises, 1683
Joseph Moxon was a hydrographer with a wide number of interests, which included typography. In the 1680s, he produced what is possibly the first handbook on the craft of printing— published as a kind of part-work.

autem pecuniæ cupiditate uicti manifesta dederũt supplicia:Cuius rei
exépla etsi quotidie uidemus:unũ tamen ex priscis referre operæpreciũ
duximus.Dicunt igitur qui foetidos sacrum bellum cõscripserũt quũ
lex esset aut præcipites ex alto deiici:aut i mare submergi:aut igne cre
mari sacrilegos:quumq; Philomelus Onomarchus & Phaylus tres isti
Delphicum spoliauerint templum:secũdũ legem diuinitus supplicia
dedisse.Alterũ eim quum per aspera scanderet loca præcipité decidisse:
ac ita expirasse.Alterum quum eques per littora ferretur in profundo
lapsum una cum equo fuisse aquis demersum.Phaylum aũt alii sacro
morbo consumptum:alii quũ templũ Inabis incéderet una cõcrematũ
fuisse tradiderũt.Nemo profecto hæc casu nisi amés accidisse putabit.
Omnes enim hos tres eisdem temporibus propter idem delictum non
aliis suppliciis q̃ lex uolebat iure punitos non a fortuna & casu sed di
uinitus credere debemus:Quod si nõnulli rapaces & factiosi homines
qui non alienos solummodo populos sed patrias etiam suas subiece
rũt impune id fecisse uidétur:mirandum non est.Primum enim non
similiter deus atq; homines iudicant:homines enim de manifestis tan
tũmodo cognoscunt:deus uero in aĩum igressus ipsũ nudos uolũtatis
perspicit motus.Quare nunq̃ humana iudicia diuino tanq̃ meliora &
iustiora præponenda sunt.Multis eim hoies fallunt sensibus corporis
atq; turbatiõibus animi.Iudæo autem nihil est quod fallat:sed sũma
iustitia una cum ueritate cuncta geruntur.Deinde recte illud imprimis
fert id esse apud populũ tyrannos quod sunt in lege supplicia.Quãdo
igitur in ciuitatibus adeo abundant ut nulla legum reuerétia sit:tunc
deus ut uitia repellat & ad uirtutem homines cõuertat crudelibus atq;
tyrannic s uiris non in uriam potentia præbet:uitiorum enim cumulus
sine crudelitate mundari nõ potest:& quéadmodũ uindices publicas
rerum ad homicidas proditores & sacrilegos interficiendos publice a
luntur:non quia tale hominis exercitium laudetur:sed quia populo
necessarium est:eodem profecto pacto huius mundi gubernator quasi
cõmunes uidices tyrãnos in ciuitates exsuscitat:ut iniuriã atq; ĩpietaté
aliaq; huiusmodi ui & crudelitate istorum puniat:qui quoniam non
recto aĩmi ,pposito sed crudelitate cõmoti diuinæ uolũtati submistra
runt:ut ignis consumpta materia demum extĩguitur:sic & ipsi quum
ciuitates prauas ianes hominum fecerit:tunc demũ in pnicié iacidunt.
Quid autem miramur si tyrãnoꝛ interdum ministerio effusas hoium
iniurias deus cõpescit:quum etiã sæpius nõ alioꝛ ope sed p se ipsum
fame terræmotu peste aliisq; huiusmodi qbus multas urbes desolatas
uidemus id factitet?Satis dictum esse puto neminem qui male iuiat

esse fœlicem:unde maxime prouidentia esse probatur.Et post aliqua.
Ventorum inquit impetus & pluuiæ uis non ad pniciem nauigátiũ
aut agricolaꝛ:sed ad utilitatem humai generis diuinitus mittit:Aquis
eim terrã uentis uero regioné quæ sub luna est inundare solet:& utrisq;
aialia & plantas alit auget perficit.Quod si nauigátes aut agricolas nõ
nunq̃ pdit mirari nõ debes.Minima eim quædã isti particula sũt:cura
uero totius humani generis deo est.Vt ergo in editione ludorum atq;
certamis ædiles ,ppter aliquos rei. p. usus die certamis mutato secerũt
nõnullos luctatorum non affuisse:Sic & deus quasi magnæ cuiusdam
ciuitatis totius orbis curã gerens humidioré æstatem & uernalé hyemé
ad utilitatem totius effecit:q̃uis nonnulli hac temporum iæqualitate
magna dãna patiantur.Elementorũ igitur inter se transmutationes ex
quibus mũdus cõstat & quibus coseruat tanq̃ necessarias ipse instituit:
pruinæ aũt & niues cæteraq; huiusmodi ad frigiditaté aeris cõsequunt
sicuti ad cõcussionem nubium fulgura & tonitrua:quorũ nihil forsan
& prouidentia sit.Pluuiæ uero ac uenti quum uitæ alimenti cremétiq;
causa plantarum atq; animalium sint prouidétia certe siunt & ex istis
illa cõsequuntur:ut si editoris munerum liberalitate atq; magnificétia
magna unguétorum copia proponatur:unde guttis quil usdã in terrã
deflexis lubricus ualde locus effectus sit:nemo non insanus prouidétia
editoris munerum lubricitatem facta esse cõtenderet:sed ad magnificé
tiam abundantiáq; unguentoꝛ confecutam concederet.Iris similiter &
alia huiusmodi nõ sunt naturæ o pa principaliter sed nubibus naturali
quadam ratione accidentia:& tamen etiam hæc prudétioribus cõserũt:
tranquillitatem eim aeris motus uétorũ hyemes et serenitaté his signis
prædicere solét:fornices porticusq; nũ uides quoꝛ plurimi ad meridié
respiciunt ut de ãbulantes in hyeme calefiãt & in æstate op aco frigore
utantur?quã rem illud consequitur non ab ædificatoris sentétia factũ
q̃ umbris quæ a basi excidunt horæ significãtur.Ignis similiter naturæ
opus est necessarium:quem quasi accidens quoddam fumus cõsequir.
Qui tamen est quando non paruam attulit utilitatem.Interdiu enim
non igne sed fumo aduentum hostium significamus.Talis ratio etiam
in Eclipsibus dici potest quæ solem atque lunam consequĩtur:& aut
mortis regum aut urbiũ desolationes prudétibus signa solent afferre.
Lacteus uero circulus stellas habet eius substantiæ cuius cæteræ.Cuius
rei causam quis difficilis sit nõ tamen negligũt sed diligenter quæritãt
philosophantes:putant enim & recte iucundissimam rem per se ipsam
esse scientiam.Sicut igitur sol & luna cæteræq; stellæ per prouidétiam
factæ sunt:sic profecto cælestia omĩa q̃uis nos naturam atq; uirtutem

in 1470, Jenson's Roman had only 23 letters,
since "J," "U," and "W" were not yet in use.
He used the typeface for an edition of Eusebius's
De Evangelica Praeparatione. The lowercase
alphabet is the same, except that the "v" is
used in place of "u," and, in addition, there is a
long "s" and "æ" and "œ": 15 contractions,
six double letters, and three full points: 73
punches in all.

The first Roman type
In 1469, Nicholas Jenson, a French national working in Venice, cut what is considered to be the first true expression of the Latin letterform. This appeared in an edition of Eusebius's De Evangelica Praeparatione, and it set a standard by which others would be judged.

FROM A CRAFT TO AN ART

Nicholas Jenson had served an apprenticeship at the Paris Mint, and was promoted to Master of the Mint at Tours. Charles VII sent Jenson to Mainz to learn about the new invention of printing from movable type. He may have met Gutenberg. However, he arrived in Venice and proceeded to set up a printing workshop to print in his own right. At the time of his death in 1480 he had produced about 150 editions.

In 1476, when Jenson produced a volume of Pliny's *Natural History*, he required financial support from the Venetian bankers Strozzi and Agostini. As a result, payments are recorded of 731 ducats for 86 bales of paper. Each copy was sold for seven ducats. Jenson's type has become renowned for the comfortable fit of the letters as words and the beautiful proportions of the letterforms themselves. The Victorian designer William Morris (1834–1896) was to use Jenson's type as a model for his own Golden Type. The 20th-century typographer Bruce Rogers had a sustained interest in Jenson's roman which culminated in his typeface Centaur, released by Monotype in 1929, and discussed later in this book. In 1996 Robert Slimbach of Adobe designed an excellent digital version of Jenson's roman that is lighter in color than the heavy period quality of Morris's design. Jenson is admired above all other Venetian printers and typecutters of the 15th century because he is considered to have raised type design from a craft to an art form in its own right.

William Caxton
Printing was brought to the British Isles by William Caxton in 1476 (right). He set up his printing press in the Abbey Precinct at Westminster. His first book in English was printed in Bruges, Belgium, in 1475.

Dance of death
Printing soon became part of mainstream culture. The 15th-century scene below depicts the medieval allegory of the universality of death, no matter what one's station in life. This is one of a series, and is set in a printer's workshop.

ALDUS MANUTIUS *& the Italian Old-Face*

Aldus Manutius
An engraving of the publisher Manutius (above), who was known for his energy and kindness.

Some 15 years after Nicholas Jenson's death, another high-quality roman typeface was created in Venice that was to inspire type design for the next century and a half. This was the result of Aldus Manutius's remarkable qualities as a publisher, and the superb skills of his punchcutter, Francesco Griffo of Bologna.

Teobaldo Manuzio, now better known by his Latinized name, Aldus Manutius, studied Greek and Latin in Rome. He developed a love of Greek, believing (in common with many other scholars) that a thorough knowledge of Greek literature was the way to a greater appreciation of the culture and knowledge of antiquity. He was a teacher until, in his forties, he decided that he should attempt the printing and publishing of classical Greek literature in the original language.

When Manutius arrived in Venice in 1489 the market for Latin books was well provided for, but for Greek books there was less demand, since most of Greek literature could already be found in Latin translation. Manutius made contact with writers and scholars. His research rewarded him with suitable manuscripts to convert into printed books. Venice had had a resident Greek community since the fall of Constantinople in 1453, and members of this community were able to help with the editing and publishing of the texts. Finally, Manutius needed printers and financial backing for his plans. Aldus Manutius's first book in Venice was a Latin grammar printed by Andrea Torresani in 1493.

Aldus Manutius's device
Venice in the late 15th century was a hive of printing activity. The academic printer Manutius was also a businessman, and was aware that his books should be clearly identified by his device, which showed a dolphin and anchor.

EARLY TEXTS

Using the engraving skills of Francesco Griffo (d.1518), it was Aldus's primary intention to produce a satisfactory Greek typeface for his publications. Typographically speaking, ancient Greek had not gone through the process of revision and development in the same way that Latin had. This made it a complex project for type designers. For their Greek typeface, Manutius and Griffo chose to adapt the calligraphic hand used in Venice at the time, rather than a more formal manuscript hand. Griffo's type influenced subsequent Greek types for many years, although it never received the same acclaim as his roman typefaces. The first volume from the Aldine Press was an introduction to Greek grammar, with parallel Latin translation, which appeared in 1495.

Towards the end of the century Manutius turned to Latin editions as well as Greek, since his Greek publications never reached the level of popularity that he had hoped. In 1495, Griffo cut the type used for a Latin text, *De Aetna*, by Pietro Bembo. This was to become the typeface that made the names of Manutius and Griffo part of printing history.

ITALIC TYPE

Manutius added a series of pocket books to his list of publications. This was not a totally original idea, since small books had been produced before. However, for his small-format editions Manutius commissioned Griffo to cut a typeface based on the humanist script that was current—a similar concept to the Greek types he had already cut. Consisting of lowercase only (roman was used for the capital letters), this typeface is what we now call italic. The fact that it was more condensed than a roman face made it more economical in terms of space and thereby reduced the number of pages—an important consideration for cost and weight. These compact volumes of Latin literature were not intended for academics, but for general readers to carry with them to be read when time allowed. They proved to be extremely successful: the first volume, published in 1501, was an edition of Virgil which ran to two editions of 3,000 each.

Aldus guarded his publications and types jealously and claimed copyright and monopolies from the College of Venice. This resulted in a dispute with Francesco Griffo as to the true authorship of the Aldine set of types. Griffo claimed that he had not been given enough credit for his part in their creation and was restrained legally from cutting further types in the same style, reducing his ability to trade.

Virgil's Opera
In 1501, Manutius produced the first of his octavo classics, which was set entirely in italic type. In this book he praises his typecutter Francesco Griffo.

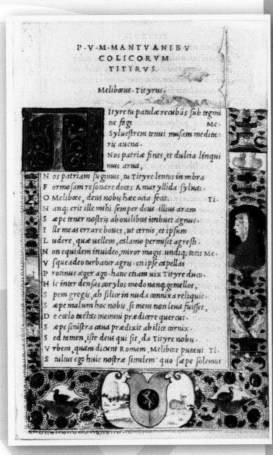

Contextualizer

Aldus Manutius
1451–1515

Venice

Venice during the Renaissance was a powerful city state with vast trading connections throughout Europe and the East. By the end of the 1480s, Venice had an extremely well-organized printing industry, and was far more advanced in the production and distribution of printed works than any of the other Italian centers of trade.

The early Renaissance italic

In the 1600s, the majuscule (upper case) and miniscule (lower case) alphabets were viewed as independent components of a roman typeface, rather than as companions to roman faces. The upper case of a Renaissance italic is often smaller than the upper case of a roman font of equivalent size, and are, in fact, small caps. During this time, the separation of roman and italic lowercases was logical since the two were kept entirely separate; entire books would be set in roman or italic but never mixed both. Consequently, authors of modern Old-style revivals have had to artificially match independent designs, often created by different typographers and in different centuries, to compose a complete font family with roman and italic faces.

BEMBO: *the Italian Old-Face*

ABCDEFGHIJKLM

abcdefghiklmnopqrs

abcdefghiklmnopqrstv

Erotemata by Constantine Lascaris
This reprint of the popular introduction to Greek grammar was the first publication of the Manutius Press in 1495.

Bembo is classified as an Old-face; an Italian Old-face, to be more precise. It is characterized by full, generous forms, and is light in color as a page of text. The serifs are large but delicately bracketed and give the letters a sound base. The capital "N" and "U" are particularly wide, and there is a generous flourish to the tail of the "J" and "Q," and in the widely extending leg of the "R." The ascenders are taller than the capitals, which tends to make the x-height (the height of the lower case) appear small. The accompanying italic alphabet conveys the style of a pen script in the sharp change of stroke thickness and the serifs.

The typefaces of Manutius and Griffo were to become successful because of their plain and simple readability, which expressed so well the importance that humanists attached to practicalities. Their beauty is to be found in the structure of the letterforms and the proportions of the page, not in the elaborate ornamentation that was so important in Gothic manuscripts. Griffo's highly skilled interpretation of the classical roman alphabet was to be a standard for punchcutters to follow for the next two hundred years.

NOPQRSTUVWXYZ
tvxyz& 1234567890
xyz& 1234567890

Hot-Metal Bembo
*A specimen sheet of
Monotype's 20th-century
revival of Francesco
Griffo's types.*

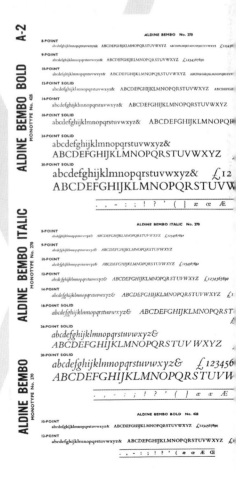

BEMBO REVIVAL

The revival of Bembo was part of the Monotype Corporation's program of recutting a series of historic typefaces, under the supervision of Stanley Morison (1889–1967). Many of the intended historic specimens, like Bembo, were only available as printed books. This created problems for the redesign. The texture of the paper and the ink spread caused by the impression made it a process of interpretation of form when drawing for a new cutting. There were two types cut originally by Griffo considered for revival. They were Poliphilus, drawn from the text of *Hypnerotomachia Poliphili* of 1499, and Bembo, the typeface used in the printing of *De Aetna* in 1495, which takes its name from the author, the humanist scholar and poet Cardinal Pietro Bembo.

Poliphilus was cut first and released in 1923, and an italic alphabet to accompany it was based on a Chancery type used by Antonio Blado in 1539. The types were acclaimed for the authenticity of the design, which retained many of the original irregularities. Poliphilus has

been digitized, as has the italic, being identified separately as Blado. In the case of Bembo, not cut and released until 1929, a modernizing approach was taken: the irregularities were eradicated, the capitals lightened, and the serifs refined. Bembo has proved to be a very successful book face throughout the 20th century, and its simple elegance continues to make it one of the most popular fonts for a wide range of books and publicity material. The italic design to accompany the roman was based on a Chancery type of Giovantonio Tagliente. The current 1980 digitized version of Bembo has been considerably extended in seven weights, including roman, semibold, bold, and extra bold, and incorporates expert fonts that contain small capitals, ligatures, superior alphabet, and Old-style figures. It should be noted that the style of the digital version is somewhat of a departure again from that of the hot-metal Bembo. There are also two weights of Bembo Schoolbook with bold and italics; and a Bembo Titling with italics. Although conceived as a text typeface, digitization makes it possible to use Bembo as a very effective display font.

Francesco Griffo's romans at work

Hypnerotomachia Poliphili
Produced in 1499, the page on the left is from a bestseller of the Renaissance that shows Griffo's elegant poliphilus type set against the book's woodcut illustrations. The scene shows the triumph of Jupiter and Semele. The page below illustrates how Manutius uses a device for the close of chapters that tapers the lines of text until a point is created by star ornaments. Note the tight word-spacing and interlinear spacing, creating a strong image on the page.

Now

Francesco Griffo's romans at work

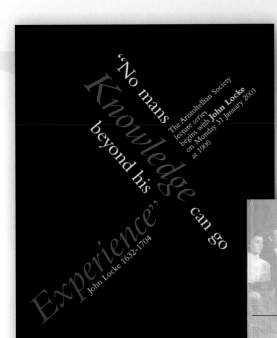

Educational poster
This 2002 student design for the event at the University of London (left) uses Bembo throughout. The digital arrangement plus the large italic and interlocking display types create a dynamic image.

Elegant capitals
This piece of graphic ephemera (right) from 1999 promotes the events at an educational institution. The use of the full forms of Bembo to create a compact typographic design. The open strokes of the letters allow the pale halftone photograph to show through and contrast with the squared-up halftones below.

Bembo usage

Tracking, kerning, and H&Js

When the Monotype Corporation revived Bembo in 1929 it was intended to be a text face. The capitals are generous; the capital "N" is almost the same width as the "M." It has excellent word fit so standard tracking does not require alteration. If it is to be reversed out of black or a color, then there should be a small increase in the tracking.

Text sizes

The ascenders are slightly taller than the capitals, so there is a small x-height and short descenders. In normal circumstances only a little leading is required; 20 percent of body size is sufficient. Bembo was designed originally for printing on a fairly coarse, surfaced paper, so it can look rather light on smooth-coated paper.

Display sizes

Although not intended as a display face, as a digital font with the facility to generate display sizes, this typeface's elegant authority makes a stylish display face at any size. During the 20th century, bold and extra bold have been added to create a family. Reduce tracking incrementally in relation to size.

On-screen display

Screen resolution makes the detailed character of Bembo hard to appreciate. It is best used only for display, as its small x-height and only light stem contrast mean font fidelity below 14-point is compromised by the screen resolution. For Web site design, the character of Bembo is best conveyed within a GIF or JPEG.

CLAUDE GARAMOND *& the French Old-Face*

ABCDEFGHIJKLMNOPQRS
abcdefghiklmnopqrstvwxyz&
abcdefghiklmnopqrstvwxyz&

During the 16th century, French printing gained prominence over that of Italy. The middle years of the century have been called the Golden Age of French book arts.

Claude Garamond
An engraving of Garamond (1480–1561), the typecutter who helped to bring French printing to prominence early in the 16th century.

CLAUDE GARAMOND

Some of the important printers of this period were Simon de Colines, Jean de Tournes, Robert Estienne (son of Henri, the father of the dynasty of printer/publishers), and Geoffroy Tory, whose skills and learning were rewarded by promotion to become the first Imprimeur de Roi, the king's printer. This was a period when the printer still took responsibility for deciding what to print, so that printer/publishers were well-educated in the classics of Greek and Latin literature as well as in their native language.

Claude Garamond's types were among those that supported the advance of French printing. Garamond had been apprenticed to Antoine Augereau, a Protestant printer/scholar who, like Geoffroy Tory, had been instrumental in promoting the use of the humanist Aldine roman types rather than the Gothic blackletter, which still maintained favor with some French printers.

In Paris, Garamond worked for several printers at first, but was taken up by his contemporary Robert Estienne, when Estienne commissioned a set of punches from the ambitious young punchcutter. After his father Henri died, Robert Estienne continued to be trained by Simon de Colines, who had married his widowed mother and taken over responsibility for the Estienne Press. Eventually, in 1526, Robert took over the running of the press from his stepfather and became the royal printer of Hebrew, Latin, and Greek.

Garamond took the opportunity to become independent, and established himself as the leading French typecutter. The new roman that Garamond cut was used in Estienne's edition of *Pharaphrasis in Elegantiarium* by Erasmus, which appeared, together with several other publications in the series, in 1530.

TUVWXYZ

1234567890

1234567890

K

K

Garamond Roman
As can be seen in this comparison, the uppercase letters of Garamond (top) show greater contrast of stroke thickness compared with that of Bembo (above). Note the subtle swelling of the rising arm of the "K," as it meets the serif. Garamond's Roman has a lighter color on the page. The serifs, while being larger, have smaller bracketing than the more austere Aldine Roman.

A HARMONIOUS SET

There is little doubt that Garamond gained inspiration from Francesco Griffo for his own designs. However, Garamond introduced refinements to the Old-face which he maintained and modified over the years. The italics that Griffo had cut for Manutius were only lowercase letters. Garamond took up the idea to cut a companion italic alphabet, with italic capitals that would partner roman fonts, a concept that is now a basic feature of all text faces. The combination and balance of capitals with a lowercase and italic alphabet provided the printer with a comprehensive and harmonious set of letterforms for the first time.

The success of Garamond's types results from their technical brilliance as well as from the quality of the design. His ambition to set up independently and make full use of his skills and connections helped to establish the cutting and casting of type as a specialized skill separate from printing.

After the death of Claude Garamond in 1561, his punches and matrices were sold. The biggest collection was purchased by Christopher Plantin, the French printer/publisher based in Antwerp.

Robert Estienne
Garamond was a trainee of master punchcutter and printer Simon de Colines, who was a generation older.

Contextualizer

Claude Garamond
1480–1561

Garamond revivals

The early-20th-century revivals of Garamond's designs have been subject to some confusion as a result of events in 17th-century France. At this time Jean Jannon, printer for the Calvinist Academy in Sedan, produced an excellent set of matrices. They were rediscovered a century later in the French National Printing House and attributed to Claude Garamond. Later, in 1917, they were accepted as the model for the Garamond designs produced for the American Type Foundry by Morris F. Benton with T. M. Cleland, and in 1922 for those produced by the Monotype Corporation. The italic alphabet, also from the National Printing House, was based on an italic attributed to Robert Granjon. The designs rapidly became classics for book work. However, in 1926 the historian Beatrice Warde discovered a 1621 specimen sheet and was able to make clear the mistaken identity, but it was too late to rename the faces.

Digital versions

In the current versions, the lowercase x-height varys from typefoundry to typefoundry. The Adobe version of 1989 and the Stempel version digitized from the 1925 design are on the small side, allowing for generous descenders. However, the 1977 ITC Garamond, drawn by Tony Stan, has a large x-height, so that the lower case is not immediately recognizable, as it has a distinctly different form to many of the other "Garamond" digital revivals.

Garamond at work

Garamond Title page
A 16th-century title page showing Garamond's types in use, including small capitals and italics with swash capitals, surrounded by an elaborate border composed of columns and foliage.

Garamond at work

What does it cost to send a letter

What does it cost to write and mail a business letter; and how much more would it cost on Crane, the world's finest paper

There's a lot more to sending a business letter than buying a stamp. Add the costs and you will see.

Simple good form
This 2002 direct mail from US manufacturers Crane Paper (above) uses a clean, simple layout of medium-sized Garamond to promote stationery paper.

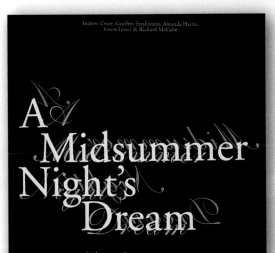

Andrew Cryer, Geoffrey Freshwater, Amanda Harris, Anton Lesser & Richard McCabe

A Midsummer Night's Dream

William Shakespeare

Monday 16 August - Saturday 28 September
The Barbican Theatre, Silk Street, London EC2Y 8DS

Recorded Information Service
071-628 2295/071-628 9760

Theater poster
In this design (left), Garamond is used to overlay a delicate script that evokes the world of magic and fairies.

Garamond usage

Tracking, kerning, and H&Js

Garamond remains a popular book face. With a fairly low contrast of stroke thickness, it is light-colored on the page. Alteration of tracking is necessary only when reversing out of a solid color background. Only standard kerning is required.

Text sizes

The ascenders are slightly taller than the capitals, which means a quite a small x-height. It is a compact typeface and therefore an efficient user of space. Normally only a small amount of leading is required—20% of body size is adequate. Garamond's original typeface was designed for textured paper, so it can look rather light on smooth paper.

Display sizes

Although not originally intended as a display face, digital versions make this possible, its elegant character giving text a polished look. It is important to reduce tracking as the size increases to maintain good word fit. Twentieth century typefounders' revivals have extended the family of Garamond by adding semibold and bold to the basic roman and italic.

On-screen display

Screen resolution makes the detailed form of Garamond difficult to appreciate. Garamond should be used display sizes of 18-point and larger, and for Web site design is best used within a GIF or JPEG.

CHRISTOPHER PLANTIN *& the Netherlands Old-Face*

Christopher Plantin
An engraving of the highly successful French printer.

After the death of Claude Garamond, a large quantity of his punches and matrices were purchased by printer and publisher Christopher Plantin. Plantin was also French, born near Tours in 1520. He had trained and worked as a bookbinder, spending a number of years in Paris and traveling around France.

The Plantin-Moretus Museum of Printing
A general view of part of the Plantin-Moretus Museum in Antwerp (above), once the press room of the Plantin publishing house. The heavy wooden presses on the left are fitted with struts from the ceiling. These steadied the presses as the continuous pulling action of the pressmen meant they were likely to move.

Plantin settled in Antwerp, which was at the time under the rule of the Spanish Habsburgs. After an injury that affected his ability to work as a bookbinder, he turned to printing and publishing in 1555. He quickly gathered around him a group of scholars, linguists and theologians, and proceeded to publish a wide range of scholarly volumes. Although produced in the Netherlands, Plantin's publications were still effectively French. Not only had he been trained in France, but from the start he acquired much of his equipment, materials, and types from France.

Plantin is said to have had as many as 21 presses operating in his workshop when at full capacity, with a team of men to each press, each man carrying out his allotted function: one inking the type, one feeding paper in, one operating the lever to pull the impression, one removing the printed sheet.

Apart from his collection of the acclaimed Garamond types, Plantin was successful enough in his publishing enterprise to be able to commission types from other typefounders, in particular Robert Granjon of Lyon, who was resident in Antwerp also for a period. Granjon provided several of Plantin's civilité types (a cursive type based on the hand of the period, which could be described as a kind of French italic) and the Greek and Syriac for Plantin's master work, the *Polyglot Bible*. The *Polyglot Bible* was a massive eight-volume production, including texts in Hebrew, Greek, Latin, Chaldaic, and Syriac, produced between 1569 and 1572 under the patronage of King Philip II of Spain.

The typecutter Hendrik van den Keere started working for Plantin in 1568 and from 1570 was responsible for the typefoundry work and 40 sets of punches and matrices, which are still with the Moretus-Plantin Museum in Antwerp to this day.

The *Polyglot Bible*
A page from Plantin's mammoth work, the Polyglot Bible *(right), an eight-volume edition containing texts in Hebrew, Greek, Latin, and Chaldaic. Completed in the late 1560s and early 1570s.*

REGNI NEAPOLITANI
PRIVILEGIVM.

PHILIPPVS DEI GRATIA REX
CASTELLÆ, ARAGONVM, VTRIVSQVE
SICILIÆ, HIERVSALEM, VNGARIÆ, DALMATIÆ, ET CROATIÆ, &c.

ANTONIVS Perrenotus, S.R.C.tit. Sancti Petri ad Vincula Preſby-
ter, Cardinalis de Granuela, pręfatæ Regiæ & Catholicæ Maieſtatis
à conſiliis ſtatus, & in hoc Regno locum tenens, & Capitaneus ge-
neralis, &c. Mag^co viro Chriſtophoro Plantino, ciui Antuerpien-
ſi, & præfatæ Catholicæ Maieſtatis Prototypographo fideli Re-
gio, dilecto, gratiam Regiam & bonam voluntatem. Cùm ex præ-
clarorum virorum literis certiores facti ſimus, opus Bibliorum quinque linguarum,
cum tribus Apparatuum tomis, celeberrimum, reique publicę Chriſtianæ vtiliſſimũ,
eiuſdem ſereniſſimæ Maieſtatis iuſſu, ope atque auſpiciis, ad publicam totius Chri-
ſtiani orbis commoditatem & ornamentum, typis longè elegantiſſimis, & præſtan-
tiſſimi viri Benedicti Ariæ Montani præcipua cura & ſtudio. quàm emendatiſſimè
à te excuſum eſſe, eiuſdemq; exemplar ſanctiſſimo Domino noſtro PP. Gregorio XIII.
oblatum, ita placuiſſe, vt præfatæ Maieſtatis ſanctos conatus, & Regi Catholico in
primis conuenientes, ſummopere laudarit, & ampliſſima tibi priuilegia ad hoc opus
tuendum Motu proprio conceſſerit; Nos quoque cum naturali genio impellimur ad
fouendum præclara quæque ingenia, quæ inſigni quopiam conatu ad publica com-
moda promouenda atque augenda aſpirant; primùm quidem longè præclariſſimum
hoc ſuæ Maieſtatis ſtudium, vt verè Heroicum & Ptolomęi, Eumenis, aliorumque
olim conatibus in Bibliothecis inſtruendis eò præſtantius, quòd non vanæ ſtimulo
gloriæ, vt illi, ſed rectæ Religionis conſeruandæ & propagandæ zelo ſuſceptum, meri-
tò ſuſpicientes; deinde eximiam operam doctiſſimi B. Ariæ Montani, ac immortali
laude dignam admirantes, rebuſque tuis, quemadmodũ tuo nomine expetitur, pro-
ſpicere cupientes, ne meritis frauderis fructibus tantæ operæ, & impenſæ, quæ ſumma
ſolicitudine & induſtria in opus ad finem feliciter perducendum à te etiam inſumpta
eſſe accepimus; cumque certò conſtet, opus hoc nunquam hactenus hoc in Regno excuſum eſſe, dignumque ipſo S. ſedis Apoſtolicæ ſuffragio ſit iudicatum vt diuulgetur
ac priuilegiis ornetur. Tuis igitur iuſtiſſimis votis, vt deliberato conſilio, ita alacri &
exporrecta fronte lubenter annuentes; tenore præſentium ex gratia ſpeciali, præfatæ
Maieſtatis nomine, cum deliberatione & aſſiſtentia Regij collateralis conſilij, ſtatui-
mus & decreuimus, ne quis intra viginti annos proximos, a die dat. præſentium dein-
ceps numerandos, in hoc Regno dictum Bibliorum opus, cum Apparatuum tomis
coniunctis, vel Apparatus ipſos, aut eorũ partem aliquam ſeorſum, citra ipſius Chri-
ſtophori, aut cauſam & ius ab ipſo habentis, licentiam imprimere, aut ab aliis impreſ-
ſa vendere, aut in ſuis officinis vel aliàs tenere poſſit. Volentes & decernẽtes expreſsè,
quòd

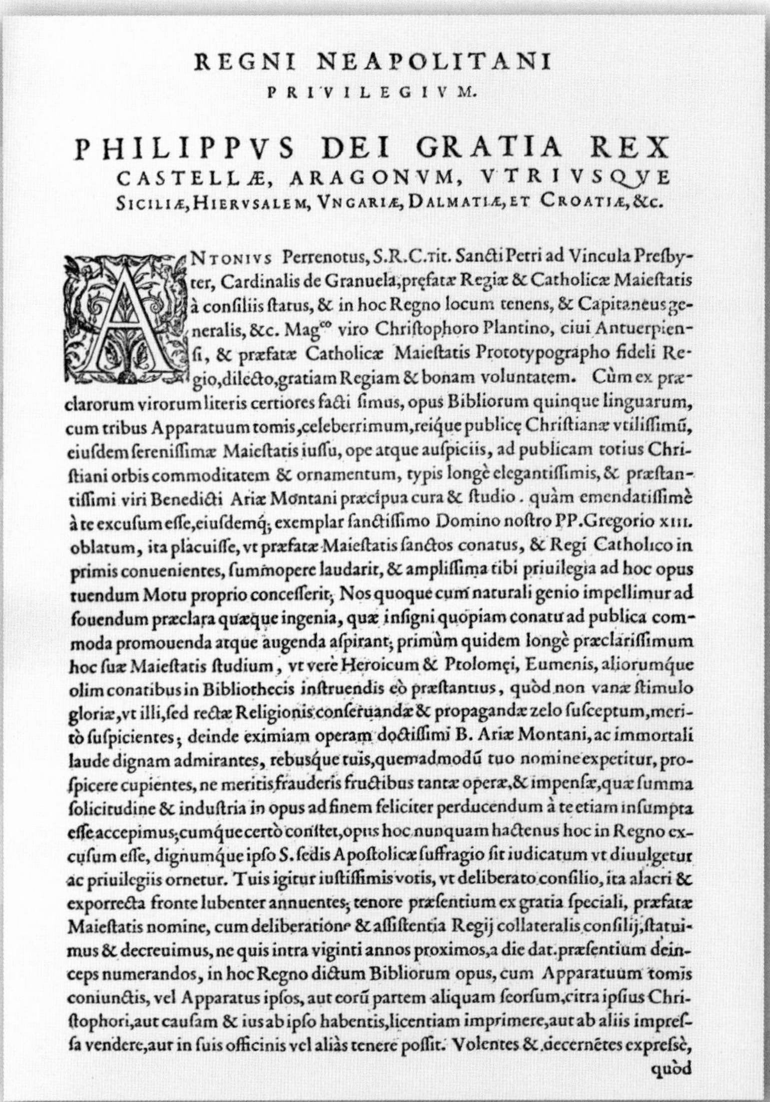

DUTCH RISE TO PROMINENCE

After Plantin's death in 1589, his son-in-law Johannes Moretus continued to run the business, and was succeeded by his son Balathasar. The business remained in the Moretus family until 1867.

The prominence of French printing gave way to the Netherlands largely through the efforts of the Moretus-Plantin dynasty and later, in the 17th century, the Elzevir dynasty. There was also a demand in continental Europe and Britain for the work of a number of remarkable Netherlands typecutters: van den Keere, Christoffel van Dyck, and Dirck Voskens.

The Plantin typeface issued by Monotype in 1913, although named after the printer, was based on a Robert Granjon type used by Plantin's successors. This was found in use in Frankfurt, Germany, and Basle, Switzerland, at the end of the 16th century. Plantin is a stocky face compared with most Old-faces, with a large x-height, which makes it suitable for printing on glossy-coated papers. The current digital range of Plantin includes a light as well as roman. There is also semibold as well as bold, all with accompanying italics, plus a single bold condensed.

Galliard Roman
The Plantin font of today is not a serious representation of Plantin's letterforms. Mathew Carter's Galliard, shown here on the right, is one of the best-known modern interpretations.

ABCDEFGHIJKLMNOPQR
abcdefghijklmnopqrstuvwxyz
1234567890$¢£€¥ƒ 1234567
ABCDEFGHIJKLMNOPQR
abcdefghijklmnopqrstuvwxyzæœ
1234567890$¢£€¥ƒ 123456789

3   The Enlightenment

The demand for books and other reading material increased throughout the 18th century, and the period became one of increasingly widespread enquiry. The ability to read was empowering as it permitted access to knowledge, and the educated members of the population became more confident in themselves and less deferential to the authority of the crown and the church. Belief in the divine right of kings and trust in God was giving way to more independent attitudes.

Benjamin Franklin
An important figure in the American struggle for independence from Britain, Franklin (1706–1790) had worked as a printer and had contacts in France, including other printers. He is shown below conducting his most famous experiment, in which he proved lightning to be electricity.

During the latter part of the 17th century, Isaac Newton had begun to lay the foundations of science as a modern discipline. He discovered the law of gravity, the fact that light is composed of many colors, and he also defined the laws of motion. Humankind was no longer at the center of the universe. By 1705, Newton was President of the Royal Society and the father of modern science.

The attention of philosophers also turned to dealing with the issues thrown up by this new sense of humankind and its surroundings. John Locke published his *Essay Concerning Human Understanding* and *Letters on Tolerance*. In France, similar issues occupied thinkers. Voltaire, the trenchant critic of French authoritarianism, returned to France after a period of exile in Britain and wrote his *Philosophical Letters* (1734), expressing his appreciation of the British way of life. Possibly Voltaire's most famous book today is *Candide* (1758), a satire on Gottfried Leibniz's assertion that the progress of science need not clash with Christian teachings but will result in "the best of all possible worlds." His observation became the refrain of Leonard Bernstein's 1956 musical *Candide*.

Another French philosopher, Charles Louis Montesquieu, wrote his satire *Persian Letters* on French society as observed by foreigners. His treatise on politics, society, and legal issues, *The Spirit of the Law*, became the basis of several liberal constitutions. Yet another major work was published in 1751: the first volume of the *Encyclopedia* or *Analytical Dictionary of Sciences, Arts, and Crafts* edited by Denis Diderot and Jean d'Alembert. The 28 volumes took over 20 years to complete and contained 72,000 entries. The publication caused the committee of the Académie des Sciences some embarrassment, as their *Descriptions of the Arts and Trades* did not appear for another ten years.

Declaration of Independence
This handwritten document shown on the right was first printed by John Dunlap in 1776, set in Caslon Roman.

REVOLUTIONARY DEVELOPMENTS

Humankind's relationship with the environment was changed by far-reaching practical developments. A first step toward the machine age was made in Britain in 1712, when Thomas Newcomen invented and built the first steam engine. Scottish engineer James Watt made improvements to Newcomen's design. There were agricultural advances that led to much greater efficiency: Jethro Tull developed a drill to plant seeds mechanically, while Robert Bakewell made improvements in breeding farm livestock, and Viscount Charles Townsend developed methods of crop rotation and innovations in the production of winter feed for cattle. In 1767, James Hargreaves built the first spinning jenny, a machine that twisted fibers into yarns for weaving, a process previously carried out by hand.

In the visual arts, Sir Joshua Reynolds did much to raise the status of painters and sculptors and he became the first president of the newly chartered Royal Academy of Arts in 1768. Reynold's 15 discourses set out the ideals for academic art, while James Gillray and Thomas Rowlandson produced caricatures of political and social life. The Venetian painter Antonio Canaletto gained an unsurpassed reputation as a landscape artist. He specialized in the then new form of painting the city view.

In 1774, the First Continental Congress was held in Philadelphia and was marked the beginning of the American War of Independence. In 1786, the first performance took place of Mozart's opera *The Marriage of Figaro*, based on Beaumarchais' radical comedy that mocked the upper classes. Finally, in 1789, the storming of the Bastille in Paris marked the beginning of the French Revolution.

William Hogarth
An English painter who trained in London as an engraver, Hogarth (1697–1764) rose to become an important painter of portraits and strongly moralistic genre pictures, The latter include this one from the series The Rake's Progress *(above).*

Samuel Johnson
Johnson (1709–1784, right) is widely regarded as the father of the English dictionary and was a dominant figure in 18th-century literary London. His opinions and wit were recorded by his famous biographer, Boswell in A Life of Samuel Johnson, *1791.*

WILLIAM CASLON *& the English Old-face*

In 1586, the Archbishop of Canterbury and the Bishop of London were empowered by the Privy Council to control the number of printing presses, printers, and apprentices in Oxford, Cambridge, and London.

William Caslon
Caslon (1692–1766, above) was the father of British typography and his work is the typographic embodiment of the English Baroque.

Printing was not allowed elsewhere in England. The restrictions on the number of printing presses and therefore the size of the industry had a damaging effect: the quality of printed work declined, and English printers became dependent on types imported from the Netherlands, either as metal type or as matrices to be cast locally. These restrictions were lifted during the mid-17th century, although censorship remained in place. In the 1670s, however, when Dr John Fell and his committee set about improving print quality at Oxford University, it was still necessary for him to buy a collection of types and punches from Holland for the university's press to use. Due to these restrictions it was natural that William Caslon chose the Dutch Old-face as his model when cutting his first English Old-face types.

Caslon has been called the greatest British typecutter and founder. The establishment of his typefoundry was a landmark in English printing because, with the quality of his types, he was able (almost single-handedly) to eliminate the need for imported Dutch types.

SKILLED CRAFTSMAN

Born in Worcestershire in 1692, Caslon started his working life as an engraver. He set himself up in business engraving hunting guns and cutting punches for bookbinders' tooling. His fine work brought him to the attention of the printers John Watts and William Bowyer, who were impressed with the quality of Caslon's skills—so much so that they offered Caslon financial support to set up a typefoundry. In the same year of 1720, as a result of Caslon's growing reputation, the Society for the Promotion of Christian Knowledge used Caslon in a Psalter in 1725 and a New Testament in 1727, for its overseas mission. At the foot of Caslon's proofs for this font, he added his name cut in a pica roman. Bowyer was so impressed by these few letters that he encouraged Caslon to cut a complete roman font in that style. As a result, Caslon produced a roman and italic font, as well as one of Hebrew that was used by Bowyer for a folio edition, published in 1726.

Caslon cut several other faces required by his patron, Bowyer, including Coptic and other exotic types. It was possibly due to the intensity of his workload that he did not issue a specimen sheet of his types until 1734, 14 years after opening the typefoundry for business.

His designs soon achieved acceptance by many of the major printing houses, including King George's printer, who used his types to the exclusion of others. Caslon's reputation also spread abroad, but his English types marked the end of the historical Old-face. On the European continent the turn of the century had brought about changes in type aesthetics, and by the mid-century in Birmingham, England, John Baskerville was exploring new forms.

Caslon died at the age of 74 in 1766, and the business was continued by his son, William Caslon the second. He was also an excellent craftsman and he maintained his father's standards, expanding the company still further. The Caslon Foundry continued until 1937, when it became part of the Sheffield Foundry, Stephenson, Blake, & Company, which was to become Britain's last metal typefoundry.

Isaac Newton
In laying the foundations of modern science, Newton (1643–1727) was a major influence during the enlightenment and beyond. He defined gravity, and discovered that white light is composed of the color spectrum. The form of his Philosophiae Naturalis Principia Mathematica *(1687) (below), is typical of the publications to appear throughout the enlightenment.*

Contextualizer

William Caslon
1692–1766

The Industrial Revolution

Caslon's typefaces were cut during the growing upheaval of the Industrial Revolution; the movement born in Britain as rapid developments in methods, ideas, and machinery dramatically changed the way people lived.

The Baroque letter

Baroque art featured exaggerated motion and clearly interpreted detail to give a sense of drama and grandeur. The Baroque letter was popular throughout Europe in 17th century, mixing roman and italic letterforms on same line for the first time. Modern fonts classified as Old-face include Elzevir, and Janson Text as well as Caslon.

Caslon Foundry specimen sheet
Caslon was the first internationally known British typefounder. The Caslon Foundry's type specimen sheet (above) did not appear until some ten years after he established his typefoundry.

CASLON: *the Last Old-Face*

abcdefghijklmnopqrstuv

ABCDEFGHIJKLMNO

abcdefghijklmnopqrstuvw

Type ornaments
*A range of boarders
from Caslon's specimen
book of 1764.*

Caslon's first roman rapidly became a success when it appeared in the 1720s. This was largely because it was the first opportunity British printers had to use an unrivaled British typeface instead of those imported from Holland. It is a typeface that has a uniquely friendly individuality, with many quirks and inconsistencies, making it remarkably readable; it has endeared itself to generations of English-speaking printers, publishers, and readers. Indeed, the leading English dramatist George Bernard Shaw insisted that all his books were printed in Caslon. In its stocky geometry, freehand curves, and modest baseline serifs, it maintains the practical qualities that made the Dutch types so popular. The lower case at the x-height have wedge-shaped serifs on "i," "j," "m," "n," and "r," but not on the "u," which has a lighter serif, square to the x-height. The distinct contrast of thick and hairline strokes can seem uneven when examined on individual letters, but strangely, when set in words, this works well.

Caslon became established in the 18th century and spread over the English-speaking world as part of the instruments of colonial rule. When it was first printed in 1776 by John Dunlap, the American Declaration of Independence was typeset in a Caslon type exported to the United States. Caslon's popularity faded for a while at the end of the 18th century because of competition from a new style of face, the transitional, led by Baskerville and Fournier. But in the mid-19th century there was a revival of interest in the Old-face, and it appeared again in the specimen books in 1857. Almost simultaneously, there was a revival in the United States when it was issued by the Philadelphia Foundry of L. J. Johnston.

TWENTIETH-CENTURY CASLON

The popularity of Caslon Old-face is evident from the number of versions available throughout the 20th century. The original Caslon was available from Stephenson, Blake, & Company for handsetting as recently as 2001. There were two hot metal Caslons: Monotype cut a version in 1915 and Linotype cut one in 1921. The ATF Caslon 540 (1905) was an adaption of the Johnston Caslon. The Haas Foundry in Switzerland cast Caslon from original matrices, casting larger sizes in 1944.

wxyz& 1234567890

PQRSTUVWXYZ

xyz& 1234567890

n r
u

Late Old-face
*Caslon's types were
a great achievement
but the last of a line
of Old-faces. These
three lowercase letters
show the heavier,
triangular serif on
the "w" and "r" not
applied to the "u."*

DIGITAL CASLON

There are at least nine digital versions of Caslon available. Most supply a full range of sizes, but Adobe Caslon, designed by Carol Twombly in 1990 and consisting of 20 variants including swash capitals with the italics, is suitable only for text setting, since the design has modified Caslon's original characteristics by reducing the contrasts and increasing the weight of the serifs. It functions well in smaller sizes, but the loss of the unique Caslon character is very noticeable in display sizes. Matthew Carter's Big Caslon is a crisp, geometrically refined design that expresses the contrasting stroke thickness of Caslon with elegance, designed specifically for display work. Linotype's ATF Caslon is a combination of two American designs, Caslon 3 and Caslon 540, and offers a sensible range of weights; these are all identified as roman but Caslon 3 would function well as a bold. ITC Caslon, digitized by Justin Howes, was released in 1998. It consists of four versions of Caslon, each covering a specific range of sizes, and it closely follows Caslon's original metal designs. This is a range for the Caslon connoisseur and is an attempt at following the founder's traditional practice of making modifications to letterforms by way of optical corrections to suit a particular size. Founders 12 is for text based on a pica Caslon, and has noticeably uneven edges and more irregularities than the larger display sizes. Founders 30 is based on two-line English Caslon and 42 on a two-line double pica Caslon. Following 18th-century conventions, there are no bolds, and figures are Old-style (like lower case, they align with the x-height); there are italics and small capitals. ITC also has a Caslon range designed in 1982 by Edward Benguiat. Caslon Classico, designed by Franko Luin in 1993 and available from Linotype, is a modest range of roman and bold, italics, and roman small capitals. Berthold offer two ranges of Caslon: Caslon 471 in regular, and italics, and Caslon Book in regular, medium, and bold with expert fonts. William Caslon is well served by the heirs to his art.

Adobe Caslon™ Regular

24 pt OHamburgefonstiv

36 pt OHamburgefonstiv

48 pt OHamburgefonstiv

60 pt OHamburgefonst

72 pt OHamburgefo

84 pt OHamburge

96 pt OHambur

Adobe Caslon is a trademark of Adobe Systems Incorporated which may be registered in certain jurisdictions. For further information please contact: info@linotype.com

Adobe Caslon
*A specimen sheet of
the digitized Caslon
released in 1990.*

Caslon at work

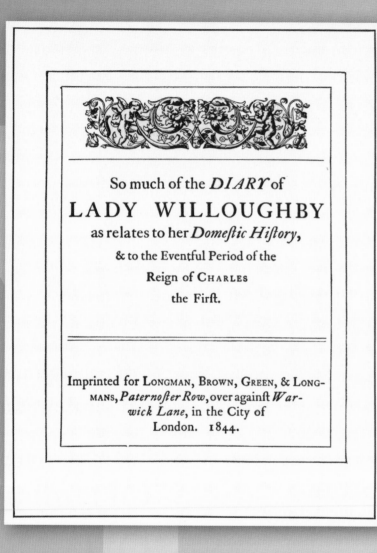

So much of the *DIARY* of
LADY WILLOUGHBY
as relates to her *Domeſtic Hiſtory*,

& to the Eventful Period of the

Reign of CHARLES

the Firſt.

Imprinted for LONGMAN, BROWN, GREEN, & LONG-
MANS, *Paternoſter Row*, over againſt *War-
wick Lane*, in the City of
London. 1844.

Lady Willoughby's Diary
*As the 18th century
became the 19th, Caslon's
Old-face gave way to
the new fashion for the
transitional letterforms
introduced by Fournier and
Baskerville. However, there
were those who valued the
Caslon types. Among these
were the printer Charles
Whittingham and the
publisher William Pickering.
This diary was printed by
Whittingham using Caslon
at the Chiswick Press in
1844, for Longman, Brown,
Green, & Longman in
London. Note the use
of the long "S."*

Lady Willoughby.	77

1641.

her Cheeke by ſome Query reſpecting a particular Piece of Needle-work in hand; and
added, on perceiving the Effect ſhe had produced, ſhe had heard S^r. *Eraſmus de la Fountain* much commend the delicate Paterne:
whereat poore *Margaret* attempted to look up
unconcern'd, but was obliged to ſmile at her
Siſter's Pleaſantry. I was diſcreet, and led the
Converſation back to the Spinning.

The Days paſſe ſmoothly, yet Time ſeemeth
very long ſince my deare *Lord* departed on his
Journey. We heare no News. *Armſtrong* will
perchance gain ſome Tydings at *Colcheſter:*
and I muſt await his Return with ſuch Patience
I can.

Since my little *Fanny's* long Sickneſſe I have
continued the Habit of remaining by her at
night, ſometime after ſhe is in Bed: theſe are
Seaſons peculiarly ſweet and ſoothing; there
ſeemeth ſomething holy in the Aire of the
dimly lighted *Chamber*, wherein is no Sound
heard

Now

Caslon at work

Caslon Italic
This book jacket to the left uses predominantly Caslon italics in a combination of sizes and color to give a sense of action.

Caslon Style
This 21st-century magazine page uses the elegant digital Caslon Italic design of Matthew Carter for an effective display.

Caslon usage

Tracking, kerning, and H&Js

Caslon is an excellent text face, following the Dutch style of Old-face that tended toward greater contrast of stem thickness than earlier Old-faces. Close word spacing is preferable, and no additional tracking. Caslon was designed to print on a coarser surface than modern coated paper.

Text sizes

In the last century Caslon was a greatly loved typeface for lengthly texts. Adobe Caslon fulfills this role with a useful range of weights, and the typeface prints well on smooth, matt-coated paper. As Caslon has a good sized x-height, it can be leaded generously, although generally it is not. Sizes below 9-point will benefit from minimally increased tracking.

Display sizes

The true splendor of Caslon can be appreciated at display size. ITC Founder's Caslon offers three fonts of authentic Caslon especially for display. Matthew Carter's crisply engineered Big Caslon, although a single weight, has some ligatures that add elegance to a design that does not have the bookish quality associated with Caslon. Adobe Caslon offers semibold and bold weights, including two of swash capitals that can be also used as initial capitals.

On-screen display

As a text face, Caslon has a comparatively good-sized x-height but a strong contrast between the thick and thin stems, so it is best used for display only and should not be used in sizes below 18-point. Owing to the screen resolution, much of the type's character cannot be appreciated. Thus, if it is essential to use Caslon, it is best displayed within a GIF or JPEG.

THE KING'S ROMAN: *The Transition Begins*

The King's Roman
Grandjean's types for the French King Louis XIV, shown below, were first used in 1702, although the complete range was not finished until 1745.

Although William Caslon's typefaces met with success in Britain, they were based on the types of the 16th century. As Caslon's typefoundry expanded, almost simultaneously there was a development in France that moved type design into a new age; this was the first of the transitional typefaces.

In 1692, Louis XIV of France commissioned a new collection of types to be created for the exclusive use of the *Imprimerie Royale*. A committee was appointed by the *Académie des Sciences* to supervise this project, under the leadership of Jacques Jaugeon.

The formation of a committee to consider the requirements of a typeface was a break with the traditions of past centuries. These were the early years of the new scientific age, and the committee studied a considerable quantity of writing on letterforms and type from previous generations, including those of Albrect Dürer and Geofroy Tory, as well as contemporary writing masters. The results of their deliberations were drawn using a grid of 2,304 small squares,

to determine the proportions of each letter. A series of copper plates engraved with the final letters was executed between 1695 and 1718 as the committee's work proceeded slowly. The calligraphic flow, or the forms echoing the movement of the broad pen, was no longer evident: these forms were determined by mathematics rather than craft.

Jaugeon's committee took some time to agree on the requirements of the new Royal type. The first cutting of the punches was entrusted to Philippe Grandjean de Fouchy, a typecutter with a growing reputation, and his assistant Jean Alexandre. Work started on cutting the first punches in 1693 and continued until 1745. Grandjean and Jaugeon seem to have had disagreements from time to time during this period, because Grandjean was not altogether convinced by the mathematical certainty of the forms as presented on the copper plates. This point of friction and other revisions resulted in punches being destroyed and others remade. Among the issues tackled

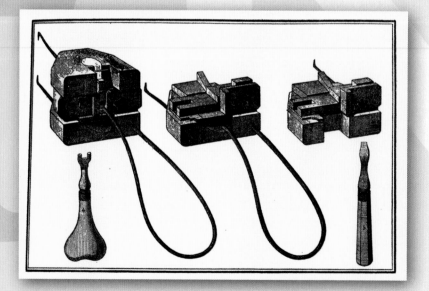

The typecaster's mold
This engraving to the right illustrates the typefounder's mold used in the 17th and 18th centuries. The matrix was fitted into the mold, which could be adjusted to receive any letter width.

by the committee was the rationalizing of type body sizes. A system was devised to standardize a unit of type measurement based on the *pied du roi*, the unit of linear measurement at the time. This made it possible to establish collections of types with interrelated body sizes—an important rationalization for letterpress printing, which was not fully implemented in France until 1775.

ROMAIN DU ROI

When completed, the resulting type design, *Romain du Roi* (King's Roman), consisted of 21 sizes of roman and italics, and 21 roman and italic initial letters—a total of 84 fonts. The serif brackets are less prominent than on Old-face types. Ascenders are designed with serifs on both sides at the head of the stem, adding horizontal emphasis. The contrast between thick and thin strokes is more pronounced compared to the types of Garamond and his school, and the overall appearance is of a lighter weight than Old-face. The engraved plates show that a sloped roman was intended rather than the eventual cursive italic. It has been said that the design appears to be influenced by engraving rather than calligraphy.

Recent research suggests that the work the committee undertook on the creation of a new typeface was only the beginning of a more ambitious project. The intention seems to have been to produce a kind of database for the *Descriptions of Arts and Trades*, but the committee's slow progress rendered it unable to complete the project before Diderot and d'Alembert published their encyclopedia in the 1750s containing similar information. Not until 1761 did *Descriptions of the Arts and Trades* appear in 73 parts, although a section on printing and allied trades was not included.

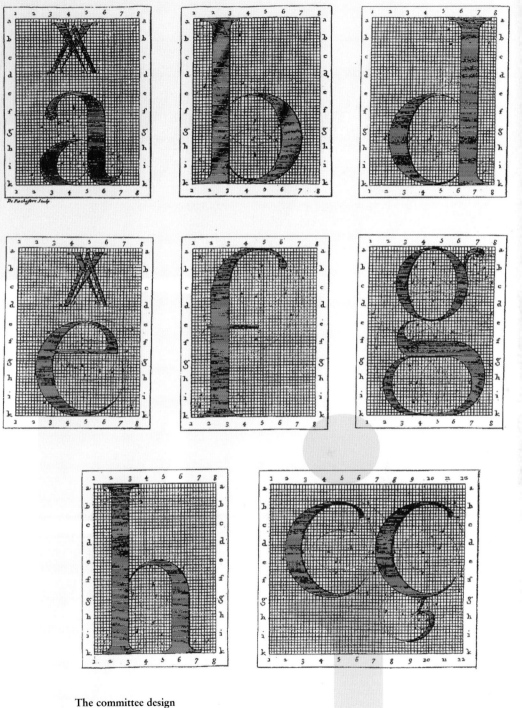

The committee design
Engraved plates of each letter design were prepared to show how its individual shape related to the grid.

PIERRE SIMON FOURNIER *& the Point System*

The new *Romain du Roi* had many admirers, among them the typefounder Pierre Simon Fournier (1712–1768), known as "the younger." He later claimed that his business was the first in France to carry out every aspect of typefounding: designing, cutting punches, striking matrices, making molds, and casting type. Fournier was a very close contemporary of Caslon.

Heavenly typefoundry
The engraved frontispiece shown above is from the second volume of Fournier's Manule Typographique, *printed in 1766.*

Fournier's transitional
A specimen of the 1925 revival of the French founder's transitional roman (right).

Unlike Caslon, Fournier was born into a family of typefounders and printers. His father Jean-Claude had been the manager of the Paris typefoundry LeBé for almost 30 years. His older brother Jean-Pierre Fournier (1706–1783), known as "the elder," was a typecutter and founder who bought the LeBé in 1730. His second brother François was a printer in Auxerre, the birthplace of his father.

Pierre Simon Fournier had studied drawing as a child, which was most likely the beginning of his attraction to letterforms. At first he worked for his older brother at the typefoundry, and as he gained experience he was allowed to engrave punches for capital letters (large initial letters normally cut from wood). In 1736 Fournier set up in business in his own right. He quickly gained a reputation for his technical brilliance as a typecutter and founder, and for the technical innovations he introduced. As a type designer he was not an innovator; his ability lay in the adaption and developments he made to the ideas of others. This accounts for his appreciation of the *Romain du Roi* types, which he emulated despite the king's prohibition.

supreme, and the *éditions à tirage restreint* almost without exception employ the wood engraving. For an example of a most successful book illustrated with fine new engravings, the collector may be referred to André Gide's *La Tentative Amoureuse* with the compositions of Marie Laurencin, published by the "Nouvelle Revue Francaise" in 1923. In nearly every respect this fine French book offers its possessor a greater interest than that yielded by the banal and bankrupt period typography given us by too many London publishers.

MEASUREMENT SYSTEM

In 1737, Fournier began to formulate a system of comparative type body sizes. The typeface body sizes of early typefounders were not standardized; founders cast their type on bodies of their own specification. Any given typeface was generally only cut in a limited number of sizes. Names were used to give an indication of size, some were derived from a historic publication in which the type of that size had first been used: for example, Cicero, the continental 12-point, is said to originate from Fust & Schoeffer's edition of Cicero's *De Oratore*, printed in a type close

Pierre Simon Fournier
An engraved portrait
(right) of the typefounder
shortly after he had
began to formulate his
type-sizing system.

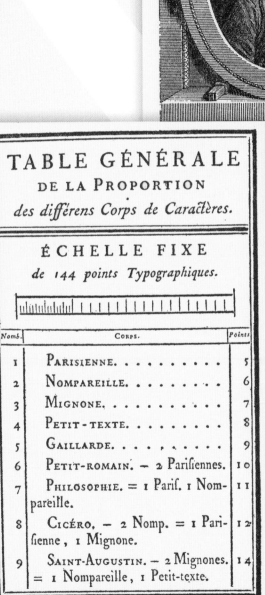

to 12 Didot points in about 1466. Other examples are Brevier, a size between 7.7- and 7.9-point, and Great Primer, a size between 16.6- and 16.9-point.

Fournier based his standard on two inches; each inch divided up into 12 lines and each line into six typographic points, making 144 typographic points overall. Therefore two *nonpareils* (a *nonpareil* being equivalent to six points) equals one Cicero. This offered a measurement system that was of great practical benefit, although it was not taken up by other foundries for another decade or so.

Fournier's most remarkable achievement, and the culmination of many years dedicated to the perfection of his art of typography, was his two-volume *Manuel Typographique*. The preface to the first volume, published in 1764, was set in his remarkable italics. The following pages contained example after example of types set in an elegant display of the typography of the period, many borrowed from his brother's typefoundry collection, including a number of large, simple initial letters not commonly available. Also displayed, with great elegance and refinement, were a large variety of typographic ornaments modified to the taste of the day. These were intended to replace the copperplate engravings used by many printers.

Fournier's two-volume set explained the mysteries of the practice and art of typefounding and was the most authoritative publication available at the time. Volume II appeared in 1766, two years before he died (from what some have described as overwork). In a span of 28 years he had cut over 80 fonts of type, as well as carrying out his duties managing the daily work of the typefoundry.

Type sizing
Fournier spent many years devising a system of interrelated type sizes, which he put into practice in his own typefoundry. The chart (left) explained his ideas.

BASKERVILLE *& Typography as an Art Form*

John Baskerville
A true perfectionist, Baskerville (1706–1775, above) took great pains with his type designs.

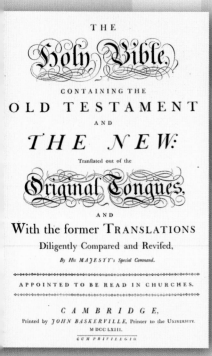

Cambridge University Press bibles
Baskerville achieved one of his dearest wishes in 1758: the opportunity to print bibles and prayer books for Cambridge University Press, an example of which is shown above.

During his lifetime John Baskerville was considered something of an eccentric, and in Britan his ideas on type design were not met with much enthusiasm initially. Some critics even suggested that his type was bad for the eyes. However, in continental Europe his innovations were received with greater appreciation.

John Baskerville was born in Worcestershire, England in 1706 and moved to Birmingham at the age of 19, where he trained as a writing master and stone engraver. After some years, he was able to invest in the manufacture of "Japanned Goods," which utilized a method of varnishing furniture, screens, and smaller items such as tea trays and snuff boxes to achieve a hard, brilliant finish. Baskerville found success in this very lucrative activity and after a number years achieved financial security, becoming a established figure in Birmingham. In 1750, his achievements allowed him to turn his attention to printing, and he set up a printing press at the age of 44.

Baskerville's typeface, cut by his employee John Handy, was completed after many false starts owing to Baskerville's perfectionism. The complete set of punches took approximately three years to complete. His first book, and edition of classic poetry by Virgil, appeared in 1757. In his striving for perfection Baskerville explored ways of improving the printing press, to make it capable of greater precision, more subtle impressions, and the printing of more delicate types. He also devised improvements in the quality of his printing ink. He had paper woven to his specification, he developed a method of further smoothing the paper, and he lent a brilliance to type by passing the printed sheets between heated copper plates. With this attention to detail Baskerville was able to produce books of great elegance.

BASKERVILLE'S LEGACY

Baskerville's perfectionism tended to hinder his financial success. Shortly before he died he tried to sell the printing press and his punches, without success. After he died, his widow maintained the business for a while, but eventually sold the complete Baskerville typefoundry to the French Pierre Augustin Caron de Beaumachais in 1779. Beaumachais was a playwright, secret agent, and

ABCDEFGHIJKLMN
abcdefghijklmnopqrstu

The Psalter
From the Book of Common Prayer, *printed by Baskerville in 1760 for Cambridge University, England.*

John Baskerville
1706–1775

The transitional letterform

The general characteristics of Baskerville are the full, open and generous letterforms that give the page a light gray appearance. The transitional face reflects the influence of the copperplate engraver of the period. Possibly the most distinctive capital is the "Q," with its sweeping tail that tucks under the following letter. In the original metal it would actually rest on the shoulder below the following letter and would cause a clash if the next letter had a descender. The lowercase has a number of other identifying characteristics: the open loop of the "g" is unmistakable, the cross bar of the "e" is high above the center, providing a generous open counter below, and the "J" has a tail which curves below the baseline to create a descender.

American neoclassicism

Benjamin Franklin, the printer, inventor, and politician who helped draw up the American Declaration of Independence and Constitution, was a great admirer of the Baskerville typeface. The clean lines and easy symmetry of American neoclassical federal architecture shares the same style as that of the typeface, in that both enjoy a sense of delicate order and simple, uncluttered elegance.

visitor to the London house of John Wilkes (a friend of Baskerville). He was also a friend of Benjamin Franklin and supporter of American independence from the British king. He acquired the contents of the Baskerville typefoundry with the intention of printing the collected works of the French enlightenment philosopher, Voltaire, whose work was prohibited in France.

Beaumachais was also the author of *The Barber of Seville* and *The Marriage of Figaro*, better known today as the 18th-century operas by Rossini and Mozart respectively. The surviving 2,750 punches from Baskerville's original collection was presented to Cambridge University Press in England, in 1953, after being lost for many years.

OPQRSTUVWXYZ
vwxyz& 1234567890

Baskerville at work

PUBLII VIRGILII

MARONIS

BUCOLICA,

GEORGICA,

ET

AENEIS.

BIRMINGHAMIAE:

Typis JOHANNIS BASKERVILLE,

MDCCLVII.

Baskerville's Virgil
After several years of experimentation, Baskerville was satisfied with his design. The punches were cut by John Handy, under Baskerville's close supervision. In 1757, his first printed book appeared, a Latin volume of Virgil (left).

Aeneid
Baskerville's typography was influenced by a revival of interest in the classical. His page layout below has a pure simplicity, with letter-spaced capitals and generous margins. Such simplicity needs great attention to the details of proportion

P. VIRGILII MARONIS

AENEIDOS

LIBER SEXTUS.

Sıc fatur lacrymans: claffique immittit habenas,
Et tandem Euboicis Cumarum allabitur oris.
Obvertunt pelago proras: tum dente tenaci
Ancora fundabat naves, et litora curvæ
5 Prætexunt puppes. juvenum manus emicat ardens
Litus in Hefperium: quærit pars femina flammæ
Abftrufa in venis filicis: pars denfa ferarum
Tecta rapit, filvas; inventaque flumina monftrat.
At pius Aeneas arces, quibus altus Apollo
10 Præfidet, horrendæque procul fecreta Sibyllæ   {que
Antrum immane, petit: magnam cui mentem animum-
Delius infpirat vates, aperitque futura.
Jam fubeunt Triviæ lucos, atque aurea tecta.
Dædalus, ut fama eft, fugiens Minoia regna,
15 Præpetibus pennis aufus fe credere cœlo,
Infuetum per iter gelidas enavit ad Arctos;
Chalcidicaque levis tandem fuperaftitit arce.
Redditus his primum terris, tibi, Phœbe, facravit
Remigium alarum; pofuitque immania templa.
20 In foribus lethum Androgeo: tum pendere poenas
                                              Cecropidæ

P. VIRGILII AENEIDOS LIB. VI. 235

Cecropidæ jufli (miferum) feptena quotannis
Corpora natorum, ftat ductis fortibus urna.
Contra elata mari refpondet Gnofia tellus:
Hic crudelis amor tauri, fuppoftaque furto
25 Pafiphae, miftumque genus, prolefque biformis
Minotaurus ineft, Veneris monumenta nefandæ.
Hic labor ille domus, et inextricabilis error.
Magnum Reginæ fed enim miferatus amorem
Dædalus, ipfe dolos tecti, ambagefque refolvit.
30 Cæca regens filo veftigia, tu quoque magnam
Partem opere in tanto, fineret dolor, Icare, habeores.
Bis conatus erat cafus effingere in auro:
Bis patriæ cecidere manus. quin protinus omnia
Perlegerent oculis; ni jam præmiffus Achates
35 Afforet, atque una Phœbi Triviæque facerdos,
Deiphobe Glauci; fatur quæ talia Regi:
    Non hoc ifta fibi tempus fpectacula pofcit.
Nunc grege de intacto feptem mactare juvencos
Præftiterit, totidem lectas de more bidentes.
40 Talibus affata Aenean (nec facra morantur
Juffa viri) Teucros vocat alta in templa Sacerdos.
Excifum Euboicæ latus ingens rupis in antrum;
Quo lati ducunt aditus centum, oftia centum:
Unde ruunt totidem voces, refponfa Sibyllæ.
45 Ventum erat ad limen, quum Virgo, Pofcere fata
Tempus, ait: Deus, ecce, Deus. Cui talia fanti
Ante fores, fubito non vultus, non color unus,
Non comtæ manfere comæ; fed pectus anhelum,
Et rabie fera corda tument: majorque videri,
50 Nec mortale fonans; afflata eft numine quando
Jam propiore Dei. Ceffas in vota precefque

G g 2   Tros,

Baskerville at work

"WHEN I READ A GOOD BOOK I WISH THAT LIFE WERE THREE THOUSAND YEARS LONG."

Ralph Waldo Emerson

www.waterstones.co.uk

W

Bookseller publicity material
To the left, this promotional bookmark of the 1990s makes good use of the formality of an arrangement of Baskerville's generous capitals.

Film company
The German film production company Expofilm has combined Baskerville Roman and italic for their eye-catching, yet restrained logotype, shown above, right.

Concert programs
Monotype digital Baskerville is used as text and display for these two concert programs on the right. The type's form works effectively with the period illustration.

Baskerville usage

Tracking, kerning, and H&Js

Baskerville works well for publicity material and remains a popular bookface. Its generous x-height and open letterforms make it very readable. Standard tracking is good for most situations, and this is also the case for kerning. Baskerville, size for size, will occupy more space than Garamond and Bembo.

Text sizes

Ascenders align with the capitals and have a well-proportioned x-height. Baskerville can be leaded more generously than a standard 20 percent of body size, if desired. It is at its best on smooth-surfaced paper, but it also functions, albeit less well, on rougher paper.

Display sizes

Baskerville exhibits a warm elegance when used in display sizes. The capitals can stand some increased letter-spacing, which should be done visually, but reducing tracking as the text increases with size will provide better word form.

On-screen display

As with many serif typefaces it is not possible to fully appreciate individual detail on screen. Baskerville is best used as display text within a GIF or JPEG.

THE DIDOT FAMILY *& the Modern Face*

François Ambroise Didot
Above is a portrait of the father of Pierre and Firmin Didot, François Ambroise Didot (1730–1804). He established what became known as the Didot Point System, a type-sizing system still in use today.

In the later part of the 18th century, the Didot dynasty was an important presence in French printing. The patriarch of this family of remarkable printers, publishers, typecutters, and papermakers was François Didot (1689–1757), printer and bookseller. Both his sons, François Ambroise and Pierre François, made significant contributions to the development of French printing.

François Ambroise (1730–1804) was a highly skilled printer and typefounder, and he introduced France to the fine-surfaced paper favored by Baskerville. He was commissioned in 1783 by Louis XVI to produce an elegant collection of classical French authors. The types were cut by his former apprentice Pierre-Louis Vaflard to François Ambroise's specification, which expressed the classical mode.

François Ambroise established the Didot point system, the type body-sizing method that had first been contemplated by the *Académie des Sciences* in the 1690s and developed subsequently by Fournier. François Ambroise standardized the point at 72 points to the French inch, and with royal authority Didot's rationalization became the accepted standard in France by the end of the century. When the metric system was introduced by Napoleon in 1801, however, Didot tried to adapt his system, without success— another change so soon was unacceptable to printers and foundries. When the grandson of

Typecasting machine
The engraving shows the machine invented by Henri Didot, son of Pierre François Didot. It was taken over by his nephew Marcellini Legrand and patented in 1829. One of these machines was taken to London by the typefounder Louis Pouchée a few years later.

Benjamin Franklin, the American scientist and diplomat, wished to take up an apprenticeship in printing, it was François Ambroise that Franklin recommended he contact.

A FAMILY BUSINESS

François Ambroise's two sons, Pierre and Firmin, both continued the family business. Pierre took over the running of the printing office and Firmin distinguished himself as a typefounder. While still working for his father in 1784, he had cut punches for a letterform that has since been claimed to be the first Modern type. His design reduced serifs and the thin strokes to fine lines, and increased the contrast of the thick strokes. Fermin printed his work on smooth-surfaced, woven paper, which was possible through improvements in the presswork. Firmin's father proudly used his son's creation for a fine edition of the Renaissance poet Tasso's *Gerusalemme Liberta*.

Pierre's printing and publishing skills were admired greatly, so that his printing office was allocated premises in the Louvre. From this location, he produced a series of elegantly illustrated volumes of French and Latin classics known as *Editions du Louvre*. In 1818 he bought, from the Beaumarchais family, the sets of punches for 22 Baskerville types.

Firmin's two sons, Ambroise Firmin and his brother Hyacinthe, maintained the publishing side of the family firm as Firmin Didot Brothers into the 19th century. Pierre Didot's son Henri was highly regarded for his cutting of microscopic types. His brother Saint-Léger, a paper manufacturer, was responsible for supporting the early developments of a papermaking machine, later perfected in England.

Firmin Didot gained great prominence for the quality of his types and they represented the cool elegance of the neoclassical age in France. He was also an inspiration to others, particularly the great genius of the Modern letterform, the Italian printer Giambattista Bodoni. Didot was made director of the typefoundry of the *Imprimerie Impériale* by Napoleon, and died in 1836 having received many honors.

Firmin Didot
A page from Didot's prospectus showing his version of the Modern Roman; this was to become the style of the 19th-century text face.

Horace Flacci
A page from Pierre Didot's 1799 edition of Horace, *the Roman poet and satirist, 65–68 BC. This gives an example of the vertically stressed French Modern type style.*

QUINTI
HORATII FLACCI
CARMINUM
LIBER QUARTUS.

ODE I.
AD VENEREM.

Intermissa, Venus, diu
Rursus bella moves. Parce, precor, precor!
Non sum qualis eram bonæ
Sub regno Cinaræ. Desine, dulcium
Mater sæva Cupidinum,
Circa lustra decem flectere mollibus
Iam durum imperiis. Abi
Quo blandæ iuvenum te revocant preces.

167. *Page of folio Horace: Pierre Didot, Paris, 1799*
(reduced)

LE VINGT ET UN.

Couplets chantés par une des élèves
DE MADAME HÉMART,
DONT LE PENSIONNAT EST ÉTABLI RUE DE LA PÉPINIÈRE.

Un beau modèle est sous nos yeux;
C'est Minerve, c'est la prudence:
Qu'il seroit pour nous glorieux
D'en bien prendre la ressemblance!
Saisissons cet ensemble heureux,
Et ces détails remplis de grace:
Le succès, quoique un peu douteux,
Peut favoriser notre audace.

Oui, Madame, à la Vérité
Rendons cet hommage sincère,
Nous trouvons en vous la bonté
Et les tendres soins d'une mère.

GIAMBATTISTA BODONI *& the Modern Face*

Giambattista Bodoni
Above is an engraved portrait of Italy's most celebrated type designer and printer. Bodoni (1740 –1813) was creator of the Modern typeface that still bears his name.

The Manuale Tipografico
To the right is a page from Bodoni's master work, which contained specimens of his enormous collection of types, and his views on the art of type design, printed in 1788. The second volume was published posthumously by his wife in 1818, five years after his death.

The brilliant printer and punchcutter who, more than anyone, brought the Modern face to the height of elegance and sophistication was the Italian, Giambattista Bodoni. The typeface classified as Modern reached a peak of perfection in the late 18th century, although as a style it remained popular throughout the 19th century.

By the end of the 18th century Modern itself had come under attack as a poor face, being described as an adulterated construct that was lacking the qualities for good legibility, and so began its fall from favor. However, the Modern letterform at the close of the 18th century was one created by the aesthetics and technical refinements of a new Classical age, far from the calligraphically-derived forms of the Renaissance.

Bodoni was born in Saluzzo, northern Italy, in 1740. He was the son of a printer, so he came into contact with printing at an early age, and soon picked up skill in the practice of engraving woodblocks. At the age of 18, he became a compositor in the Vatican Printing Office in Rome. He was ambitious and quick to learn, and having shown an interest in Oriental languages, he was put in charge of the Vatican Oriental typefaces. Many of these had been cut some two centuries earlier by such names as Garamond and Grandjean, and they now required organizing and cataloging, since they were in a bad state of neglect. It was this experience that broadened Bodoni's interest in letterforms. He took great pleasure in this work, at times designing and cutting typographic ornaments for use in the department.

GIAMBATTISTA BODONI

A CHI LEGGE.

Eccovi i saggi dell'industria e delle fatiche mie di molti anni consecrati con veramente geniale impegno ad un'arte, che è compimento della più bella, ingegnosa, e giovevole invenzione degli uomini, voglio dire dello scrivere, di cui è la stampa la miglior maniera, ogni qual volta sia pregio dell'opera far a molti copia delle stesse parole, e maggiormente quando importi aver certezza che

Bodoni italic
*A page from
Signora Bodoni's*
Manuale Tipografico,
Parma, 1818.

FROM CRAFTSMAN TO ARTIST

John Baskerville's reputation and printing
achievements had reached Italy, and in 1768,
at the age of 28, Bodoni decided that he should
travel to England and meet Baskerville for
himself. However, when preparing for his journey
to Birmingham in Britain, he fell sick with
malaria and was forced to spend time recovering
at his family home in Saluzzo. It was while
convalescing that he received a proposal from
the Duke of Parma, who had learned of Bodoni
from contacts at the Vatican. The Duke was the
patron of a library and academy of art in Parma.
and he was planning to increase his prestige by
setting up a printing office with the intention of
printing fine books. He asked Bodoni to become
the director, which Bodoni was keen to do. He
started work at the Stamperia Reale, Parma, in
1768, and would spend the rest of his working
life there. The first types he chose to print with
were the transitional types of Pierre Simon
Fournier. However, Bodoni was ambitious, and
soon designed his own types that fully expressed
his concept of elegance. These were demonstrated
in his specimen book, prepared in 1771.

Large capitals
A page from the the
Manuale Tipografico
*showing the use of the
largest and smallest of
Bodoni's collection of
roman and italic capitals.*

Contextualizer

*Giambattista
Bodoni*
1740–1813

Patronage and sponsorship

The prestige of the Vatican's
Propaganda Fide printing house
and the Duke of Parma's printing
office suited Bodoni's perfectionist,
scholarly inclinations, and allowed
him to elevate the letterform to
an art in his work. He labored
endlessly to refine the design of his
neoclassical and romantic fonts,
safe in the knowledge that his
patronage allowed him to disregard
all commercial considerations.

Form over function

The vertical strokes of the letters
contrast dramatically with the thin
serifs and horizontal strokes—a style
inherent to Bodoni's letterforms.
The typefaces lack the rhythmic,
calligraphic flow of the Renaissance
forms, but have a static formality,
which can be at the expense of the
text's readability. Bodoni was no
scholar, yet his books were published
as objects of artistic merit in their
own right.

abcdefghijklmnopqrstuvw
ABCDEFGHIJKLMNOP

BODONI

B*B*

TYPEFOUNDRY AMSTERDAM

Typefoundry publicity
In the early 20th century Bodoni's elegant, delicately hairlined forms returned to favor, and every typefoundry was required to offer a version of Bodoni in its catalog.

Punchcutting for typefaces with such fine serifs required enormous skill, not only in cutting, but also in striking matrices and casting. Bodoni would plan each project in detail, often cuttiing new punches for each project, rather than using his existing stock. This often required months of thought, interspersed with test cuttings and castings, until he was satisfied. This was possibly Bodoni's greatest luxury, as he had the comfort of knowing that he was not working to commercial demands.

Bodoni was no scholar, although among his printed titles were many of the classics of great literature: Horace in 1791, Virgil in 1793, Catullus in 1794, and Homer's *Iliad* in 1808. Bodoni's main concern was the perfection of his book concepts. In 1810, he presented Napoleon with a copy of Homer's *Iliad* printed on vellum. He would also print for outside commissions, with the Duke's agreement, since this raised the profile of the Duke of Parma as well as that of his printer. From 1791, Bodoni was printing Greek and Latin editions for a London bookseller, James Edwards.

WORKS OF ART

Bodoni's goal was to produce spectacular visual experiences for his reader; he created brilliant examples of the skills of punchcutting and presswork that were to became objects of great fascination for their aristocratic owners. His books were objects of great typographic beauty

xyz& 1234567890

QRSTUVWXYZ

that were seldom read, rather they were collected and admired in themselves as works of art.

Bodoni died in 1813 before the second edition of his *Manuale Tipografico*, which was issued by his widow in 1818. This contained specimens of his beloved Modern typefaces; all, he claimed, planned and cut by himself. The book held over 200 typefaces in a variety of sizes.

Bodoni Ultra Bold
Below is a typefoundry promotional display of Bodoni with the dominating presence of Bodoni Ultra Bold framing the range of sizes.

Hairline Serifs
Compared with the more organic forms of an Old-face, the unbracketed hairline serifs of Bodoni are thrown into strong contrast, as shown to the right.

IJKLMN*O*PQRS*T*U*V*WXY*Z*

BODONI SEMIBOLD

Balanced
Melodia so
Here this line
Unas melodias
Here are lines with
Melodia sostenida con
This large range of types
Una melodia sostenida con
This large range of a carefully
Es una melodia sostenida con un
This large range of carefully balance
Es una melodia sostenida, con un tema
This large range of carefully balanced grades of boldness

ABCDEFGHIJ
KLMNOPQRS
TUVWXYZ&ç
abcdefghijkl
mnopqrstuvw
xyzç.,:;'"·-*/!?
1234567890†§

BODONI ITALIC

This large range of carefully balanced grades of boldness is
Es una melodia sostenida, con un tema sostenido, sostenida

Es una melodia sostenida, con un tema vari
This large range of carefully balanced gr
Es una melodia sostenida, con un tema
This large range of carefully balan
Es una melodia sostenida con un
This large range of carefully
Es una melodia sostenida,
This large range with
Con una melodia

ABCDEFGHIJ
KLMNOPQRS
TUVWXYZ&ç
abcdefghijkl
mnopqrstuvw
xyzç.,:;'"·-/!?*
1234567890†§

BODONI SEMIBOLD ITALIC

Here we show so
Melodias con un tema
This large range of care
Es una melodia sostenida,
This large range of carefully
Es una melodia sostenida, con un
This large range of carefully balan
Es una melodia sostenida, con un tema
This large range of carefully balanced grades of bold
Es una melodia sostenida, con un tema sostenida, sostenido

ABCDEFGHIJ
KLMNOPQRS
TUVWXYZ&ç
abcdefghijkl
mnopqrstuvw
xyzç.,:;'"·-/!?*
1234567890†§

BODONI BOLD

This large range of carefully balanced grades of
Es una melodia sostenida, con un tema var
This large range of carefully balance
Es una melodia sostenida con un
This large range of carefully
Con una melodia sostenida
This large range of cares
Una melodia sostenida
This large range so
Con unas melodias
This large rang
Es una melo
Here come
Melodias
Balance

ABCDEFGHIJ
KLMNOPQRS
TUVWXYZ&ç
abcdefghijkl
mnopqrstuvw
xyzç.,:;'"·-*/!?
1234567890†§

BODONI BOLD ITALIC

Here we
Con tema
Violon and
Es una melo
Fine violon has
Melodia con un te
This large range so
Melodia con un tema?
This large range of a car
Con una melodia sostenida
This large range of a carefully
Es una melodia sostenida, con un
This large range of carefully balance
Es una melodia sostenida, con un tema vari
This large range of carefully balanced grades of

m n o p q r s t u v w *x y z* & *1 2 3 4 5 6 7 8 9 0*

Bodoni at work

BODONI *a famous type face, cut by Giambattista Bodoni who was active as a printer and designer successively in Rome & Parma, has developed itself in the course of time into a complete series of the same magnificence and charm which marks the original.*

TANTA EST HOC TEMPORE in toto terrarum orbe linguarum varietas, ut qua ætate hominum animi ad mutuam intelligentiam et societatem inter se ineundam impensius feruntur, graviora eorum studiis impedimenta obstare videantur communi quodam fato

Immortal Bodoni
Although the popularity of Modern types declined towards the end of the 19th century, the early 20th century saw a restoration of Bodoni's refined creations to a position of honour in printing houses throughout Europe and the United States, and reproductions of his types became the personification of style.

You love flowers?
But spring is a most incalculable thing.
Get your bulbs from Holland,
the country which makes spring
in a range of exciting colours

P. Gérard

CONSULT YOUR SEEDSMAN FOR FULL DETAILS AND PRICES

*E*in richt'ger Wirt
wird immer klüger werden
je mehr die Gäste trinken.
Wenn aber er kopflos wird
sodaß im Maße er sich irrt
wird der Wirt wohl ruiniert

This is real
Old English Ale
at its very, very best

CBH

CERES
BREWERIES
HARROW

Bodoni at work

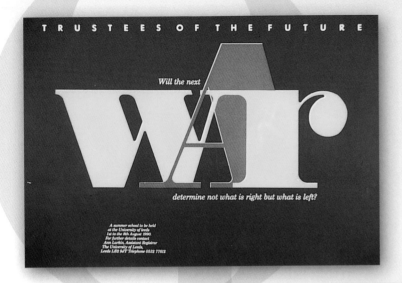

Bodoni usage

Bodoni Ultra

The 20th-century typefoundries added to their range of Bodoni typefaces by taking up the 19th-century concept of the fat-face. As an extra bold, the Bodoni fat-face became known as Ultra. It is used for the word "WAR" in the poster to the left here.

Photographic exhibition

The exhibition poster to the right designed by Malcolm Frost composes the vertical stress of Bodoni against the slim horizontal line of the distant landscape.

Asymmetric design

The 20th-century concept of asymmetric layout uses the classic forms that Bodoni created in the 18th century on the left; the design confirms that the typeface still retains its elegance.

Tracking, kerning, and H&Js

There are quite a number of digital versions of Bodoni to choose from. All versions have high contrast, thick and thin stems that vary slightly in weight, and character word fit from font to font. A minimal increase in tracking is recommended to overcome the visible vertical stress the face creates—a strategy preferred by typefounders in the 19th century. Bodoni prints best on smooth, matt-coated paper, but avoid high-gloss surfaces with Bodoni text.

Text sizes

Berthold Bodoni needs to be leaded, otherwise the descenders tangle with capitals and ascenders on the line below. Bauer Bodoni tends to be wider set than Berthold, this could be significant over a number of pages. Use ITC Bodoni Six for small-sized text, such as captions.

Display sizes

It was the fashionable style of the Modern-face that became the basis for the first true display fat-faces. Adobe Poster Bodoni, and Monotype Bodoni Ultra bold are revivals of this style. ITC Bodoni 72 has been released in two weights, book and bold, specifically as display fonts with swash fonts for both italics. The capitals can be heavily letter-spaced.

On-screen display

By the end of the 19th century, Bodoni had become a controversial design to use as a text face. Although it was revived in the 20th century, it remains far more popular in the role of a display face. The same is true of the face for layouts that are dedicated for screen display. The fine hairlines, high stem contrast, and the low resolution of the screen do not mix well. It is advisable to use this type within a GIF or JPEG.

4   The Machine Age

The 19th century was a period of great change and development. Many of the discoveries and inventions of the 18th century had been absorbed and put to practical use, and, by 1800, agriculture in Britain and the Netherlands had become a great deal more commercialized and efficient.

In Britain, the portion of the labor force engaged in agriculture had dropped to 33 percent causing the unemployed to move into the towns to find work in the mines, ironworks, and factories. British farming practice had been made more efficient by the introduction of the iron plow, Jethro Tull's seed drill, and improved animal husbandry.

A major contributing factor to the rapid developments in the 19th century was the arrival of new forms of power. Water power had been used ~r centuries to drive mills and water hammers, but was location-dependent. The steam pump—first invented to pump out water from mines, had been improved by the Scottish engineer James Watt in 1769. By 1802, Richard Trevithick had developed a road steam locomotive, and in 1804 he unveiled the first steam locomotive to run on rails. In 1821, George Stephenson built the first public railway, the Stockton and Darlington Railway. At that time, the land speed of a trotting horse pulling a carriage was between four and six miles per hour. Tarmacadamed road surfaces increased these speeds to 12 mph, but the first railways increased this again to at least 40 mph. In 1885 Karl Friedrich Benz, a German engineer, built the first gasoline-driven motor vehicle.

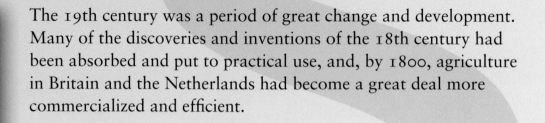

Volta's battery
Alessandro Volta was an Italian physicist who invented the first electric cell—known as the Volta Pile, and the electrophorus, an electrostatic form of generator.

BUILT BY GEORGE STEPHENSON

The Rocket
The English engineer George Stephenson constructed the first successful steam locomotive, the Rocket. He was responsible for the Stockton and Darlington Railway in 1821, which was the first of its kind.

In 1800, Alessandro Volta invented the first electric cell, and in 1831 Michael Faraday constructed the first electric dynamo. Samuel Morse initiated the advance of telecommunications by inventing the electric telegraph. In 1843, he was granted $30,000 by US Congress to set up an experimental telegraph line between Washington and Baltimore. In 1876, the Scottish scientist Alexander Graham Bell invented the telephone.

THE ARTS

In the early years of the century, Romanticism was the dominant aesthetic ideology informing literature, music, and the visual arts; it emphasized the importance of imagination, emotion, and creativity, emerging as a reaction to the restrained objectivity of the neoclassical enlightenment. Among those typifying this movement were the French painter Eugène Delacroix, the Polish composer and pianist Frederick Chopin, the French composer Hector Berlioz, the Scottish novelist Sir Walter Scott, and the Russian poet Aleksandr Pushkin.

The visual arts witnessed change toward the middle of the century. The heroic neoclassicism of the painter Jacques-Louis David, seen in such painting as *Napoleon Crossing the Alps* (1800), and the cool lusciousness of the portraits by Jean Auguste Dominique Ingres, met a challenge from the scenes of rural life by Jean-François Millet and Gustave Courbet in the 1850s. These in turn made way for the "painters of modern life" in the 1870s. Manet and his fellow Impressionists broke away from academic respectability to take the first steps toward the so-called modern art of the 20th century.

In terms of architecture, the early 19th century was a time of renewal for London. John Nash submitted plans for the development of the capital, these transformed the West End into the great squares, terraces, and mews that now represent London's most characteristic architectural identity. Mid-century saw a Gothic revival led by Augustus Pugin, the architect responsible for the Houses of Parliament (1840–1860). In France, Baron Haussmann, the French administrator during the period 1850–1870, supervised the planning and construction of the *étoiles* (vantage points such as the Place de la Bastille, from which streets radiated), parks, and boulevards of modern Paris.

The telephone
The Scottish scientist Alexander Graham Bell patented his invention, the telephone, in 1876. Later he worked on an early type of gramophone.

Paris in 1882
A view of Paris after the great upheaval of Haussman's planning and construction. The city was designed to be physically revolution-proof.

THE FAT-FACE *& the Slab-Serif Egyptians*

The Compositors
A 19th-century typesetter stands at a "frame," setting type from a typecase.

Playbill
A typefoundry's specimen page demonstrating the sizes available. This is a 20th-century revival of a 19th-century slab-serif Egyptian in which the serifs have the appearance of being heavier than the letterform itself.

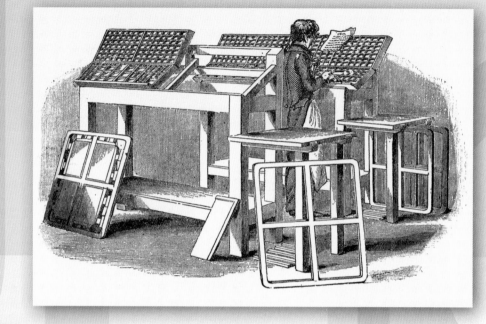

By the early 19th century typefoundries had a new kind of client, demanding a new sort of typeface. The new client was the jobbing printer, and his demand was for "display" typefaces. The jobbing printer's role emerged from increasingly sophisticated commercial activity and its accompanying need for publicity materials.

In towns and cities the advertising needs of all kinds of businesses, ranging from patent medicine vendors to auctioneers, were served by the local jobbing printer.

Large poster types were needed. The large decorated and engraved letters that were in existence in the 18th century, especially those of Pierre Simon Fournier, were only intended for the title pages of books. The manufacture of display types was an area of enterprise that gave British typefoundries an opportunity to develop their range of typefaces.

The first design to successfully fulfil the requirements of display type became known as the "fat-face," the invention of which is credited to Robert Thorne (1754–1820). Thorne's simple but ingenious concept was to make use of the current vogue for the continental Modern face, such as Bodoni. By increasing the thickness of the stems to an enormous degree, while maintaining the thin strokes and the thin, unbracketed serifs, he produced a fierce blackletter of enormous power. It was extremely popular with advertisers, but filled many typographic commentators with horror. Nonetheless, the idea soon gained favor with other foundries and their customers.

Robert Thorne, one of the outstanding typefounders of the 19th century, had been apprentice to Thomas Cottrell. Nine years after Cottrell's death in 1794, Thorne bought the typefoundry and its collection of punches and matrices, and proceeded to expand the range of types on offer. His 1798 specimen book contained 45 pages of romans, italics, titlings, shaded letters, flowers, and one font of two-line script. Thorne's fat-face designs were greatly admired. Their reputation spread to the continent, with the result that he received an unprecedented request to cut a fat-face font for the *Imprimerie Royale* in Paris.

DOUBLE PICA No. 2.

How far, O Catiline, wilt thou abuse our patie
How long shall thy frantic rage baffle the effo
Justice? To what height meanest thou to carr
daring insolence? Art thou nothing daunted a
nocturnal host to secure the Palatium? Nothi
the City Guards? ABCDEFGHIJKLMNOPQRSTUVV
ABCDEFGHIJKLMNOPQRSTUVWXYZA

THE FIRST SLAB-SERIFS

The new display faces were outsized types that were measured by "lines." A line was the equivalent of one pica (12-points). A common size, six-line for example, would be 72-points. Many display faces were only available as titlings—fonts of capital letters only, that were enlarged on the body, taking up the space normally allocated to the descenders, in order to achieve greater impact.

Just before his early death in 1820, Thorne had been in the process of cutting a slab-serif display type for which he coined the name "Egyptian." The name seemed appropriate since there were parallels drawn between the square black serifs and the relics of ancient Egyptian architecture. It was only a short time after Napoleon's fleet had been defeated in the Battle of the Nile in 1798, and there was a considerable amount of public interest in Egypt due to the Rosetta Stone and other antiquities that had been found there.

It was, however, Thorne's competitor Vincent Figgins, who created the first slab-serif face in 1815. He named his face "Antique" and produced it in four sizes, all titlings. This was possibly Britain's first truly original contribution to the art of type design. Figgins, a prominent London typefounder, had been apprentice to

Joseph Jackson, who himself had been apprentice to William Caslon I. Figgins had managed Jackson's typefoundry during the last years of the latter's life, although he did not manage to take it over after Jackson's death. He was forced to start up on his own, with encouragement from a John Nichols, to whom he later expressed his enormous gratitude. A very capable man, Figgins set up in Holborn, London, soon gaining a reputation as an outstanding, creative typecutter.

The Egyptian slab letterform was a great success, and was soon in use on the continent and in the United States. Over the coming years, the slab-serif was subjected to numerous variations that condensed it into narrow vertical forms or stretched it out to forms that were much wider than they were high. At least two versions, Playbill by Stephenson, Blake & Company and Barnum by the American Type Foundry (ATF), featured serifs more dominant than the body of the letterforms.

The first of many
Thorne's concept of fat-faces was met with great approval by his jobbing printer customers, and was soon copied by many other foundries. ITC's Fat Face Western (below) is a descendant of Thorne's design.

abcdefghijklmnopqrstuvwxy
ABCDEFGHIJKLM

SLAB-SERIFS: *the Types*

Pouchée's display types
The French typefounder set up a short-lived typefoundry in London to produce these elaborately decorated display types. They were produced with the aid of the casting machine invented by Henri Didot.

A 20th-century type
Slab-serifs have now become more refined than the 19th-century Egyptians. Due to the aesthetics of the 1920s, the designs of the 20th century generally have a single-line thickness with more traditional serif proportions.

Two important forms survived the 19th century's exuberant typographic inventions that went on to be developed in the 20th century: the sans-serif and the resilient slab-serif.

The popularity of slab-serifs faded in the latter part of the 19th century, largely because of competition from new developments of the typecutter's art. However there was a revival of the slab-serif form during the 1930s. These new versions maintained the Egyptian theme. The first to appear was Memphis, from the Stempel Foundry of Frankfurt in 1929. Then came Karnak from Ludlow, and Beton from Bauer in 1931; Cairo from Intertype, and Pharaoh from Deberny & Peignot in 1933; Rockwell from Lanston Monotype in 1934; and Scarab from Stephenson, Blake & Company in 1937. The 20th-century slab-serifs were not the extremely assertive extroverts of the 19th century. The new types were designed for a modernist aesthetic, and were refined, monolined forms with the same kind of geometric purity of the sans-serifs of the same generation. The serifs are without brackets

ABCDEFGHIJKLMN

abcdefghiklmnopqrs

abcdefghiklmnopqrstu

and have the same thickness as the body strokes, which are modified as the weight increases. These types were designed to be used for text in publicity material, rather than books, but they are also capable of functioning as display fonts.

The slab-serif, like the sans-serif form, was not only a vigorous survivor of the hot-metal and photosetting periods, but now retains great popularity in the present digital age. The characteristics can be found in the metal typefoundry updates such as Berthold's Beton, Stempel's Memphis, Monotype's Rockwell, and Morris F. Benton's Stymie for ATF, but they can also be found in some new-generation digital fonts. The digitized slab-serif Beton of the Baur Foundry has five weights and no italics; an extremely delicate light, demi-bold, bold, extra bold, and bold condensed. There is an outline shadow version that has not been digitized as yet. Monotype's Rockwell family consisted of light, roman, bold, extra bold, condensed, and bold condensed, each with slanted roman rather than italics. The hot-metal family included a display titling outline shadow form and a shaded form cross-hatched with fine lines which seem to be a remnant of the 19th century. Stempel's Memphis

digitized family provides light, medium, bold, and extra bold. The full hot-metal range included three weights of condensed, an outline version called Open, and Luna, a shadow version. Morris F. Benton's ATF Stymie consists of light, medium, bold, black, and two weights of condensed, medium, and bold. As yet there are no italics or slanted romans. Also not included in the digitization is an outline shadowed form cross-hatched with fine lines, similar to the one in Beton.

ARG
ARG

Rockwell
the quick brown fox jumps over the lazy dog

Memphis
the quick brown fox jumps over the lazy dog

Futura
the quick brown fox jumps over the lazy dog

Slab-serifs compared
At first sight Rockwell and Memphis are the same face (see left). However, closer inspection reveals Rockwell has a traditional two-storey "a" while Memphis has a single-storey "a," which is favored by the 1927 Futura. The terminal of the vertical stroke of the lower case "t" also differs, while for Rockwell the dot on the "j" is round, when the Memphis "j" it is square.

Capital comparision
The differences are more obvious when comparing Rockwell Regular capitals (top), with Memphis Medium capitals (above).

Slab-serifs at work

Theater publicity
These typical 19th-century posters are a riot of letterforms, slab-serifs, and fat-faces; each shouting for attention.

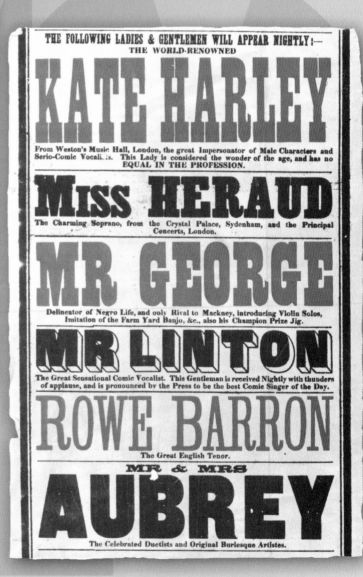

Now

Slab-serifs at work

Text and Display
This 21st-century design makes use of many of the Rockwell range of weights and italics, aiding the structure of information.

Effective contrast
The forceful impact of this combination of large, condensed slab-serif forms with smaller sans-serif forms, gives added visual meaning to the text.

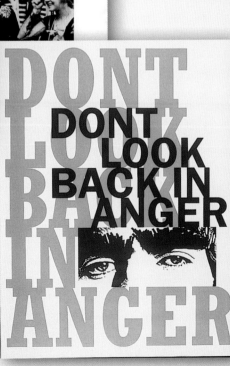

Design Tips

Slab-serif usage

Tracking, kerning, and H&Js

There are four 20th-century slab-serif faces which offer a extensive family of weights: Rockwell, Stymie, Memphis, and Beton. The geometric style of these slab-serifs engenders good letter fit. Slab-serif capitalized words have naturally good letter fit, although capitalized headings can be overbearing if used too extensively.

Text sizes

The light and medium weights of these faces are underrated as fonts for text setting. All three tend to have short descenders. Beton and Stymie have a smallish x-height so their tight letterfit makes more than slight leading unnecessary. Conversely, Rockwell has a comparatively large x-height and can stand more leading.

Display sizes

The extra bold and condensed weights that are available in all three of these typefaces make useful display fonts, and the compact fit of capitalized headings means letter-spacing can be flexible. In most cases the tracking should be reduced incrementally as the size is increased.

On-screen display

Rockwell has a large x-height, which is a required characteristic of fonts designed for on-screen text display. The digital screen seems to be sympathetic to the slab-serif form, although web design best practice would advise avoiding sizes below 14-point. It is also best that all sizes are displayed within a GIF or JPEG.

CLARENDON: *the Fann Street Foundry*

ABCDEFGHIJKLMN
abcdefghijklmnopqr

TWO LINES ENGLISH CLARENDON

tandem abutere Catilina, patientia
quamdiu nos etiam furor iste tuus
uem ad finem sese effrenata jactabit
tua? nihilne te nocturnum præsi-
atii, nihil urbis vigiliæ, nihil timor
£1234567890
ROPOLITAN IMPROVEMENT.

Two Clarendon examples
First produced by Thorowgood's Fann Street Foundry in 1845. Robert Besley, a foundry worker, later to become a partner, is credited with the design.

Synopsis in 24 Point

ABCDEFGHIJKLM
NOPQRSTUVWXYZ&
abcdefghijklmnop
qrstuvwxyzfififlffffiflæœ
£1234567890ÆŒ
.,:;!?''-([*†‡§$/%—

ABCDEFGHI
JKLMNOPQRSTUV
WXYZ&ÆŒ
abcdefghijklmnop
qrstuvwxyzfififlffffifl
£1234567890æœ
.,:;!?''-([
*†‡§$/%—

The following Accents
ÀÁÂÃÄÅÇÈÉÊËÌÍÎÏÑÒÓÔÕÖÙÚÛÜ
àáâãäåçèéêëìíîïñòóôõöùúûü
now available in all sizes

The slab-serif emerged as a new form due to typefounders' search for fresh, eye-catching display letterforms. During the 19th century, as the founders' technical skills improved, more and more elaborate inventions of typographic novelty were created, although many were short-lived. Typefounders had answered the challenge that the jobbing printers set. The 19th century set the fashion for the celebration of technical extremism that has been with us ever since. There began an insatiable need to create novelty letterforms, coupled with an equally insatiable appetite for them. Despite this creativity, however, only a handful survived to serve generations to come.

During the early years of the century, the new typeforms were subject to considerable confusion regarding terminology. Foundries invented their own names until later in the century, when many of the more popular forms became part of the jobbing printer's stock of types.

In 1820 Robert Thorne's Fann Street Foundry was taken over by William Thorowgood, who bought it when it was put up for auction. He had no previous connection with type-founding, but threw himself into the business, determined to make a success of his new acquisition. It was said that he had bought the typefoundry with winnings from a state lottery. Thorowgood soon re-established Fann Street on the typographic map, so that by 1822 he had been appointed letterfounder to King George IV. Thorowgood enlarged his collection of punches and matrices, not only by creating his own designs, but also by acquiring the stock from Dr Edmund Fry's typefoundry when he retired. This collection included Greek, Hebrew, Russian, and German (blackletter) typefaces.

A MUCH NEEDED ADDITION

In 1845, Thorowgood registered a new type called Clarendon. It is actually Robert Besley who is credited with the origination of this letterform. Besley had worked at the Fann Street Foundry for some ten years and was made a partner in 1838. This was a face that had its origins in the Egyptian slab-serif, but displayed far more refinement. It showed the thick and thin modeling of a roman, a slight narrowness, and finely bracketed, heavy serifs. It was a bold type cast in text sizes, for Clarendon was designed to emphasize type. The Modern roman was the text face in common use (though the color may have varied from one cutting to another) and was only produced as roman and italics. At this time text typefaces were not cast with a range of different weights, as now. The new typeface was intended

OPQRSTUVWXYZ
stuvwxyz& 1234567890

AaRr

AaRr

to be used with a roman text face in order to emphasize words as required—for example, in dictionaries and similar listings, or to give more impact within the text of advertisements. The bracketing of the serifs was intended to blend the bolder face with the delicate Modern form.

Clarendon proved to be a much needed addition to the printer's range. This was the first typeface design to be registered under England's Designs Copyright Amendment Act. The act prevented the copying of the type for three years. However, because of the popularity of this design, the ban had little effect on the plagiarists; certainly after the three years the specimen books of most foundries carried a version of Clarendon. Among printers, the name "Clarendon" came to be used as a generic term to describe boldness.

Clarendon has maintained an almost unchanged presence in typefounders' specimen books. It is one typeface that has not been extended with numerous variants. In digitized versions, Hermann Eidenbenz's designs for the Linotype library has three weights, while the Clarendon carried by the Adobe library has a light, medium, bold, and two extra versions; extra bold, and extra bold expanded. Monotype's Clarendon also has three weights, plus a condensed bold. There is no italic form of Clarendon.

Bracketed slab-serif
Clarendon and other similar types are described as bracketed slab-serifs, although the curl in the the lowercase serif of the "a" and in the leg of the "R" are more organic than typical brackets. The ball terminating the "a" and "r" stand out as typical of the voluptuous forms of the 19th century. These traits are more obvious when Clarendon (right, above) is compared Rockwell (right).

Text and display
This letterpress specimen sheet to the right shows sizes from 6-point up to 48-point.

Series 617: 6 to 48 point
(60 and 72 point to follow)

6 point
With the dead there is no rivalry. In the dead there is no change. Plato is never sullen. Cervantes is never petulant. Demosthenes never comes unseasonably.

8 point
Coleridge holds that man cannot have a pure mind who refuses apple-dumplings. I am not certain but he is right in his opinion.

10 point
When an equerry related a questionable story at Windsor, the royal reply was "We are not amused".

12 point
To travel hopefully is a better thing than to arrive, and the true success is to labour.

14 point composition
By appointment to His Royal Highness

14 point display
A Penny Plain and Twopenny Coloured

16 point
An Englishman's house is his castle

18 point
Oliver Twist has asked for more

24 point
Repeal of the Corn Laws

30 point
George Stephenson

36 point
The Lost Chord

42 point
Savoy Operas

48 point
Alton Locke

Series 618: 6 to 48 point
(60 and 72 point to follow)

6 point
Sherlock Holmes composed a little monograph on the ashes of one hundred and forty different varieties of pipe, cigar and cigarette tobacco.

8 point
The liberty of the individual must be thus far limited; he must not make himself a nuisance to other people. (Mill)

10 point
Mr. Gladstone mentioned that decision by majorities is as much an expedient as lighting by gas.

12 point
Hazlitt said, as we advance in life, we acquire a keener sense of the value of time.

14 point composition
I dreamt that I dwelt in marble halls

14 point display
The Charge of the Heavy Brigade

16 point
Stockton and Darlington Railway

18 point
The Walrus and the Carpenter

24 point
Victorian Music Halls

30 point
Idylls of the King

36 point
Arts & Crafts

42 point
St. Pancras

48 point
Exhibition

Clarendon at work

For emphasis

*Because text typefaces of
the 19th century seldom
had an accompanying bold,
Thorowgood's Clarendon
was intended to act as a
means of emphasis in text.
It was a device that became
common throughout the
rest of the century.*

86
Decoy: Sandpiper
John Glover
Duxbury, Massachusetts; c. 1890
Painted wood, metal, glass;
4 × 6¼ × 2in. deep
Gift of Alastair B. Martin. 1969.1.90

Sandpipers are so small (only six to eight inches in size), that it is remarkable that they were hunted. However, their unwary nature and willingness to return to a hunter's decoys made them the easiest of targets. Still, most hunters preferred the more marketable wild birds.

87
Decoy: Long-Billed Curlew
Mason Decoy Factory
Detroit, Michigan; c. 1900
Painted wood, metal, glass;
7¼ × 17¾ × 4¼in. deep
Gift of Alastair B. Martin. 1969.1.88

William J. Mason founded the decoy company that bore his name in 1896 and ran it continuously until 1924. During that time, no other factory made as many species and few attained its standard of quality. Mason decoys are known for their signature painting style. Paint was always applied with a deep texturing and in a swirl pattern unlike any other maker's. This shorebird, with its fully developed body and expert paintwork, represents the highest grade of Mason factory decoy.

ENGLISH CLARENDON ON GREAT PRIMER BODY.
Cast to range with ordinary Great Primer, the Figures to En Quadrats.

PIRACY is the great sin of all **manufacturing** communities:—there is scarcely any Trade in which it prevails so generally as among **TYPE FOUNDERS**. Messrs. **BESLEY & Co.** originally introduced the **Clarendon Character**, which they registered under the **Copyright of Designs' Act**, but no sooner was the time of Copyright allowed by that Act expired, than the **Trade was inundated** with all sorts of **Piracies and Imitations**, some of them **mere effigies of letters**. Notwithstanding this, nearly all the **respectable Printers** in **Town and Country** who claim to have either **taste** or **judgment**, have adopted the **original Founts**, and treated the Imitations with the contempt they deserve.

SMALL PICA CLARENDON ON PICA BODY.
Cast to range with ordinary Pica, the Figures to En Quadrats.

PIRACY is the great sin of all **manufacturing communities**:—there is scarcely any Trade in which it prevails so generally as among **Type Founders**. Messrs. **BESLEY & COMPANY** originally introduced the **Clarendon Character**, which they registered under the **Copyright of Designs' Act**, but no sooner was the time of Copyright allowed by that Act expired, than the **Trade was inundated** with all sorts of **Piracies** and Imitations, some of them **mere effigies of letters**. Notwithstanding this, nearly all the **respectable Printers** in **Town and Country** who claim to have either **taste** or **judgment**, have adopted the original Founts, and treated the **Imitations** with the contempt they deserve.

LONG PRIMER CLARENDON ON SMALL PICA BODY.
Cast to range with ordinary Small Pica, the Figures to En Quadrats.

PIRACY is the great sin of all **manufacturing communities**:—there is scarcely any Trade in which it prevails so generally as among **TYPE FOUNDERS**. Messrs. **R. BESLEY & Co.** originally introduced the **Clarendon Character**, which they registered under the **Copyright of Designs' Act**, but no sooner was the time of Copyright allowed by that Act **expired**, than the **Trade was inundated** with all sorts of **Piracies** and **Imitations**, some of them **mere effigies of letters**. Notwithstanding this, nearly all the **respectable Printers in Town and Country** who claim to have either **taste** or **judgment**, have adopted the original Founts, and treated the **Imitations** with the contempt they deserve.

R. BESLEY & CO., (late W. Thorowgood & Co.,) LONDON.

One hundred years later

*In the 1980s, Derek
Birdsall designed this
book on American folk
art (above). The design
echoes the 19th-century
device of emphasizing text
using Clarendon alongside
a Modern face. Birdsall
has chosen a sympathetic
typographic style to suit
the illlustrations.*

Now

Clarendon at work

Tourist publicity
The above 21st-century promotion for visitors to Britain makes effective modern use of the 19th-century survivor, Clarendon. It manages to reflect Britain's individual, historic appeal, while the layout conveys its contemporary dynamism.

Barcelona
This Catalan street poster associates Clarendon with modernist aesthetics.

Design Tips

Clarendon usage

Tracking, kerning, and H&Js
Today Clarendon remains a support to text fonts rather than functioning as a text face itself. Its strong identity allows for increased tracking, although this works better for the capitals at most sizes, than for the small sizes in lowercase.

Text sizes
Clarendon can only be used to a limited degree as a text face because it has no italic—this is a basic requirement for a fully acceptable text face.

Display sizes
Clarendon is an excellent, extrovert, and friendly display face, as its generous basic weight and x-height make it extremely readable and eyecatching.

On-screen display
Clarendon is less likely to be rendered unreadable than some typefaces, but for effective and full use of its character it is best conveyed within a GIF or JPEG.

THE 19TH CENTURY: *Technical Developments*

The 19th century was one of energy and innovation, not least in the printing industry. The general economic expansion stimulated more change in this industry throughout the century than there had been in the previous 350 years. There was a growing demand for printed material of all kinds—including reading material for entertainment and education, as well as commerce. There were developments in paper manufacturing, reproduction techniques, type-founding and typesetting.

Casting machine
In 1838, the 19th-century New York typefounder David Bruce invented this machine on the right to increase the speed of typecasting.

Machine typesetting
By the early years of the 20th century, many printers were installing mechanized typesetting plant. The photograph below is of a typical range of Monotype keyboard operators during the 1930s.

In the closing years of the old century, Nicholas-Louis Robert, an employee at the Didot family papermill in France, experimented with a means of making paper by machine. He took his invention to England, where it was improved with the help of John Gamble and the engineering skill of Brian Donkin. It was put into production in 1803 for the Fourdrinier brothers, Henry and Sealy. The Fourdrinier machine is the forerunner of the modern papermaking machine, which produces a continuous web (reel) of paper rather than the individual sheets of the handmade method. The machine was also ten times faster. The web can then be cut into sheets or printed on first. The machine was able to produce paper at ten times the rate of the handmade method.

The need for faster and cheaper typesetting encouraged innovation. This was initially tackled in two ways: by improved rates of casting, and by improved setting methods. Between 1820 and 1883, about 200 experimental machines were patented, mostly in America. In 1838 the New York typefounder David Bruce invented a device that speeded up the handcasting process. In 1881, John Mair Hepburn constructed an improved casting machine for the German Bauer typefoundry. The first typecasting machine to produce a finished product ready for use was developed in France by Foucher Frères in 1883. In 1880, Frederick Wicks built a rotary typecasting machine that was of great use to newspapers and journals because it was able to produce large quantities of type daily, which could be melted down and re-used.

In 1822, Dr William Church of Vermont devised a typecaster that distributed letters to a supply chamber or magazine, from which they were selected by keyboard action; after use the letters were melted down. This highly innovative typecaster did not achieve wide commercial use, but a more successful machine was invented by Charles Kastenbein, which was used by *The Times* newspaper from 1872 until 1908. The machine was not fully mechanized: the lines of type were assembled by a keyboard fed from a amagzine above it, but needed to be justified by hand. After printing the type was distributed by hand back into the magazine.

TYPECASTING MACHINES

Two different solutions to the need for faster typesetting were invented and became commercially successful by the end of the century. In 1890, the Linotype machine, invented by Ottmar Mergenthaler, was demonstrated in New York. An operator sat at the keyboard and, by depressing the keys, assembled a line of matrices from a magazine above the keyboard. The line of matrices were then cast as one piece of metal, called a "slug," by the injection of molten metal. This was delivered to a galley, while the matrices were redistributed by the machine back to the magazine ready for use again.

In 1885, Tolbert Lanston patented his Monotype machine, and by 1898 the first machines were functioning in Washington and London. The Monotype machine, like the Linotype machine, cast type as well as assembling it in lines, but as individual letters rather than slugs. The Monotype had two units, requiring two operators: a keyboard unit that recorded the text as a code of punched holes on a reel of paper tape, and a caster unit that was instructed by the paper tape. The caster unit was driven by passing compressed air through the perforations in the tape, this positioned the matrix case over the body mold, to be injected with molten metal.

The Fourdrinier papermaking machine
The first successful machine to produce paper as a web, rather than in individual sheets.

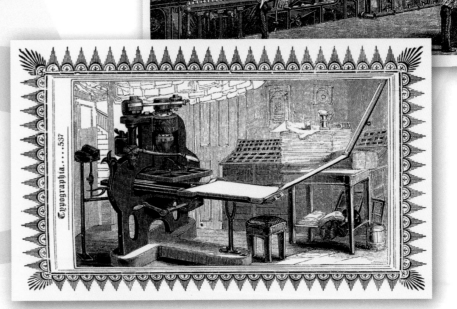

The matrix case—a metal frame roughly 100mm square—contained a grid of matrices containing all the characters of a single size of a specific typeface. The type was cast as individual letters in lines as directed by the perforated paper tape.

Both the Linotype and the Monotype machines were in general use for textsetting of all kinds throughout most of the 20th century. They were eventually superseded by photosetting machines, although many remained functioning even after this latter-day innovation.

The Stanhope printing press
The above engraving illustrates the first radical design that was an all-iron press, although it was still hand-operated. It appeared at the beginning of the 19th century.

Linotype machine
The above images illustrate the machine that solved the need for faster typesetting at the end of the 19th century. The first model appeared in 1890 and combined a keyboard to assemble the matrices and the casting process in one unit. The type was cast as a solid line of letters, called a slug.

IMAGE PRODUCTION METHODS

Stereotyping was an important process that was developed over many years. Records of the process go back to the 17th century, but it was not perfected until 1829. Stereotyping was a process for making copies of the made-up pages of text and illustrations, known as a "foundry forme." The foundry forme would be coated with papier-mâché. When dry, the papier-mâché could be used as a flexible mold to make a stereotype of the original forme. This would be used for long print runs when type was likely to wear out; for multiple copies; or for making curved plates for rotary printing presses.

Illustrations in books and periodicals were in high demand as the reading public grew. Woodcuts and copper engravings had been used for illustrations for centuries. Wood engraving developed in the 18th century and remained popular for advertising well into the 20th century.

However, the photograph provided a more accurate record of reality. Since the invention of photography earlier in the century, there had been numerous attempts to reproduce photographs for printing. This was not achieved until George Meisenbach made the process effective in 1881. There were more attempts to improve the technique, including those by Frederick Ives of Chicago, who, in 1888, was credited with the introduction of the squared screen. This was later perfected by Max Levy. The continuous-tone, original photograph is transferred onto a metal plate by being projected through a squared glass screen that converts the image to a grid of regularly spaced dots. In light areas the dots are small and widely spaced, in dark areas the dots are larger, and in very dark areas they join together. Since the dots are small, the optical effect is of a range of tones similar to the original. The process allows for a single uniform inking by the printing press.

PRINTING PRESS ADVANCES

The printing press itself had had few radical changes since the model that is presumed to have been devised by Gutenberg, although there had been many modifications and refinements over the centuries. A radical improvement to the hand platen press came when Earl Charles Stanhope designed his all-iron press. This had a compound lever action, and an enlarged platen that could print a larger sheet at one pull. An American, George Clymer, patented his Columbia Press in London in 1817.

The first successful machine press was Frederick König's steam-driven stop-cylinder press, constructed in 1812. The pages of type fitted the machine bed, while the paper was wrapped around the cylinder as it passed over the inked type. It was capable of printing 800 copies per hour. König went on to make improvements to his invention. In 1816, he developed the "perfecting machine" which was capable of printing both sides of the sheet in one operation. In New York in 1845, Richard Hoe patented a rotary sheet press, on which pages of type were fitted round the cylinder. In 1848, in London, Applegath & Cowper built a vertical rotary sheet press. Stereotyping was used to make plates that fitted round the cylinders. By 1865, William Bullock had developed the rotary printing press, which used stereotyped plates and printed on a continuous reel, or web, of paper.

König's powered cylinder press
Invented in 1814, the above press used an impression cylinder to apply pressure to the typeforms. Everything was mechanized, except for the feeding of sheets of blank paper for printing.

The Monotype caster
The caster was the second unit that made up the Monotype typesetting system as shown below. The two-unit system consisted of a keyboard copy-entry system and a stand-alone caster.

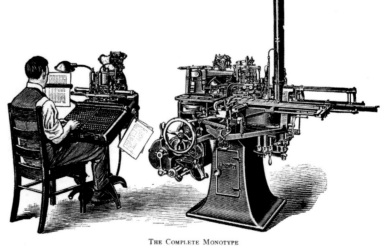

THE COMPLETE MONOTYPE

WILLIAM MORRIS *& Looking Back for the Way Ahead*

William Morris (1834–1896) is a germinal figure in the history of modern design. A man steeped in Greek and Latin texts, medieval legends and Nordic sagas, his energy and enthusiasm were legendary. He was a poet and a novelist, a craftsman, a weaver, a designer of wallpaper patterns and textiles of brilliant originality, a calligrapher and book designer, a social and political activist, a medievalist, and a latter-day Renaissance man.

THE ARGUMENT.

UCIUS Tarquinius (for his excessive pride surnamed Superbus) after hee had caused his owne father in law Servius Tullius to be cruelly murd'red, and contrarie to the Romaine lawes and customes, not requiring or staying for the people's suffrages, had possessed himselfe of the kingdome: went accompanyed with his sonnes and other noble men of Rome, to besiege Ardea, during which siege, the principall men of the Army meeting one evening at the tent of Sextus Tarquinius the king's sonne, in their discourses after supper every one commended the vertues of his owne wife: among whom Colatinus extolled the incomparable chastity of his wife Lucretia. In that pleasant humor they all posted to Rome, & intending by theyr secret and sodaine arrivall to make triall of that which every one had before avouched, onely Colatinus finds his wife (though it were late in the night) spinning amongest her maides, the other ladies were all found dauncing and revelling, or in severall disports: whereupon the noble men yeelded Colatinus the victory, and his wife the fame. At that time Sextus Tarquinius being enflamed with Lucrece beauty, yet smoothering his passions for the present, departed with the rest backe to the campe:

55

Jenson revival
An example of Morris' Golden Type in use. Morris chose Nicolas Jenson's Venetian types used in 1476 as a model for his own Golden Type.

Hand-operated press
The Albion press was a popular printing press during the 19th century. During the eight-year existence of the Kelmscott Press, all the work was carried out on machines like this.

Morris' writings and lectures on the arts, design, and society made major contributions to the issues that concerned generations of designers and manufacturers to come. Born in Walthamstow, London, into a wealthy family, Morris was financially independent. While at Oxford University he met Edward Burne-Jones and became associated with the Pre-Raphaelite Brotherhood, a group of artists whose inspiration was the Middle Ages and early Renaissance. The group included Dante Gabriel Rossetti, Holman Hunt, and John Everett Millais.

Morris' original intention was to enter the church, but on leaving university he became an architect, working for the London architect G. E. Street. He was soon diverted from this to fine art in 1857, when he was persuaded by Rossetti to help him complete the murals for the Oxford Union. In 1861, his interest in the arts and architecture led him in 1861 to set up in business with friends as Morris, Marshall, Faulkner, & Company in order produce stained glass, furniture, wallpapers, and printed textiles. The company first made an impact at the South Kensington International Exhibition in 1862. Morris' wallpapers and textiles became so successful that he received the accolade of being Britain's greatest pattern designer. In 1875, he became the sole proprietor of the renamed firm Morris and Co., with a shop in London's Oxford Street.

Morris was among the growing number of thinkers who were concerned with the growth of 19th-century capitalism and urbanization,

Kelmscott Press
Morris' private press in Hammersmith, London, was named after the house he and his family had occupied in Oxfordshire, Kelmscott Manor. The colophon is shown to the left.

and the alienating effect it had on the individual and society in general. He was of the opinion that industrialization had ravaged the natural environment and the repetitious nature of factory production had destroyed the opportunity for workers' satisfaction and fulfilment from work, providing poor quality of life in exchange. Morris had developed strong political views which came to the fore in 1876 when he attacked the government's Bulgarian policy in a letter to the press. He declared himself a socialist and in 1879 became the Treasurer of the National Liberal League. In 1883, he was elected to the executive committee of the Democratic Federation.

THE ARTS AND CRAFTS MOVEMENT

In Morris' day, "Decorative Arts" was the term that described the activities that today would include design. The phrase is apt, since in the 19th century the application of ornament and decoration on all manufactured goods—from wallpaper and textiles to furniture and household utensils, was mostly without thought of form or function. Morris and his circle were appalled by what they considered the shoddy and tasteless results of mass production.

Morris' response to this state of affairs was inspired by his love of Gothic art and architecture. He turned to tradition, looking back to previous centuries for traditional working methods and materials. With John Ruskin and C. R. Ashbee, he formed a movement that was

to reestablish the idea of craftsmanship as an alternative to mass production and other aspects of industrial society. It was a movement that was also to have equivalents in other countries.

The Arts and Crafts Exhibition Society was formed in 1887, and the members' aims were to foster the neglected arts and crafts by creating craft guilds and communities of craftsmen. The Arts and Crafts movement was subject to the criticism that it was escapist and avoided the economic realities of the modern world. Morris himself had to admit that the products of his workshop were expensive compared with their mass-produced equivalents and were not within the reach of the average consumer. However, the movement continued to attract new members and drew international attention.

Golden Type
Although Morris seemed to prefer a more Gothic letterform for his types, the Golden type met with approval from other designers and printers.

INCIPIT LEGENDA YPERMIS

GRECE WHYLOM WEREN brethren two,
Of whiche that oon was called Danao,
That many a sone hath of his body wonne,
As swiche false lovers ofte conne.
Among his sones alle ther was oon
That aldermost he lovede of everichoon.
And whan this child was born, this Danao
Shoop him a name, and called him Lino.
That other brother called was Egiste,
That was of love as fals as ever him liste,
And many a doghter gat he in his lyve;
Of which he gat upon his righte wyve
A doghter dere, and dide her for to calle
Ypermistra, yongest of hem alle;
The whiche child, of her nativitee,

Woodcut patterns
*William Morris' aesthetics
were deeply rooted in the
Middle Ages. He acquired
a formidable reputation for
his inventive use of pattern,
which he also applied to
the pages of his books.
This can be seen in the
initial word engraved in
wood to the right.*

CALLIGRAPHY

William Morris had a practical interest in calligraphy and a great love of books, in particular those of the 15th century. He attended a lecture by Emery Walker on printing at the Arts and Crafts Society, and became so enthusiastic that he decided to start a printing press of his own. He said his intention in designing and printing books was to produce pieces of printing and arrangements of type that would be a pleasure to look at.

Like Bodoni in the 18th century, Morris was not in the habit of doing things by half measures. This adventure, as he called it, led him to consider a number of things: the paper, the form of the type, the relative spacing of the letters, the words, and the lines, and lastly, the position of the printed matter on the page. He decided to commission special handmade, laid paper, rather than using the standard wove. This would have the texture and quality of pre-Baskerville paper, in keeping with 15th-century printers. Morris was critical of the strongly contrasting strokes of the current Modern face, as he thought it difficult to read. He therefore decided to design his own typefaces based on those of the 15th-century printers. Using photographic enlargements from a Nicholas Jenson book of 1476, Morris drew over the prints, increasing the weight until he was satisfied with the forms. Later he decided that he also wanted a more distinctly Gothic typeface. He based the resulting alphabet on a type by the German printer Gunther Zamier of Augsburg, from a book of 1475.

illu
efti
erú
m uít
feíp abcdefghíjklmnopqurstvwxyz
uc e abcdefghíjklmnopqurstvwxyz
done
at: A
t aími   d

THE KELMSCOTT PRESS

Morris set up the Kelmscott Press close to his home in Hammersmith, West London, in 1890. The first of the types was based on Jenson's 1476 typeface. He named it "Golden Type" because it was used in an edition of *The Golden Legend*, a 13th-century text popular with early printers. The second typeface was intended for an edition of *Recuyell of the Historyes of Troye*, a text that Caxton had also published. This was an attempt to produce a readable form of blackletter. It was cut in two sizes, 18-point Troy for text and 12-point Chaucer for contents and glossary. Morris designed all the Kelmscott books, including 644 initial letters, borders and ornaments, and initial words. In eight years the press, with a full staff of up to 12, produced 52 titles in 66 volumes, typesetting by hand and printing on manual presses. Morris suffered from ill health from 1891 and when he died in 1896, at 62, his doctor said that he died simply from being William Morris, and having done more than ten average men.

The Kelmscott Press was among the first of the private presses that were commonly set up with similar aims to the Arts and Crafts movement; it produced limited quantities of fine typography, printed on high-quality materials. The private press movement was one that spread to many countries. Notable private presses included the Doves Press run by Emery Walker and Thomas Cobden-Sanderson in Hammersmith, London; the Merrymount Press in Boston, USA, run by Daniel Berkeley Updike; and in Germany in Weimar, the Cranach Press run by Harry Graf Kessler. It is a movement that continues to be active to the present day.

Manuscript forms
Morris studied early printed books and modelled his type designs on these. Above are studies by Morris for his Troy typeface.

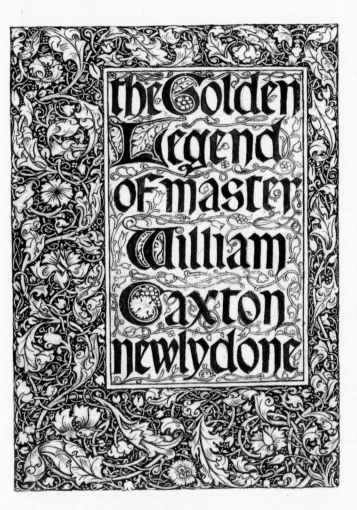

The Golden Legend frontispiece
Morris designed this highly ornamented book as a tribute to Britain's first printer, William Caxton. The Golden Legend was originally an incunabula bestseller, and is still in print to this day.

CHELTENHAM: *the Old-Style*

Aa Gg

Cheltenham Old Style letterforms
Bertram Goodhue's design became popular immediately and sparked off a number of similar designs.

12-point Old-style
This specimen page of 19th-century Old-style is an example of the type that influenced the forms of Bertram Goodhue's later creation, Cheltenham.

TWELVE POINT OLD STYLE

NOT all type faces are as successful in the sizes below eleven-point as in those above it. Caslon and Garamond seem to many to improve as the sizes increase, while the Bembo face is one of the few old styles that preserves all its freshness and charm in the smallest sizes. Fournier and Plantin, for different reasons, are highly successful in the smallest settings as well as in and over the normal sizes. Centaur is a fine type in any size, but certain subtleties of cutting cannot be fully appreciated below twenty-four-point, and these details go to make it as successful an upper and lower-case for display work as has ever been designed.

If the quality of the paper is known in advance, as it should be in most cases, and especially where illustrations are used, this will influence the choice of a type face. Old-face was not designed for calendered paper, which did not exist until Baskerville's experiments; the difficulty arises from the fact that the smooth-finished surface of paper takes the inked copy with such facility that little or no impression into the fabric of the paper is necessary, and, therefore, the only ink which comes off the type is that on the actual printing surface. In general, calendered or shiny surface paper needs such a face as Plantin, which is not noticeably thinned down by such treatment.

In the old days a printer had no reasons such as these for stocking different type faces. He worked on only one kind of paper: hand-made pure rag, with the corrugated surface left by the wires of the paper mould, a surface now known as antique. He had only one process by which pictures and type could be printed at the

199

The term "Old-style" should not be confused with "Old-face;" Old-style is a 19th-century type form. The term "style" is significant and should be understood in the sense of "in the style of," meaning not the genuine thing, but emulating or similar to it. Although the Modern face dominated most publications—especially early in the 19th century, it was not used exclusively.

In about 1840, Charles Whittingham, of the Chiswick Press near London, took to using Caslon cast from the original matrices. He printed *Lady Willoughby's Diary* for Longmans book publishers in 1844. While this gained some attention, the revived use of Caslon was considered by some commercial printers and publishers as a retrograde venture. Caslon was not viewed with the same favor as the Modern face. However, Whittingham and a bookseller, William Pickering, went on to use the face for several books, which encouraged others to try it. A decade or so later, Caslon Old-face, which had been forgotten by the Caslon typefoundry, appeared again in the specimen book.

In 1860, the first named "Old-style" type was issued by the Edinburgh typefoundry, Miller & Richard. The publicity assured the reader that the new type design had "removed the distasteful qualities of the Old face while retaining the fundamental characteristics of a pre-Modern face."

Alexander C. Phemister, an employee of the Edinburgh typefoundry, was responsible for the cutting of the Old-style series. He had attempted to adapt the Old-face form to the current aesthetic of the Modern face. The serifs were bracketed and gradual stress was reintroduced, modified to become more vertical, following the modern preference. His typecutting skills gave a uniform keenness to the forms, eliminating the irregularities of the 18th-century typeface. Shortly after he completed the series in Edinburgh, Phemister settled in America. Working in Boston for the Dickinson typefoundry he cut, among other faces, Franklin Old Style, a similar version to his earlier Old style.

The lighter, more open forms of the Old style gained in popularity over the next few years—aided by some dissatisfaction with the ubiquitous Modern face, and as a result of the more spectacular activities of William Morris and his experiments with the Venetian Old-face of Jenson. There were many copies developed into the early 20th century. There was a tendency for the later Old-styles to emphasize the archaic. They now seem rather mannered. When the machine typesetting companies began their revival of many excellent versions of Old-faces and transitionals, it was with a new respect for the punchcutters of the earlier generations.

CH. PLANTIN has a foremost position in PLANTIN deserves

Bertram Goodhue was an architect by training, with an interest in typography. In 1894, he designed a typeface for the Merrymount Press of D. B. Updike, based (like Morris' designs) on Jenson's type of 1475. Goodhue had also been involved with the production of a "Chapbook" journal printed by the Cheltenham Press in New York. He was commissioned to design a typeface for the Press's own use. Goodhue set to work on the design with the intention of taking a methodical approach to produce a highly legible typeform influenced by Old-style characteristics.

Cheltenham Old Style, as it was named, became possibly the most popular American typeface of its time, more for its qualities as a display face than as a text face, and, to a large degree, because of the range of variants available.

Cheltenham has a light, condensed appearance, proportionally short, stubby serifs and an interesting mixture of 20th-century geometric precision and mannered organic forms. This is most noticeable in the vertical stems of the capitals, which contrast with the curved letters of the lowercase "a," "g," "f," "r," and "s." The capital "A" has an overhang at the apex, while the capital "G" has a spur on the lower curve of the bowl which is not quite a serif. It is suitable for publicity texts that need character, since it has a very strong personality on the page.

Cheltenham Old Style
Goodhue's design to the left has a distinct character and is rather condensed, with stubby serifs and a small x-height. In this italic cut the lowercase "e" and "p" have open counters, and the "s" has the characteristic terminating teardrop forms rather than serifs.

Large family
Cheltenham's popularity was, in some part, owing to the large range of weights and other related forms available. This was a fairly new concept at the time.

CHELTENHAM

6 Point
THE QUICK BROWN FOX JUMPS Over the lazy dog the quick brown fox jumps at   90 A. 190 a.; about 5 lb.
8 Point
THE QUICK BROWN FOX JUMPS over the lazy dog the quick brown fox   90 A. 190 a.; about 8 lb.
10 Point
THE QUICK BROWN FOX jumps over the lazy dog the bold   70 A. 155 a.; about 11 lb.
12 Point
THE QUICK BROWN Fox jumps over the lazy dog   60 A. 140 a.; about 13 lb.
14 Point
THE QUICK BOLD fox jumps over the dog   48 A. 100 a.; about 14 lb.
18 Point
THE QUICK Brown fox jumps over   36 A. 70 a.; about 16 lb.
24 Point
THE BIG Brown foxes jump   24 A. 50 a.; about 19 lb.
30 Point
THE BIG brown fox 5   14 A. 34 a.; about 19 lb.
36 Point
THE BIG grey fox   12 A. 24 a.; about 23 lb.
42 Point
THE Bold black   7 A. 14 a.; about 21 lb.
48 Point
FOX Jumps 5   7 A. 14 a.; about 24 lb.
60 Point
Past the idle   5 A. 10 a.; about 24½ lb.
72 Point
Red Dog!   5 A. 8 a.; about 29 lb.

ABCDEFGHIJKLMNOPQRSTUVWXYZÆŒ&
abcdefghijklmnopqrstuvwxyzæœ ﬀﬁﬂﬃﬄ
1234567890£ .,:;!?-'"{}

Contextualizer

Bertram Goodhue
1869–1924

Cheltenham Old Style as trendsetter

The most popular typeface in America of its time, Cheltenham Old Style set a trend for similar Old-style faces with "New England" names such as Gloucester, Winchester, and Windsor. The ATF (American Type Foundry) applied the "family" principle to Cheltenham, and by 1915 Morris Benton had extended the variants of the face to 21.

Goodhue's theory of legibility

Goodhue regarded the upper half of a line of type as the most important for clarity, so the ascenders and descenders were adjusted accordingly. More recent experiments have suggested that legibility is improved by a proportionally larger x-height.

The Merrymount Press

A scholarly, craftsmanlike American printers, The Merrymount Press was founded and run by Daniel Updike in Boston from 1893 to1941. It was the finest representative of the Arts and Crafts movement in American book arts, and was founded "to do common work well."

The Neo-Gothic

Neo-Gothic was the American branch of the Gothic revival movement transplanted from England in 1830s; as championed by William Morris, who based his type designs on those from the late 1400s. The movement favored medieval designs instead of the then-prevailing love of classicism of the time. Goodhue's best-known architecture was in this style.

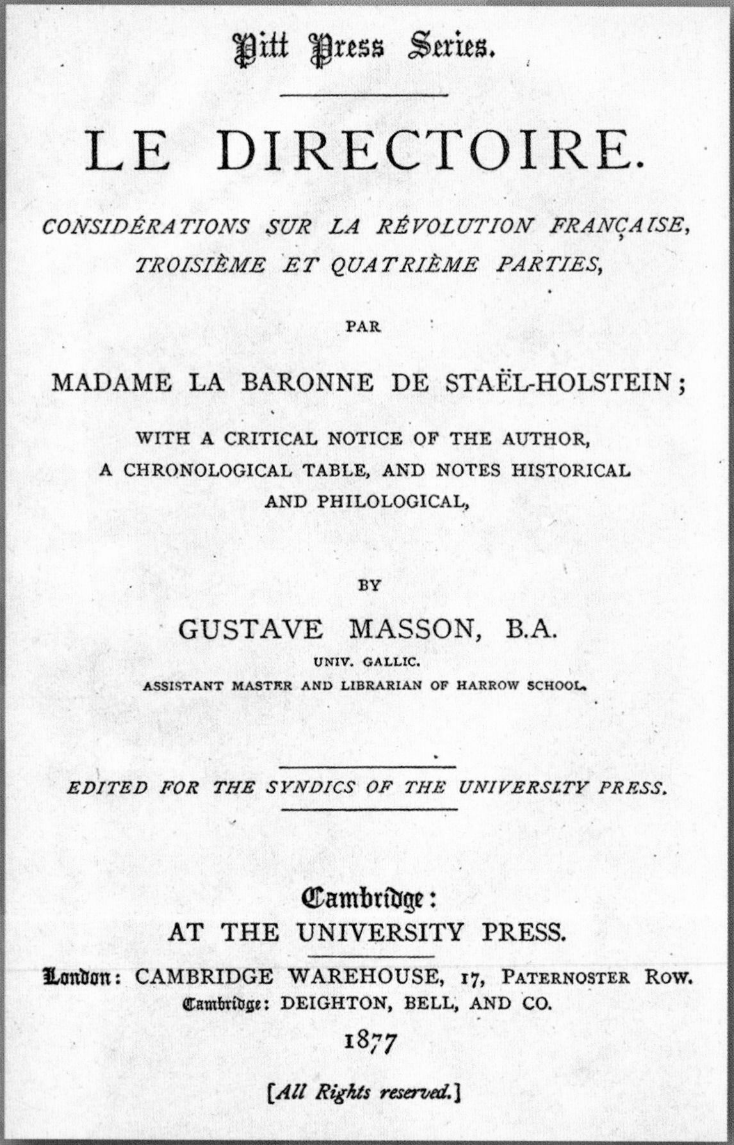

Pitt Press Series.

———

LE DIRECTOIRE.

CONSIDÉRATIONS SUR LA RÉVOLUTION FRANÇAISE,
TROISIÈME ET QUATRIÈME PARTIES,

PAR

MADAME LA BARONNE DE STAËL-HOLSTEIN;

WITH A CRITICAL NOTICE OF THE AUTHOR,
A CHRONOLOGICAL TABLE, AND NOTES HISTORICAL
AND PHILOLOGICAL,

BY

GUSTAVE MASSON, B.A.

UNIV. GALLIC.

ASSISTANT MASTER AND LIBRARIAN OF HARROW SCHOOL.

———

EDITED FOR THE SYNDICS OF THE UNIVERSITY PRESS.

Cambridge:
AT THE UNIVERSITY PRESS.

———

London: CAMBRIDGE WAREHOUSE, 17, PATERNOSTER ROW.
Cambridge: DEIGHTON, BELL, AND CO.

1877

[*All Rights reserved.*]

Title page set in Old-style
*This title page of an 1877
University Press edition
of Madame de Stael's* Le
Directoire, *is a good example
of the alternative to the
ubiquitous Modern type of
the period. The letterforms
feel a little mannered today,
but their lighter, more open
forms were originally
very appealing.*

Old-styles at work

Cheltenham Old Style usage

Tracking, kerning, and H&Js

Despite Goodhue's legibility theories, more recent digital versions of Cheltenham are produced with a larger x-height, which reduces the length of the ascenders and descenders. In small sizes it benefits from a small increase in tracking. Standard kerning may need adjustment in display sizes.

Text sizes

Cheltenham, although originally intended for use in books, works best for publicity. This is due to its development as a family of types, and its very distinct character.

Display sizes

Cheltenham has flourished as a display face since its arrival on the typographic scene. Although it has not had the attention that some revivals have experienced, its considerable number of condensed weights make it useful for newspapers and newsletters, where narrow columns limit the use of normal width fonts.

On-screen display

Like most serifed letterforms, the distinct visual character of Cheltenham is subject to loss of font fidelity when displayed on screen. Only display sizes are recommended, these are therefore best conveyed by GIF or JPEG.

Architecture began like all scripts. First there was the alphabet. A stone was laid and that was a letter, and each letter was a hieroglyph, and on each hieroglyph there rested a group of ideas, like the capital on a column. Thus, until Gutenberg architecture is the chief and universal "writing." This granite book, begun in the East, continued by the Greeks and Romans—its last page was written by the Middle Ages. Until the fifteenth century, architecture was the great exponent and recorder of mankind. In the 15th century everything changed. Human thought discovered a means of perpetuating itself which was not only more lasting and resilient than architecture, but also simpler and more straightforward. Architecture is superseded. The stone letters of Orpheus have been succeeded by the leaden ones of Gutenberg. The book will destroy the edifice. The invention of printing is the greatest event in history. It is the fundamental revolution. Under the printing form, thought becomes more imperishable than ever; it is volatile, elusive and indestructible. It mingles with the very air. Thought derives new life from this concrete form. It passes from a lifespan into immortality. One can destroy something concrete, but who can eradicate what is omnipresent? VICTOR HUGO

Cheltenham display
This page from Upper and Lowercase, *the ITC typography magazine, was designed by the American graphic designer and art director Herb Lubalin.*

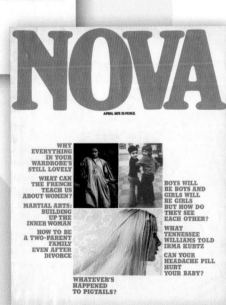

Nova
A monthly magazine, Nova *used an Old-style bold condensed for the design of its masthead.*

THE 19TH CENTURY: *Making Type*

During the 19th century considerable effort and ingenuity were devoted to the problems of casting and setting type. However, it was the innovative procedures and devices of Linn Boyd Benton (1844–1932) that contributed most to the improvement of making type.

Prior to the development of photosetting and digitization, metal type was processed in two different ways; one created foundry type and the other hot-metal type. Type metal is an alloy, primarily composed of lead with different additions of tin, antimony, and, occasionally, copper. Type alloys had been in existence from the 15th century, and were developed because lead alone was too soft: tin helps the lead to melt, while antimony is used to increase hardness and acts to stop the alloy shrinking as it cooled.

Foundry types were the traditional form of metal type that were cast as individual letters for distribution to the typecase for handsetting. The inventions of the 19th century, Linotype, the single-unit machine Linotype, and the two-unit machine Monotype, were both hot-metal systems. The initial keyboard work selected matrices in order for the type to be cast. After printing, hot-metal type would mostly be returned to the metal pot and melted down to be cast again. Foundry type used a harder alloy, and would be redistributed back to the typecase after printing or stereotyping, ready to be used again—hence the term "printing from moveable type." Today, metal type foundries are very few and far between. If type for handsetting is required, it is most likely to be cast by a Monotype Caster and then distributed to the typecase. Monotype Casters are quite difficult to find, since they are not generally used commercially today.

Linn Boyd Benton had no family connections with printing, but he became one of the most technically inventive American typefounders. In 1866, he took a job as bookkeeper at the Northwestern Typefoundry, Milwaukee. From this position he soon rose to warehouse buyer. Seven years later, with a partner, Benton bought the typefoundry. Benton's first invention in 1882 was a multiple mold for casting typespacing material. He also explored the possibilities of a typesetting machine that had automatic justification. By 1884, his typefoundry was using his most important invention, a pantograph machine for cutting steel punches, which was patented in 1885.

Benton's punchcutting machine had wider applications than those used in typefoundries —the manufacturers of the new Linotype and Monotype typesetting machines were in great need of a way of increasing their output of matrices, since every machine manufactured required multiple sets.

STANDARDIZING THE PICA IN AMERICA AND BRITAIN

France had established a standard measurement for type bodies and related spacing material in 1775, which had spread to other European countries. In America and Britain, however, no agreement about standardization in the industry had been reached, even by the late 19th century. Without pressure from some authority agreement was difficult to achieve, since this would involve many foundries disposing of their existing types and equipment, plunging them into the expensive process of retooling. A step toward standardization began in America when one of the largest typefoundries, Marder, Luce, & Company, fell

Machine punchcutter
The pantographic instrument, shown in use below, was invented by Linn Boyd Benton. It became a contributory asset to the manufacturers of Linotype and Monotype typesetting machines.

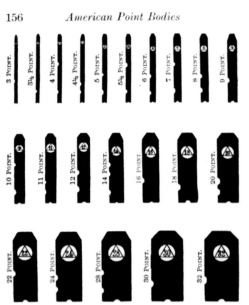

victim in 1871 to the Great Chicago Fire, which destroyed their buildings and equipment, molds and type stocks. The company was forced to rebuild and retool, and in the process the directors decided to align their type sizes with those of MacKellar, Smiths, & Jordan in Philadelphia, the biggest of America's typefoundries.

Nelson Hawks was a junior partner in the unfortunate company, responsible for the office in San Francisco. As a supplier of printers' equipment and materials he was confronted daily with the problems that non-standardization created. He devised a system of type body standardization and was keen to encourage other foundries to participate in it. Eventually his dedication paid off, in spite of resistance from some of his directors, and he was able to convince other foundries of the value of his system. His campaign reached full acceptance in 1886, and was taken up in Britain in 1898. However the MacKellar, Smiths, & Jordan point, which became the universal standard in America, Britain, and other English-speaking countries, is not exactly 72 points to an inch. One point is 1/72.27 of an inch or 0.351mm, which continues to be the standard for metal type. However, Adobe adjusted the point to exactly 1/72 of an inch (0.353 mm) when creating the computer page description program Postscript in the 1980s, and this is now the standard measurement for digital fonts.

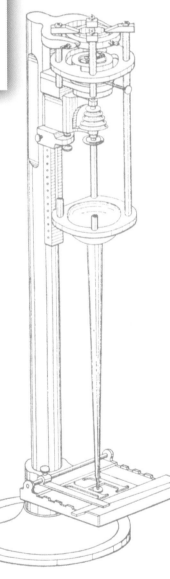

Punchcutting by machine
The drawing to the right shows an early punchcutting machine. The metal type template is sited at bench level and the cutting head is on the column above. The toggle-jointed pendulum transferred the movement around the template to the cutting head.

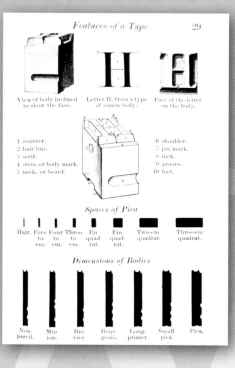

Features of a Type 29

View of body inclined to show the face.
Letter H, from a type of canon body.
Face of the letter on the body.

1 counter.
2 hair-line.
3 serif.
4 stem, or body mark.
5 neck, or beard.
6 shoulder.
7 pin mark.
8 nick.
9 groove.
10 feet.

Spaces of Pica

Hair. Five to em. Four to em. Three to em. En quad-rat. Em quad-rat. Two-em quadrat. Three-em quadrat.

Dimensions of Bodies

Non-pareil. Min-ion. Bre-vier. Bour-geois. Long-primer. Small-pica. Pica.

De Vinne on printing
*Theodore L. De Vinne
(1828–1914) was a frequent
writer on the history and
practice of printing. He
was of the opinion that the
delicate Modern types made
popular by Bodoni were
unsuitable for the faster
printing production methods
of mass-market publications.*

Theodore L. De Vinne
*A master printer of great
experience and learning,
De Vinne's opinions where
influential in the American
printing industry at the
turn of the century.*

THEODORE L. DE VINNE *& New Century*

The American printer and printing historian Theodore L. De Vinne
was concerned with the state of commercial printing. Like William
Morris in London, he had strongly held views on the general standards
in commercial printing and what he considered to be the deterioration
of the modern letterform. Unlike Morris, De Vinne was an experienced
and knowledgeable printer with a full understanding of the commercial
and practical problems of type design.

By the close of the 19th century, enormous
progress had been made in the development of
the printing industry. The demand for books,
magazines, newspapers, and other printed matter
had hastened technical innovation.

For most of the 19th century, before
mechanical typesetting became commonplace,
most newspapers and books were printed using
a variety of mediocre Modern roman faces.
By the early 1800s, British typefounders were
producing Modern romans that lacked the full
classic elegance of a Bodoni Modern. In their
pure simplicity, Bodoni's hairline serifs were not
robust enough for the rough handling of the
commercial print shop and the power-driven
presses; they could only be at their best when
given the attention that is possible with the hand
press and the smooth surface possible with wove
paper, for which they were designed.

There were three British Modern faces that
survived the 19th century but were always in the
shadow of the internationally respected Bodoni.
William Martin, brother Baskerville's apprentice
Robert, cut a type for printer William Bulmer
in 1790, revived by Morris F. Benton in 1928 as
Bulmer. Richard Austin worked for John Bell's
British Letter Foundry and cut a transitional type
bordering on the Modern that was revived as
Monotype Bell in 1932. Later, in 1810, William

Miller of Edinburgh commissioned him to cut a
Modern, revived in 1909 as Scotch Roman by the
American Type Foundry. All three of these owed
something to Baskerville, although the vertical
contrasting stress of thick and thin strokes
expresses the influence of the Modern-face. The
stress is tapered on curves and serifs carry a
suggestion of a bracket, creating a more amiable
character that is less austere than Bodoni.

De Vinne's criticism of these Modern romans
was of their poor legibility and presswork.
He believed that the uniform vertical stress
made identity of individual letters difficult. His
proposal for improvement was to increase the
thickness of thin strokes and give the serifs more
body, not only to improve legibility but also to
create a type that was better able to deal with
the stresses of the modern machine presses. He
insisted on keeping the narrow set that was
important for maintaining a high number
of words per column.

Linn Boyd Benton, as technical director
of the American Type Foundry (ATF), was
commissioned by De Vinne to cut a type for
De Vinne's *Century* magazine. Benton's final
design turned out to be a great success, which
caused the introduction of a series of variants
designed by Boyd's assistant, his son Morris
Fuller Benton. Over nearly 30 years Morris

Century Schoolbook

ABCDEFGHIJKLMN
OPQRSTUVWXYZ&
$ 1 2 3 4 5 6 7 8 9 0
abcdefghijklmnopq
rstuvwxyz.,-:;!?''
fi ff fl ffi ffl

ABCDEFGHIJKLMN
OPQRSTUVWXYZ&
$ 1 2 3 4 5 6 7 8 9 0
abcdefghijklmnopq
rstuvwxyz.,-:;!?''
fi ff fl ffi ffl

Century Schoolbook
*Century Schoolbook is
possibly the most popular
of the existing Century
family, and is admired for
its excellent readability.*

Benton developed 18 variants of Century, some
of which are now digitized. The most popular
digital version of Century is Century Schoolbook,
which was released in 1924; other versions are
Century Expanded, cut in 1903, and Century
Old Style, cut in of 1909. In 1993 Edward
Benguiat designed a range of Century hand-
tooled alphabets. Berthold recently released four
weights which retain the narrow quality of the
original Century. Century's large x-height and
generous forms provide very good legibility,
which has made it popular for press advertising
and children's books.

The Century type
*De Vinne's type design was
not so much a new design as
a technical improvement to
a Modern face that had not
kept up with technological
developments. The enlarged
image of Century schoolbook
below shows that it has
something of Clarendon in its
character, helping to maintain
it as a hard-working, versatile
typeface to this day.*

SsKk
SsKk

Contextualizer

*Theodore
L. De Vinne*
1828–1914

"Century" magazine

In order to demonstrate his ideas
on type design, De Vinne persuaded
the publisher of "Century" to invest
in a new typeface for the magazine.
This may have been the first specially
commissioned type of the century.
De Vinne entrusted the American
Type Foundry with the making of the
type, developing the design under
the supervision of Linn Boyd Benton.
Benton had recently invented the
punchcutting machine, which was
to be used on this occasion. The
monthly magazine was considered a
fine specimen of art in that period.
It featured color illustrations and
serialized fiction.

Private presses

The Industrial Revolution created a
growing literary public and mass-
produced volumes were churned out
to satisfy demand without aesthetic
considerations. It was as a response
to this that private presses with
their own particular styles sprung
up. William Morris' Kelmscott Press
in Great Britain epitomized the Arts
and Crafts movement, while Thomas
Bird Mosher's eponymous press in
the United States exemplified the
aesthetic style in America.

NELeinkophs

Century Expanded (modern)

NELeinkophs

Century Oldstyle

The Century Family

AN EXCEEDINGLY DIGNIFIED TYPE FAMILY

Century Expanded
Century Expanded Italic
Century Bold
Century Bold Italic
Century Bold Condensed
Century Bold Extended
Century Oldstyle
Century Oldstyle Italic
Century Oldstyle Bold
Century Oldstyle Bold Italic

AmericanType Founders Co.

ORIGINATOR OF THE FAMILY IDEA IN TYPES

Type specimens
*These examples highlight
the difference between
Century Expanded (top) and
Century Old Style (above).
Note the heavier, angled
serifs on the lower example.
Century Expanded was one
of the first variations on
the original Morris Fuller
Benton family design.*

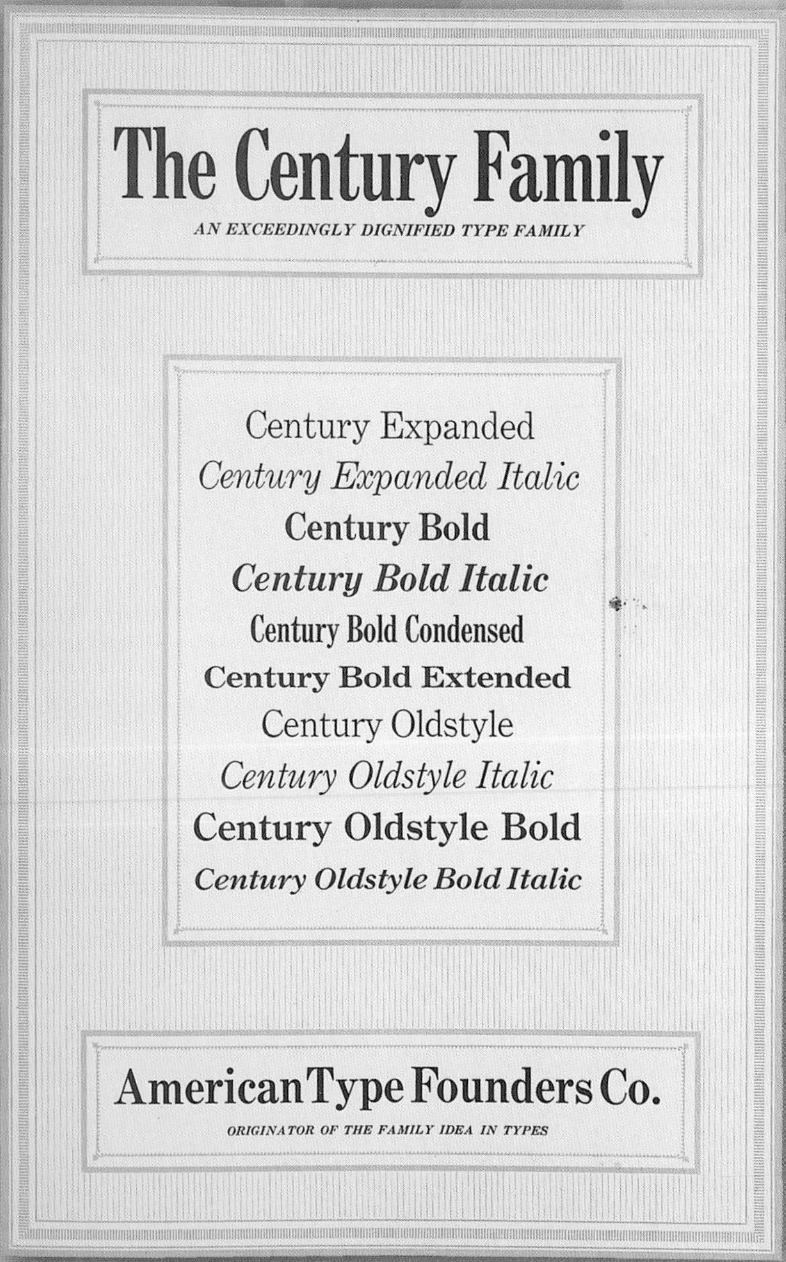

The Century family
*The American Type
Foundry promotion
of the Century range of
variants. Morris Fuller
Benton was responsible
for developing De Vinne's
1894 commission into a
family of related forms.*

Century at work

No one would have believed, in the last years of the nineteenth century, that human affairs were being watched keenly and closely by intelligences greater than man's and yet as mortal as his own; that as men busied themselves about their affairs they were scrutinized and studied, perhaps almost as narrowly as a man with a microscope might scrutinize the transient creatures that swarm and multiply in drops of water. With infinate complacency men went to and fro over this globe about their little affairs, serene in their assurance of their empire over matter. It is possible that the infusoria under the microscope do the same. No one gave a thought to the older worlds of space as sources of human danger, or thought to the older worlds of space as sources of human danger, or thought of them only to dismiss the idea of life upon them as impossible and improbable. It is curious to recall some of the mental habits of those departed days. At most, terrestrial men fancied there might be other men upon Mars, perhaps inferior to themselves and ready to welcome a missionary enterprise. Yet, across the gulf of space, minds that are to our minds as ours are to those of the beasts that perish, intellects vast and cool and unsympathetic, regarded this earth with envious eyes, and slowly and surely drew their plans against us. And early in the twentieth century came the great disillusionment. The planet Mars, I scarcely need remind listeners, revolves about the sun at a mean distance of 140,000,000 miles, and the light and heat it receives from the sun is barely half of that received by this world. It must be, if the nebular hypothesis has any truth, older than our world, and long before this earth ceased to be molten, life upon its surface must have begun its course. The fact that it is scarcely one-seventh of the volume of the earth must have accelerated its cooling to the temperature at which life could begin. It has air and water, and all that is necessary for the support of animated existence.

Century as text
This detail of a design to the left shows Century as text, and is a good example of the practical qualities of this letterform. The low contrast of stem thickness, and the generous forms combined with a fairly large x-height, result in an agreeable typeface with good readability.

Clarity
This advertising material demonstrates how Century has been and continues to be popular with advertising agencies and children's book publishers, as it has great clarity and legibility.

Century usage

Tracking, kerning, and H&Js

Century is an excellent all-purpose typeface, with good letter fit that is tight without being cramped; hence tracking is only necessary for special effects. Close word spacing is preferred for good legibility, but this is governed by line length.

Text sizes

Century has earned a reputation for good legibility and clear letter identification, making it a good choice for text. With its open, wholesome letterforms and generous x-height it is advisable to introduce leading. This sustains horizontal movement of the eye along the line for comfortable legibility.

Display sizes

Century's strong, low-contrast letterforms make it an excellent display face. Tracking should be reduced as size increases in order to maintain good word clarity. However, capitals can be letter-spaced to some degree without loss of word clarity.

On-screen display

Due to the detailed serif design Century will lose detail when displayed as a text face on-screen. It is best to use Century for display only, containing the letterforms within a GIF or JPEG.

5   Early Modernism

The years around the turn of the 20th century were a vigorous time of dissent and revolution, politically, socially, and culturally. The latter part of the 19th century had stirred up anticapitalist, anticolonialist, and antiacademic movements. There were demands for change in working conditions. Subjugated countries were demanding independence. Creative artists, from writers and musicians to painters, were breaking free from the conventional structures of their practice.

By 1880, the French Impressionist movement had become internationally influential in art, and by the end of the first decade of the new century Impressionism was the acceptable face of modern art. However, the avant garde had moved on. It was in 1905 that the Fauves ("wild beasts")

Assassination
The Archduke Ferdinand (right) was heir to the Austro-Hungarian imperial throne. His assassination in 1914 triggered a chain of events that lead to the First World War.

Revolution
Vladimir Ilyich Lenin (left) addresses a crowd at the start of the Russian Revolution in February 1917.

challenged the gallery-going public with their use of pure color. The painters Matisse, Derain, Vlaminck, and Rouault, under the influence of Gauguin and Van Gogh, experimented with color and free reference to nature. In Germany, Die Brücke in Dresden and Der Blaue Reiter in Munich were two groups of artists whose pictures responded in a violently expressive way to the times. In 1908, the first Cubist works of Georges Braque were shown in Paris, and he and Pablo Picasso went on to develop a movement that was to be a major influence on 20th-century art. The Cubists introduced words and type into their painting by pasting in pieces torn from newspapers. However, it was the provocative extrovert Filippo Tommaso Marinetti who made use of words and type in a radically new way.

The Italian Futurist group of artists were ardent enthusiasts of the mechanistic aspects of the modern world. They adored machinery, aeroplanes, fast cars, and the noisy bustle of modern city life—in fact everything that could be considered uniquely modern. Marinetti, the leader of the group, developed a technique he called "Words-in-Freedom," which ignored punctuation, syntax and other conventions of the normal printed page. Marinetti's intention was to visually record the energy of the spoken word

Zang Tumb Tumb
*A Futurist poem (right)
from 1914, by the
provocative poet and
theorist Fillipo Tommaso
Marinetti, who famously
proclaimed that war was
"the world's only hygiene."
This typographic poem
shows Marinetti's use of
type in what he called
"words in freedom."*

and to imitate sounds by use of any number of
typefaces (the more the better), by arrangement,
and by contrasts of size. In a clear break from
the past, this was one of the first attempts to free
the printed page from its historical conventions
and to create a dynamic which, by disposition
and contrast, visually added impact and emotion
to the text. Similar techniques were to became
features of the new typography.

In June 1914, Archduke Ferdinand, heir
to the Austro-Hungarian imperial throne, was
assassinated in Sarajevo by a Bosnian nationalist.
Austria declared war on Serbia, and by doing
so set in motion a disastrous chain of events:
Germany declared war on Russia and France,
and invaded Belgium, whereupon Britain
declared war on Germany and the Austro-
Hungarian empire. An estimated ten million
people were killed during the First World War.
A peace treaty was signed in June 1919 at
Versailles, but there were issues that were
not fully resolved.

During the war, an international group of
artists opposed to the politics and culture that
had created the war, and the folly of war itself,
gathered in Zurich in neutral Switzerland. Their
activities centered around the satirical Cabaret
Voltaire. Their publications used collage,

photomontage, and radical typography—similar
devices to those of the Futurists, but with a
different agenda.

In 1917, the Russian Revolution broke out,
from which emerged the Constructivist movement
that was to spread its ideas throughout Europe
during the coming years. This group of artists
were committed to the Revolution and they saw
the need for a new role for art in their vision of
reconstruction. This group was influenced by
Kasimir Malevich and his Suprematist non-
objective paintings, which were to open up a
new aesthetic for the 20th century.

The Dada movement
*Dada was a group of
artists opposed to what
they considered the
absurdity of the First
World War. They expressed
their attitudes using
satire performed at the
Café Voltaire nightclub,
in Zurich, in neutral
Switzerland, during the
war. A cover of the* Dada
*magazine, as designed
by Raoul Haussmann,
is shown above.*

g

MORRIS FULLER BENTON *& Franklin Gothic*

The search for typographic originality in the early 19th century led to the introduction of the sans-serif. At the very beginning of the 20th century, the American sans-serif Franklin Gothic was designed. It became one of the most popular Gothics in history, and it retains international celebrity to this day.

Franklin Gothic
This lowercase "g" with its full-looped descender formed into a bowl (top) is typical of the sans-serif types that originated in the 19th century. The lowercase "g" from Univers (above) is provided for comparison.

Grotesque No.9
This Stephenson, Blake, & Company foundry type shows the original forms that are characteristic of the 19th-century sans-serif.

Morris Fuller Benton began his studies at Cornell University in 1892, the same year that his father's firm, Benton, Waldo, & Company, joined up with 22 other foundries to form the American Type Foundry (ATF). Benton joined ATF as his father's assistant a few months after he graduated. Linn Boyd Benton's energy and inventive genius had made him an important asset to the new organization. Father and son and their families soon moved to New York, closer to head office. By 1900, Benton had become head of ATF's type design department. One of his first projects was the design of a new sans-serif, Franklin Gothic.

Although ATF already had a large number of Gothics in their specimen book as a result of the amalgamation, Benton proceeded to cut the first of the series of Franklin Gothic faces, completed in 1902 and released in 1905. A condensed version was released the same year, the following year saw an extra condensed, oblique fonts came in 1913, and in 1914 a condensed shaded was released. Benton gained a reputation for careful thought and for the research he carried out before commencing a new type design, so it may have been the appearance of revived sans-serifs by the German foundries of Berthold and Bauer that convinced him of the need for a revitalized Gothic. It was the pantographic punchcutting device, invented by his father in 1885 that made creating family variants a comparatively simple development.

For the new typeface, the letters were first drawn at about 40mm (1.5") high. Then each letter was produced as a enlarged outline drawing that could be studied for inconsistencies and corrected as necessary. It was also possible at this stage for the pantograph device to be adjusted to draw condensed, expanded, or oblique forms. The improved outline drawing was filled in to make a solid letterform, which was then tested for clarity of form at various

ABCDEFGHIJKLMNOPQRSTUV
abcdefghiklmnopqrstuvwxyz&
ABCDEFGHIKLMNOPQRSTUVWXYZ&

A useful family
Franklin Gothic has an extensive range of weights and italics, which include a collection of condensed designs.

BOOK

AaBbCcDdEeFf

DEMI

AaBbCcDdEeFf

HEAVY

AaBbCcDdEeFf

BOOK OBLIQUE

AaBbCcDdEeFf

HEAVY OBLIQUE

AaBbCcDdEeFf

BOOK CONDENSED

AaBbCcDdEeFf

DEMI CONDENSED

AaBbCcDdEeFf

BOOK COMPRESSED

AaBbCcDdEeFf

DEMI COMPRESSED

AaBbCcDdEeFf

BOOK EXTRA COMPRESSED

AaBbCcDdEeFf

DEMI EXTRA COMPRESSED

AaBbCcDdEeFf

sizes, by optical reduction, and again corrected if necessary. A pattern plate was made from the final drawing. This was done by a wax-coated brass plate being fitted to the pantograph machine, and an outline of the drawing being traced at a smaller size into the wax. A layer of copper was electrically deposited onto the plate in order to create a raised image of the letter. This became the pattern plate, which was used as a template by the punchcutting machine. In the 1960s, ATF develped this punchcutting principal into a machine that engraved directly into matrix blanks, providing a more practical means of making matrices. The machine could be adjusted to engrave matrices of specific point sizes.

Morris F. Benton's Franklin Gothic retained, but refined, features of 19th-century types, such as a slight overall narrowness. There is a modest reduction of line thickness at the junction of stems and bowls, and at the head and foot of circular letters. There is also the retained two-bowl, lowercase "g," which many 20th-century sans-serifs have done away with. Benton's Franklin Gothic has retained its popularity since it has a friendliness matched only by Gill Sans.

The digitized ITC Franklin Gothic consists of four weights with obliques. Franklin Gothic Condensed has three weights. Franklin Gothic Compressed, Extra Compressed, Demi Compressed and Demi Extra Compressed are four very condensed fonts.

Contextualizer

Morris Fuller Benton
1872–1948

The earliest sans-serifs

The earliest known sans-serif cut as a font for the Latin alphabet appeared in the specimen book of William Caslon IV in 1816 and was named "Egyptian." It consisted of three words of two-line titling, although no example of it in use has been found. Typefounders took some time to agree on a generic name for this form of letter. In 1832, Vincent Figgins showed three sizes of sans-serif, which he named "Antique," and in the same year, in a supplement to his specimen book, William Thorowgood showed a sans-serif described as a "Grotesque." The name reflected the response to the effect of a letterform with serifs cut off, and was the preferred name for the style in Britain. In America, the first sans-serif was released c.1837 by the Boston Type and Stereotype Company. It offered five sizes of capitals, described as "Gothic," a name normally associated with blackletter.

Typeface families

In designing Franklin Gothic, Benton was to develop the concept of type families. This was not a totally new idea, but it was an aspect of type design that he made a feature of when designing his subsequent typefaces, allowing the typographer in the age of press advertising to make use of a palette of weights and typeforms with similar characteristics.

Franklin Gothic at work

American Gothic
These advertisements in a 1902 motoring magazine are set with typical sans-serifs. Morris Fuller Benton was renowned for his carefully researched approach to type design, and he referred to similar sans-serif fonts found at the American Type Foundry, in redesigning the coherent Franklin Gothic family of weights and styles.

At work

These advertisements for an emergency road service are a typical application of Franklin Gothic's assertive but friendly sans-serif.

Break down.
Make his day.

RAC
...IGHTS OF THE ROAD.

Now there's a
hard shoulder
you can cry on.

RAC
THE NEW KNIGHTS OF THE ROAD.

Conversations

Tracking, kerning, and H&Js

Franklin Gothic offers a wide range of weights, italics, condenseds, and extra condenseds. It has a comfortable letterfit, which may benefit from a little increased tracking in the heavier weights and the extra condensed fonts. Standard kerning is sufficient, while word-spacing should generally be tighter than the default values.

Text sizes

Like many sans-serifs, Franklin Gothic has a large x-height when compared size for-size with most serifed typefaces, this means it has good legibility in small sizes. Franklin Gothic makes an excellent type for children's books and advertising.

Display sizes

Franklin Gothic is a popular display face, offering many variations. In large sizes it creates strong graphic impact with clarity and warmth characteristics that are missing from some 20th-century sans-serifs. It functions well if tracking is reasonably increased, but more impact is achieved when tracking is tightened with the increase of size.

On-screen display

Screen resolution is kinder to sans-serif than to serifed type. However, in text sizes it is preferable to use one of the sans-serif fonts more suitable for web use such as Verdana or Arial. Larger display sizes are currently best displayed within a GIF or JPEG.

Variety

This experimental poster demonstrates how a variety of weights of Franklin Gothic can create an inventive design that remains visually coherent.

MODERNISM: *20th Century Influences*

The ideas of William Morris and his circle of cultural and social theorists were responsible for stimulating debate about aesthetics, design, and manufacture. These issues were important to all industrial countries, especially the recently unified states of Germany. Since the mid-1800s, Germany's industrial power had begun to challenge that of Britain.

Hermann Muthesius (1861–1927) had spent time in London as a member of the German Embassy and had been acquainted with Morris and his views on industry and design. On his return to Germany, his interest in design and architecture led him to write *The English House*, an authoritative study of English upper-class domestic architecture. In 1904, he was employed as director of the Prussian Board of Trade for Arts and Crafts Education. In this role he was instrumental in creating the educational environment that later enabled the establishment of the Bauhaus in post-war Weimar, Germany. Muthesius was also a member of the Deutsche Werkbund. Founded in 1906 and influenced by the Arts and Crafts movement, the Werkbund were a group of artists, designers, architects, and manufacturers concerned with the quality of design, craftsmanship, and manufacture of mass-produced goods. As an organization, the Werkbund intended to advise and encourage German industry to make improvements in the

Lazar El Lissitzky
Lissitzky (1890–1941) threw himself into applying the precepts of Constructivism. From 1921 until his death, his energy was remarkable. The abstract paintings he called **PROUNS** *(below) are examples of the modernist aesthetic.*

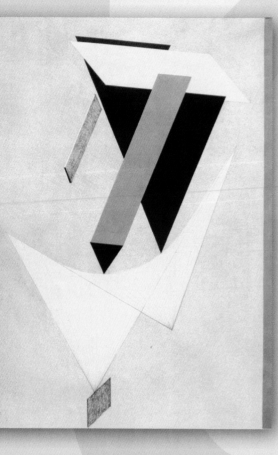

De Stijl
An example of typography from the Dutch avant-garde Modern movement, formed around the leading activist Theo van Doesburg.

design and production of German goods in order to improve Germany's position in international trade. The organization closed down under the National Socialists, but was active again after the defeat of Hitler.

A NEW TYPOGRAPHIC FREEDOM

Modern graphic design and typography were fueled by many contemporary influences. At the end of the 19th century, jobbing printing and typography were a hodgepodge of type styles and ornamentation. Avant-garde artists such as the Futurists and Dadaists, who used typography in their manifestos and publicity, recognized that reading was also seeing, in that what you see when reading affects how you respond to what you read.

From its earliest days, typesetting had been structured following ancient conventions of horizontal sentences and vertical columns. Now, in the 20th century, using techniques of photo-engraving, it was possible to paste up letters and words with no concern for the confines of horizontal or vertical, and to reproduce them by photo-chemical processes to make an engraved lineblock for printing letterpress. The Futurists and Dadaists produced publications using Marinetti's concept of "Words-in-Freedom." The use of lineblocks allowed for a more expressive use of type to convey greater visual impact.

RELATING ART TO SOCIETY

The avant-garde movements that emerged after 1918 rejected many aspects of the culture and values which they considered to have brought about the First World War. These movements were determined to create an aesthetic that was international, and so rejected national or vernacular styles. There was a strong conviction that art should make a contribution to all of society. Through manifestos and exhibitions they hoped to show how art and design could play an important part in everyday life, by recognizing the requirements of the modern urban industrial society that were spreading across Europe.

In 1917, there was a second outbreak of rioting in St Petersburg, resulting in the Bolshevik Revolution and Lenin coming to power. As part of the revolutionary events that took place, Russian artists, especially those at the Moscow Higher State Artistic-Technical Workshops (INKhUK)—a polytechnic similar to the Bauhaus, debated the role of art and artists in the new society. The term "Constructivism" first appeared in the catalogue of their 1922 exhibition. They turned away from the bourgeois concept of art to direct their attention to aspects of mass production and the needs of the new social order in Russia. They rejected the traditional materials of art, favoring timber, metal, paper and board, and photography.

20th-century modernism
The avant-garde aesthetic of the century's early decades was to strip everything down and remove ornamentation. This applied to typefaces as well, as in the simple design of this serif type, Scarab Condensed.

12 Point	57
THE QUICK BROWN FOX Jumps over	

14 Point
THE QUICK BROWN Fox jumps

18 Point
THE QUICK RED Fox jump

24 Point
THE QUICK Brown

30 Point
THE QUICK bro

36 Point
THE BIG brow

48 Point
LEAPS ove

60 Point
IDLE Bla

72 Point
DOGS

A modernist aesthetic
Laszlo Moholy-Nagy's cover design for a Bauhaus book. This is one of many that he designed in the early existence of the Bauhaus.

LISSITZKY AND DE STIJL

One of the outstanding figures of the INKhUK group was Lazar El Lissitzky, born in Smolensk in 1890. He exemplified Constructivism, his activities blurring the borders between art and graphic design. Lissitzky studied architectural engineering in Darmstadt, Germany, from 1909 to 1914, when he returned to Russia because of the outbreak of war, to work as an architect. In 1919, he was invited by Marc Chagall to join the staff of the Vitebsk Artistic-Technical Institute to teach architecture and graphic design. Here he came under the influence of Kasimir Malevich, the founder of Suprematism, a form of abstract art. He went to Berlin in 1921 to lecture on the concepts of Suprematism and Constructivism in order to promote Soviet–German links. There he made contact with Laszlo Moholy-Nagy and Theo van Doesburg.

Lissitzky created a series of compositions during the early 1920s that he called PROUNS, an acronym meaning "projects for affirmation of the new;" abstract paintings that explored space and color by the arrangement of geometric forms and reference to perspective. He helped organize the 1922 Constructivist Congress, in Weimar, Germany, and designed the Soviet journal *Veshch* ("Object"). A year later he designed a book of the poems of Vladimir Mayakovsky titled *For the Voice*, using typesetting materials in an experimental red and black design. In 1924 he moved to Switzerland, for treatment for tuberculosis. In Switzerland Lissitzky worked with Kurt Schwitters, the Dada collagist, on an edition of his journal *Merz*, and the following year he returned to the Soviet Union to continue teaching. He died in 1941 after a unique career of graphic and typographic experiment that has not been surpassed.

Among those Lissitzky influenced was the Dutch artist group of designers and architects De Stijl. They took their name (meaning "style") from the magazine that first appeared in 1917, edited by the driving force of the group, Theo van Doesburg. The group's visual philosophy was expressed through a distinctive geometric and abstract approach. Similar to that of the Constructivists, their aesthetic was the result of reducing visual constructions to the fundamental elements of simple geometric form, space, and proportion. All of their projects—painting, design, and architecture—relied on strong, pure color. Their policy, which had strong spiritual qualities, was the assertion of Modernism, the application of current technology and knowledge as a means to greater social fulfilment and unity. The energetic Theo van Doesburg traveled and lectured, promoting the De Stijl view of the future. When he died in 1931, the last issue of *De Stijl* magazine was dedicated to him.

Bauhaus Poster
Joost Schmidt's 1923 poster for the same Bauhaus exhibition as that advertised opposite. This image was to be seen in over 100 railway stations throughout Germany.

THE BAUHAUS *& the New Typography*

Jan Tschichold
A young typography teacher who was not a member of the Bauhaus staff, Tschichold (1902–1974) was nonetheless greatly impressed with the school's work. In 1945, later in life, Tschichold oversaw the redesign of British publisher Penguin, standardizing their typographic practice and laying the groundwork for Penguin to build up their reputation for faultless book-jacket design.

The New Typography
A spread (below) from Jan Tshichold's 1928 book Die neue Typographie, *which formulated the theoretical and practice background to the new approach to typography.*

The First World War was brought to an end by a revolution in Germany, which led to an armistice, the abdication of Kaiser Wilhelm, and the end of the monarchy. The Weimar Republic was inaugurated and existed from 1919 to 1933, during which time there were 17 governments. Adolf Hitler came to power in 1933. The 15 years of the Wiemar Republic were marked by political violence, assassinations, inflation, unemployment, crisis, and instability.

In 1919, the State Government of Weimar appointed Walter Gropius as director of the Art and Design School that had been installed in the old College of Fine Arts. The new institution was known as the Bauhaus. Gropius was an architect well informed in the theory and practice of the avant garde. He had been assistant to Peter Behrens, a founder member of the Deutsche Werkbund, and had established his own reputation with his advanced design for the Fagus factory building in 1911.

A NEW APPROACH

The principles by which the Bauhaus was to teach were developed from the Deutsche Werkbund, whose members believed that students of the visual arts needed a new approach to their education. Gropius invited many of the leading figures of the avant-garde in art and design to join the Bauhaus teaching staff. Among them were the Russian-born painter Wassily Kandinsky, the Swiss-born painter Paul Klee, and Johannes Itten, the Swiss painter and orientalist who was to teach the Bauhaus Basic Course. Itten's course was intended to encourage students to explore the characteristics of materials, form, and color.

Laszlo Moholy-Nagy had studied law at the University of Budapest and turned to the arts during the war. After the war he met up with the Dadaists and Constructivists, including El Lissitzky, in Berlin, which at the time was second only to Paris as a center of avant-garde arts. In 1923, following Itten's departure, Moholy-Nagy joined the Bauhaus to take over the Basic Course. He was particularly interested in the theoretical

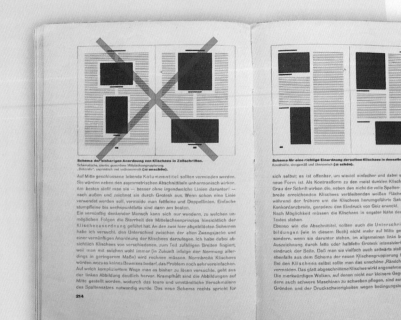

The Universal Type
A version of Herbert Bayer's design (right) for a letterform without capitals. This was a radical grammatical idea, as capitals are more frequently used in German than in English.

abcdefghi jklmnopqr stuvwxyz

Architype typefaces
During the 1990s, London digital type designers David Quay and Freda Sack of The Foundry, created a collection of fonts based on 1920s letterforms; some of which had never been available before. The fonts have been designed as faithfully as possible according to original drawings, with only essential characters added to render the font usable.

Architype Renner

ARCHITYPE VAN DER LECK

ARCHITYPE VAN DOESBURG

architype bill

architype tschichold

architype bayer

architype bayer-type is based o 1930-32 preliminary studies for face. the foundry have reconstr serif face from his experimenta alphabet following his original s as one of the collection of six a forming foundry architype 2.

architype bayer is based on alphabet which abandoned produced his first designs in charge of typography at geometrically constructed the alphabet was designed on his student thesis on the from the foundry architype archive references of origin bayer's essential ideas.

aspects of design and throughout his career wrote extensively on art and design in the new machine age. Although he designed a series of 14 Bauhaus publications, which established a kind of Bauhaus style, he was not a typographic specialist.

The Visual Communication course was not introduced until Herbert Bayer, a former Bauhaus student, returned as a member of staff after the Bauhaus transferred to Dessau in 1925. Born in 1900 in Salzburg, Austria, Bayer was the most influential graphic designer of the Bauhaus. He had strongly held opinions on letterforms, and in 1927 designed a typeface that combined capitals and lower case into a single alphabet, which he called Universal. He persuaded Gropius to allow him to remove capitals from all Bauhaus literature.

As a result of political students' influence on the curriculum, which stood to change the teaching philosophy, Bayer, Moholy-Nagy, and Gropius decided to resign, and later made their way individually to the United States.

JAN TSCHICHOLD

Another germinal figure in this period was Jan Tschichold, who was not a member of the Bauhaus, but a young teacher of calligraphy and typography from Leipzig. In 1926, he joined the staff of the Munich Master Printers' College, under the directorship of Paul Renner. Tschichold was very impressed by the Bauhaus exhibition of 1923 and was won over to what became known as "the New Typography." Unlike many of the avant-garde artists and designers, he was very knowledgeable on the subject of typography and its history, so that when in 1925 he wrote an article called "Elementary Typography," which described the new approach to typographic design, it aroused great interest. Tschichold was responsible, through his writings, for consolidating the theory and practice of modern typography. In 1928, he published his masterwork, *The New Typography*. It was a study that set graphic design and typography in the context of contemporary arts and culture. It was a theoretical, historical, and highly detailed guide to the practice of modern typography, and it has recently been republished in English.

Coming under suspicion as a left-wing radical in 1933, Tschichold spent a short time imprisoned by the National Socialist authorities in Munich. On his release, he left Germany with his family for Switzerland, which remained his home for the rest of his life.

Tschichold was a prolific writer and while in Basle in 1935, wrote *Typographische Gestaltung*, which was published as *Asymmetric Typography* in the 1960s. In the later 1960s, Tschichold designed his most important and popular face, Sabon. This was a face produced as a foundry type for handsetting and for hot metal casting, with the intention that it should be suitable for all printing techniques.

PAUL RENNER *& Futura*

For many years after the First World War, the new republican Weimar government in Germany was unstable, as was the economic situation. In the face of a collapsing, infant Republic, many people of Germany sought reassurance in strong, dynamic visions of the future. Against this backdrop, it is not surprising that there was considerable enthusiasm for, and hope in, Modernism.

Futura poster
Paul Renner (top) was inaugurated as director of Munich's Masterprinters' College, Germany in 1927.

Futura poster
Renner's poster design for the college (above) uses the letterforms that he had developed for his successful geometric sans-serif, Futura.

There was no new typeface that could express and serve this 20th-century effort to break with the past until well into the 1920s. Futura, issued in 1927 by the Bauer typefoundry, became the favorite and best known of the first geometric sans-serif typefaces that symbolize the aesthetics of early Modernism. Its very name evokes a kind of positive expectation.

Futura was the creation of Paul Renner, a teacher, graphic designer, type designer, and author. Renner was born in the German town of Wernigerode in 1878. He became director of Munich's Graphic Arts College in 1926 and from 1927 was director of the Munich Master Printers' College. During this time he was working on his alphabet design. Renner was an active member of the Deutsche Werkbund. In 1922 he wrote *Typography as Art*, and in 1932 he wrote *Cultural Bolshevism*, which later led him into trouble with the National Socialist Party and eventually led to his dismissal from his directorship. In 1933, before his arrest, he was in charge of the design of the German section of the Milan Triennale, and was awarded the Grand Prix.

The modernist aesthetic attached importance to form that derived from function, and ornament and decoration were to be stripped away. Renner took the opportunity in his early studies to explore aspects of letterform that were very different from the conventions for roman forms. At the last moment, when the finished designs were considered for production by the Bauer typefoundry, a number of modifications were recommended to the lower case because the new forms were considered too radical for general commercial use; these were replaced by more conventional forms.

During the early decades of the 20th century the sans-serif emerged as the letterform that best represented the theoretical requirements of avant-garde graphic designers and typographers of the "New Typography." The sans-serif typeface was a 19th-century invention that emerged from the needs of the industrial age. Its identity was strictly attached to commercial applications, with no connotations of bookishness. In fact, most sans-serifs were display faces, so that when Jan Tschichold was designing his book *Die Neue Typographie* he had difficulty in finding a text-size sans-serif to use.

The design of a new 20th-century sans-serif was an undertaking that occupied many type designers at this time. Jacob Erbar had claimed the sans-serif as representative of the new age

ÄBCDEFGHIJKLMNÖ
PRSTÜVWXYZ
abcdefghijklmnöpqrst
úvwxyz +!?".; * &
1234567890 ſʒ

Erbar
kpl. 1922

Erbar and Kabel
*Jacob Erbar in 1924
and Rudolph Koch in
1927 both designed
sans-serifs in the popular
geometric style, named
Erbar (left) and Kabel
(below left), respectively.*

Contextualizer

Paul Renner
1878–1956

The paradox of Futura

Renner described Futura as being not purely geometric, as it had many subtle features. However, he also believed its success was due to the purity of the idea behind it. Futura was a product of its time—in that it strongly represented the preoccupations with technology and machines of 1920s modernist design. Nonetheless, Futura also managed, and still manages, to represent a wider sense of time, in that its purity of form gives it classic appeal. Its continuing success today is proof of this.

"Die Neue Typographie"

Jan Tschichold's influential book "Die Neue Typographie" (The New Typography) was a culmination of the revolutionary approach to typographic design that developed in Europe through the 1920s and 1930s. The book drew together many of the ideas of the Constructivists and teachers at the Bauhaus, and established a new utilitarian order and simplicity. It urged designers to employ rational principles to determine use of design elements, and advocated an objective presentation of information, rejecting decoration in favor of dynamic, asymmetrical layouts. It was a typographic design handbook conceived to meet the needs of the then new technological age.

Kabel

ABCDEFGHIJKLMN
OPQRSTUVWXYZ
abcdefghijklnopqrstuv
wxyz +!?".; * &
1234567890

before the war. By 1924, he had produced a sans-serif design named Erbar for the Ludwig & Mayer typefoundry. Rudolf Koch, a highly respected German calligrapher, type designer, and teacher, contributed Kabel, a geometric sans-serif released by the Klingspor typefoundry in 1927. In England some ten years earlier, Edward Johnston, an expert calligrapher and teacher at the Central School of Arts and Crafts in London, had created a geometric sans-serif for use by London Transport. This was not released for public use until it was digitized in the 1990s.

FUTURA: *the Typeface Itself*

ABCDEFGHIJKLMNOPQR
abcdefghijklmnopqrstuvw
abcdefghijklmnopqrstuvwx

The main feature of Futura is the apparent single-line thickness of all parts of the letters, together with the rigid straightness of the stems, and the full circles that form the bowls of the letters "a," "b," "d," "o," "p," "q," "c" and "g." The letterforms appear to be created by drawing instruments, tools that eliminate the individuality of the human hand; it is this quality that earns the name "geometric." Closer inspection will reveal that where the circular forms abut the upright stems, there is an almost indiscernible thinning of the line, acting as an optical correction to avoid the heaviness that would result if lines of the same thickness met. Capital letters do not reach the same height as the ascenders, which are longer than the descenders. The x-height is comparatively small. The top bowl of "B" is noticeably smaller than the lower one. Note also that the terminals are horizontal but those on the "G" and "S" are diagonal.

In the digital range of Futura there are six weights (light, book, medium, heavy, bold, and extra bold), with companion oblique fonts. There are five weights of Futura Condensed (light, medium, heavy, bold, and extra bold), with companion oblique fonts, but no book weight. There are three special display faces: Futura Extra Bold Shaded—an outline font with a shadow to create a three-dimensional effect; Futura Black, which is a heavy stencil design that has no family resemblance to Futura; and Futura Display, an extra bold condensed font also with no family resemblance to Futura.

Futura
The typeface is constructed from geometric forms. Although there is an apparent single-line thickness for stems and bowls, subtle optical corrections at the point of contract between stem and bowl have been made.

Futura and Gill Sans
To the right here, the comparison between the two styles of sans-serif capitals—geometric (above) and humanistic (below)— can be appreciated.

BCGSM
BCGSM

STUVWXYZ
xyz& 1234567890
yz& 1234567890

Futura

the quick brown fox jumps over the lazy dog

Helvetica

the quick brown fox jumps over the lazy dog

Univers

the quick brown fox jumps over the lazy dog

Gill Sans

the quick brown fox jumps over the lazy dog

Sans-serifs
A direct comparison of four 20th-century sans-serifs makes it easier to appreciate their individual characters.

The Futura family
Futura now offers a comprehensive range of weights and styles, including special display fonts, and Futura shaded, Futura Black, and Futura display.

LIGHT

AaBbCcDdEeFf

BOOK

AaBbCcDdEeFf

MEDIUM

AaBbCcDdEeFf

HEAVY

AaBbCcDdEeFf

BOLD

AaBbCcDdEeFf

EXTRA BOLD

AaBbCcDdEeFf

LIGHT CONDENSED

AaBbCcDdEeFf

MEDIUM CONDENSED

AaBbCcDdEeFf

BOLD CONDENSED

AaBbCcDdEeFf

LIGHT OBLIQUE

AaBbCcDdEeFf

BOOK OBLIQUE

AaBbCcDdEeFf

BOLD OBLIQUE

AaBbCcDdEeFf

Then

Futura at work

Futura family
Although the basic Futura fonts became more modest in style (right), the special display font Futura Black (below right) was more extrovert.

Type design
Renner's original drawings of 1925 (below) explored radical letterforms for his 20th-century typeface. However, they were modified on the recommendation of the Bauer typefoundry.

Futura at work

Futura Bold
*This art gallery publicity
uses Futura Bold Italic.
Adjusting the stems to the
vertical is a simple device
that lends a dynamic, lively
sense to the exhibition
being publicized.*

Modern and modernist
*This design below uses the
contrast between Bodoni's
Modern-face hairline serifs,
and Futura's geometric,
monoline forms.*

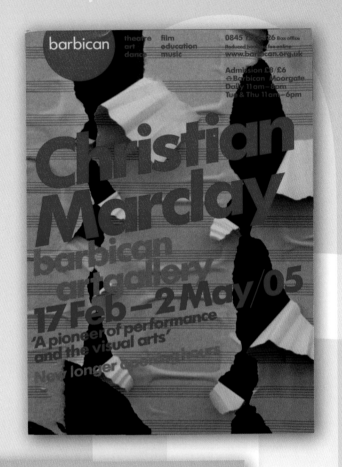

Futura usage

Tracking, kerning, and H&Js
The vertical stress that is created by the
contrast between ascenders, descenders,
and the full forms of the x-height can be
reduced by a small increase in the tracking.

Text sizes
Futura has long ascenders that are higher
than the capitals, and unless leading is
inserted they are likely to tangle with the
line above. It has a small x-height which
makes economic use of linear space, so
can be used in fairly narrow columns.

Display sizes
Futura has three special display fonts; Extra
Bold Shaded, Futura Black, and Futura
Display. These, unlike many digitized display
fonts, are rather extrovert in comparison to
their text version, which, in Futura's case,
is rather austere. Use the display fonts
judiciously therefore, or use the larger text
weights instead.

On-screen display
Futura's small x-height, tall ascenders, and
close letterfit make it a difficult typeface for
use as an on-screen font, and therefore its
use should be limited to display sizes. Set as
text, Futura loses it unique character as an
on-screen display; better to use a sans-serif
adapted for this. If it is essential to use
Futura as display, it is best done within
a GIF or JPEG.

STANLEY MORISON *& Times New Roman*

For many years after its arrival on the scene in the 1930s, Times New Roman was a typeface associated with the authority and style of the British Empire. It later became a truly democratic vehicle of printed communication, used wherever manufactured lettering was required.

Stanley Morison
Morison (1889–1967), shown above, is possibly the most distinguished British typographer of the 20th century.

While the actual creator of the design is to this day a source of controversy, it is undisputed that Morison was responsible for the introduction of this type, and it fitted the purpose beautifully.

In the 1930s, Stanley Morison was at the height of his power and influence as an authority on letterforms and type history. He was an established commentator on the art of printing and wrote extensively on the history of early printing. He has been described as possibly the most distinguished British scholar and typographer of the 20th century.

Morison started his working life as a clerk and developed an interest in printing, spending many hours at the British Museum during the weekends. In 1913, his first printing job was at the editorial office of *Imprint*, a journal that campaigned for an awareness of good printing and design. He worked there with J. H. Mason, the designer of the journal's typeface, and Gerald Meynell.

During the First World War Morison was imprisoned as a conscientious objector and on returning to civilian life in 1919 he joined the Pelican Press. By 1921, he had moved to the Cloister Press in Manchester. In 1923 he co-founded *The Fleuron*, a journal of typography which won international acclaim with its articles on typographic history and theory. Morison also took on the post of typographic adviser to Cambridge University Press and the Monotype Corporation.

Monotype was one of the leading typesetting machine companies, and as a result of Morison's scholarship it was able to carry out a series of classic typeface revivals and to commission new typefaces for its collection.

In 1929, Morison contributed to a special *Times* newspaper supplement on printing. His article, "Newspaper Types: A Study of The Times," was highly critical of the quality of the newspaper's printing and old-fashioned

The Times masthead
Morison introduced a titling version of the new type (right), to replace the traditional use of black-letter, but he emphasized the coat of arms to balance the change.

typography. In fact, Morison had already been commissioned to make revisions to the newspaper in order to bring it up to date. He produced a lengthy report, which put his case for the improvements to the paper's typefaces; making proposals in the light of type history and the qualities of various type designs, and introducing ideas from the latest research on legibility.

Several other newspapers at the time were introducing Ionic, a Linotype typeface that had connections with 19th-century typefaces. Morison rejected this. He believed that the newspaper had to improve its printing quality so that it reached the standard normal for books. Due to his interest in historic typefaces and his role of supervising the revival and commissioning of typefaces for the Monotype Corporation, Morison had in mind a modified version of the typeface Plantin, improved with sharper serifs to give the type better definition for stereotyping casting. Since he himself was no draftsman, to realize his ideas Morison made use of the drawing skills of Victor Lardent, a lettering artist employed in the advertising department of *The Times*.

The task did not prove straightforward. After many drawings and test castings, the revised style of *The Times* was launched on 3 October 1932. The previous typeface used by the newspaper had been known as Times Old Roman, so its replacement was named Times New Roman. The newspaper had sole use of the design for one year, after which it was made available to Linotype and Intertype, two major typesetting and casting machine manufacturers. *The Times* continued to use the face until a redesign in 1972, when Walter Tracy designed Times Europa.

The new type
Morison's redesign not only consisted of producing a text typeface. He wrote a detailed analysis of what were the existing faults and an explanation of what was needed. This consisted of several versions of the new type to fulfil particular functions, such the small advertisements that still appeared on the front page.

"THE TIMES" IN NEW TYPE

HOW THE CHANGE WAS MADE

The change of type completed with this morning's issue of *The Times* has involved one of the biggest undertakings ever accomplished in a newspaper office. More than two years have been devoted to designing and cutting the type charac-

"THE TIMES"

LAST DAY OF THE OLD TYPE

MONDAY'S CHANGES

The Times appears to-day for the last time in the type to which the present generation has grown accustomed.
On Monday the changes already an-

Contextualizer

Stanley Morison
1889–1967

The doubtful origins of Times New Roman

In 1994, the "TypLab Chronicle," a magazine issued at the "A Typl" Congress in San Francisco, contained an article by type specialist Mike Parker. Parker had been asked to inspect a collection of pattern plates of a roman typeface from the Lanston Monotype Company, which had closed down. They were identified as having been produced at the company in 1915. The typeface had been ordered by W. Starling Burgess, a designer of yachts and aircraft, early in the century. Parker was surprised to discover the very close similarity of the Burgess design to Morison's roman. Burgess' company closed in 1916 due to financial problems, and in 1918 its plant burned down. In his article, Parker suggested there was evidence that the president of Lanston sent details of the typeface to the English Monotype Company in England to see if they had any use for it. While there is no evidence that Stanley Morison actually knew or saw these designs, the similarity seems more than a coincidence.

Marrying Renaissance italics and romans

As typographic historian Robert Bringhurst points out, it was Morison who first paired independent Renaissance italic and roman faces, such as Griffo's Poliphilus roman with Arrighi's Blado italic, for 20th century use.

ROMAN
AaBbCcDdEeFf

ITALIC
AaBbCcDdEeFf

BOLD
AaBbCcDdEeFf

BOLD ITALIC
AaBbCcDdEeFf

ABCDEFGHIJKLMN
abcdefghijklmnopqrstu
abcdefghijklmnopqrstu

Times New Roman
**the quick brown fox
jumps over the lazy dog**

Garamond
the quick brown fox
jumps over the lazy dog

Baskerville
the quick brown fox
jumps over the lazy dog

Bodoni
**the quick brown fox
jumps over the lazy dog**

A newspaper typeface
As a serif typeface Times New Roman has a crisp, clean neutrality that has recommended it to the general printing industry. It has a large x-height and is rather narrow, which makes it very economic on space; this is an important quality for a newspaper type. Its sturdy letterforms are designed to withstand the rigors of letterpress newspaper presses.

Times New Roman is classified as a 20th-century roman. It is a typeface design that has echoes of the past, but is not a direct revival of a historical typeface. Whatever the true origins of this typeface, it has served with quiet dignity to become a truly democratic worker, appearing in every possible medium of the printed word. It is a much-loved typeface in the English-speaking world and beyond; for example, its distinct forms have been applied to Cyrillic and Greek alphabets.

Times New Roman was one of the first typefaces that resulted from a serious attempt to meet all the requirements of a newspaper in one complete, integrated typographic style. Stanley Morison achieved this by studying the various aspects of a daily newspaper's contents: the main text of the newspaper, the articles, and reports. The paper's range of headline display types required typefaces with grades of importance. In addition, until the 1950s *The Times* traditionally carried small advertisements, full-length columns across the front page with only the masthead centered above, and no headlines as there are today. All these aspects of the paper were to be dealt with in Morison's scheme.

OPQRSTUVWXYZ
vwxyz& 1234567890
uvwxyz& 1234567890

TT
RR

In the days before the Second World War, *The Times* newspaper was considered the voice of the British establishment. As a result, when Times New Roman was made available to the general printing industry, it quickly became appreciated as a typeface that expressed authority and dignity. The capitals have the classical proportions associated with the Trajan square capitals, and are a supreme example of the neoclassical style. The face maintains the favored qualities of the past, but expresses them with the precision of 20th-century engineering. The ascenders and descenders are short, the x-height large, the serifs sharply cut, so that the body area has been used fully. The thick and thin stress is well-balanced so that the contrast is fairly low, supplying a firm covering of ink. The swell of the stress on the capitals is on the vertical, but on the lower case it tends to be on the diagonal, as in a conventional Old-face. The overall color is strong, causing the type to stand eloquently out from the page. The roman letterform is compact, which is essential for newspaper use, allowing it to function well in narrow columns while not being condensed. The italics have a regular, moderate slope. Times New Roman is a sturdy, well-proportioned face that, in spite of its specialized concept, has proved to be suitable for an enormous variety of uses and this flexibility is a key reason for its germinal status.

Times New Roman's practical good looks made it a natural choice for early conversion to PC use (although its popularity makes it subject to poor copies), and it has been digitized by Monotype and Adobe very successfully. The even tone and sturdiness of its letterforms have been designed to withstand the rigors of high-speed web printing. The roman is supported by italics, semibold, and bold, with related italics and extra bold. There is a related range, Times New Roman Condensed, Condensed Italic, and Condensed Bold. There are three special fonts: Times New Roman small text, italics, and bold roman, all designed with wider set, intended for very small setting, which was one of the vestiges of Morison's original concept.

An extremely practical typeface, Times New Roman has been available continuously since 1933. It can be found as a principal member of every kind of lettering system.

Economic design
The "T" and "R" of Times New Roman (above left) are compared with the same letters of John Baskerville's roman (above right). Morison was attracted to the sturdy qualities of Monotype's Plantin (below) as he searched for suitable models for the newspaper's typeface.

Plantin
ABCDEF
GHIJKLM
NOPQRST
UVWXYZ
abcdefghij
klnopqrstu
vwxyz

Times New Roman at work

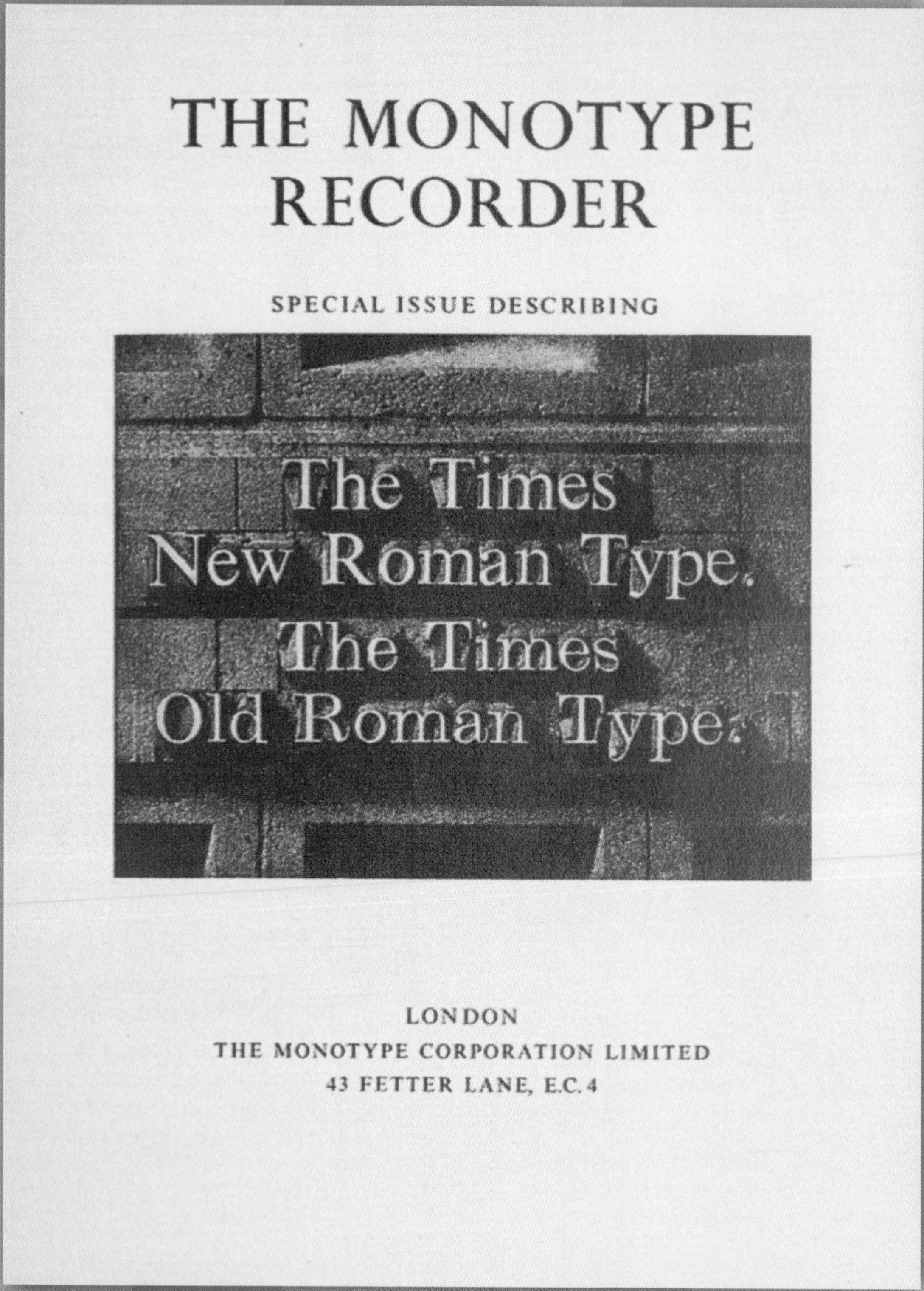

THE MONOTYPE
RECORDER

SPECIAL ISSUE DESCRIBING

The Times
New Roman Type.
The Times
Old Roman Type.

LONDON
THE MONOTYPE CORPORATION LIMITED
43 FETTER LANE, E.C. 4

Monotype Recorder
The cover of this 1932 special issue announced and reviewed the new typeface for the Times *newspaper. The photographer shows both the old and the new* Times *typefaces. The photograph has been laterally reversed so that the type can be read; in the metal it would, like all letterpress type, be reversed.*

Times New Roman at work

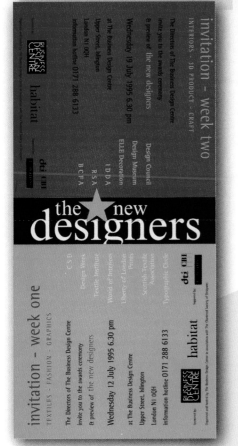

New designers
This crisp, elegant logotype, shows that good design can be created from the most commonplace typefaces, given the skill of the designer.

Go Van Gogh
Times has become a typeface for all occasions. This punning Dallas Museum of Art outreach program makes use of the clear, sharp forms of Times to promote great art.

Times New Roman usage

Tracking, kerning, and H&Js

Times New Roman has short ascenders and descenders, so it can benefit from leading whenever possible as it shows the type to good advantage. Setting solid, without additional leading, economizes on space and also promotes good legibility.

Text sizes

The typeface has gained popularity largely due to its adaptability. It lacks the exhaustive range of variants that some digital faces now offer, but it has a range of italics, semibolds, bolds, and a limited number of condensed weights, which are perfectly adequate for most purposes.

Display sizes

Times New Roman makes a excellent display face. When used in large display sizes the tracking should be reduced in proportion to increasing size. Kerning of some letter groups may be necessary.

On-screen display

An example of a well-established typeface that has been adapted for use on computer screens, Times New Roman is a default text font on most Web browsers. However, legibility is greatly reduced if it is used in sizes smaller than 12-point.

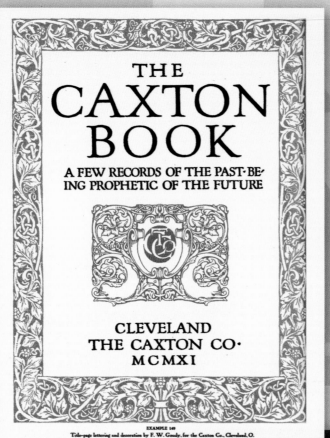

The Caxton Book
This 1911 cover design (above) shows hand-drawn capitals by Frederic Goudy, precursors of his popular Goudy Old Style designed in 1916. Note the word break to maintain even line length, possibly at the expense of meaning.

Frederic Goudy
The highly prolific typographer who famously said: "Anyone who would letterspace blackletter would steal sheep."

As the 19th century gave way to the 20th, the technological developments in type-making introduced a new kind of type designer: one who was less likely to cut punches, but more likely to draw the design, the job of punchcutting being passed to an operative. There are four Americans who developed this new approach.

FREDERIC W. GOUDY

Morris Fuller Benton's output was only challenged by that of the equally prolific Frederic W. Goudy (1865–1947). Goudy is possibly the best-known American type designer, since most of his types were named after him. He was born in Bloomington, Illinois, a 19th-century man of irrepressible energy and determination. He began work as a clerk, moving from one job to another, until he set up a small print shop with a friend. He sold his share in the business in 1896. While looking for another job, Goudy designed his first alphabet of capitals, which he called Camelot. The newly formed ATC agreed to buy the design and the next one he sent them. He started to freelance as a lettering artist, working for publishers and department stores while also teaching lettering at the Frank Holme School of Illustration. William Dwiggins (see page 116) was one of his students.

Goudy started up his second print shop, Village Press, with Will Ransom near Chicago. He moved to Hingham, near Boston, where he was joined by Dwiggins. In 1906 he moved again, this time to New York City, where two years later his printing equipment was lost in a fire. Goudy took the opportunity to concentrate entirely on type design, designing his first type for the Lanston Monotype Company, known as 38E.

In 1911 he designed Kennerley, one of his most successful types, for publisher Mitchell Kennerley. In 1915 he completed work on his 25th type design, Goudy Old Style.

Moving to Marlborough, New York, Goudy started up a typefoundry in 1925, and at the age of 62 learnt, painfully, the skill of engraving his own matrices. Goudy died at the age of 82 having produced designs for over 110 typefaces. Some were excellent, and there are a number of his fonts that have been digitized. Goudy Old Style has three weights, with italics and Old-style figures. Goudy Text is a condensed blackletter for display. Monotype Goudy Modern consists of only one weight with italics. ITC Goudy Sans, a very idiosyncratic curly sans-serif, is available in four weights with italics.

BRUCE ROGERS

Bruce Rogers (1870–1957), born in Lafayette, Indiana, was five years younger than Goudy. He studied art at Purdue University, before becoming an illustrator for a newspaper. He was greatly impressed with the work of Morris' Kelmscott Press. In 1895, he moved to Boston to work at the Riverside Press, where he established himself as a designer of fine books, with a reputation for painstaking attention to every detail.

His first attempt at type design, like William Morris', was based on Nicholas Jenson's type of the 1470s. It was to be used by Riverside Press from 1902 to 1903 for their edition of *Montaigne's Essays*, from which the typeface took its name. Although not fully satisfied with the results, Rogers left Riverside Press in 1912.

Rogers returned to the Jenson face a decade later, first making what he believed to be an improved cutting for foundry type, for use by

CENTAUR type : 72 point the largest size. SIXTY POINT follows as shown in these trial lines. FORTY-EIGHT Pt. has also been finished as you may see by this.

THIS FORTY-TWO point is a very useful size not always easy to obtain. THIRTY-SIX POINT IS furnished, as are all the founts, with the figures 1234567890. CENTAUR ON THIRTY PT. can be seen in these three trial lines which show also: ÆŒQu£$& .,:;-!?

COMPOSITION MATRICES
COMPOSITION SIZES NOW BEGIN with 24 pt, (of which this is a specimen) and include 22 pt, 18 pt, 16 pt, 14 pt, 12 pt, & 10 pt. TWENTY-TWO POINT CAN BE CAST ON 24 point bodies and supplies a convenient type for folio volumes—catalogues of art collections, etc.

Centaur by Bruce Rogers
Rogers made several versions of his typeface, which was closely modeled on Jenson's venetian types of the 15th century. Roger's Centaur was put into production by the Monotype Corporation in 1929.

New Series of the Centaur Types of Bruce Rogers and the Arrighi Italics of Frederic Warde. Cut by Monotype and here first used to print a paper by Alfred W. Pollard

the Metropolitan Museum in New York. In 1929, the face known as Monotype Centaur was prepared for mechanical typesetting, and an italic alphabet by Frederic Warde was adapted for use with it. Centaur remains the typeface for which Rogers is best known. He died shortly after his 87th birthday in 1957. Centaur has been digitized by Adobe and has two weights, regular and bold; in addition there are expert fonts and an italic swash font.

METRO

A SHOWING OF **LINOTYPE** METRO — THE **MODERN** SANS SERIF

METROBLACK No. 2 WITH METROLITE No. 2

6-point 6·0·B82 caps 121, l.c. 95 pts; figs ·055"

As customers fall into many different classes they have to be met in many different ways. Sometimes they certainly bring difficult typographical problems to a printer, for which they suggest or even dictate absurd solutions. But a printer cannot be of use to typography by dismissing their views and them. His part is to lead them into the more excellent way, by showing them what can be done to improve the work and what cannot, and by explaining to them

8-point 8·0·B72 caps 146, l.c. 108 pts; figs ·069"

As customers fall into many different classes they have to be met in many different ways. Sometimes they certainly bring difficult typographical problems to a printer, for which they suggest or dictate ridiculous solutions. But a printer cannot be of use to typography by dismissing their views and them. His part is to lead them into the more excellent way, by showing what can be done to improve their work, also

10-point 10·0·B73 caps 185, l.c. 137 pts; figs ·083"

As customers fall into many different classes they have to be met in different ways. Sometimes they certainly bring difficult typographical problems to a printer, for which they suggest or even dictate absurd solutions. But a printer cannot be of any service to typography by dismissing their views and them. His part is to lead them into the more excellent way, by showing what can be done to improve their work and what cannot, and by explaining the reason why. Thus he can avoid needlessly annoying a 'client,' and encourage him not only to have this particular piece of work printed well, but to have more work printed better; for most people will use good types if they can only be made to see the reason of their goodness. I remember once being obliged to print, for a personage dealing in

12-point 12·0·B79 caps 221, l.c. 163 pts; figs ·097"

As customers fall into many different classes, they have to be met in different ways. Sometimes they certainly present difficult typographical problems to their printers, for which they suggest or dictate absurd solutions. But a printer cannot be of service to typography by dismissing their views or them. His part is to lead them into the more excellent way by showing them what can be done to improve

14-point 14·0·B80 caps 258, l.c. 190 pts; figs ·111"

As customers fall into many different classes, they have to be met in many different ways. Sometimes they bring difficult typographical problems to the printer, for which they suggest or dictate ridiculous solutions. But a printer cannot be of use to typography by dismissing their views and them. His part is to lead them into the more excellent

---

METROMEDIUM No. 2 WITH ITALIC

6-point 6·0·D42 caps 171, l.c. 86 pts; figs ·046"

As customers fall into many different classes they have to be met in many different ways. Sometimes they certainly bring difficult typographical problems to a printer, for which they suggest or dictate ridiculous solutions. But a printer cannot be of any service to typography by dismissing their views and them. His part is to lead them into the more excellent way, by showing them what can be done to improve their work and what cannot, and by offering explanations. Thus he can avoid needlessly annoying a 'client,' encouraging him not only to have this particular piece of work printed well, but to have his work printed better; for most people will use good types if they can be made to see the reason of their goodness. I always

8-point 8·0·D43 caps 132, l.c. 97 pts; figs ·055"

As customers fall into many different classes they have to be met in many different ways. Sometimes they certainly bring difficult typographical problems to a printer, for which they suggest or dictate ridiculous solutions. But a printer cannot be of any service to typography by dismissing their views and them. His part is to lead them into the more excellent way, by showing them what can be done to improve their work and what cannot, and by also explaining the reasons. Thus he can avoid needlessly annoying a 'client,' and encourage him not only to have this particular piece of work printed well, but to have more work printed better; for most people will use good types if they can only be made to see the reason of their goodness. I always

10-point 10·0·D44 caps 167, l.c. 122 pts; figs ·069"

As customers fall into many different classes they have to be met in many different ways. Sometimes they certainly bring difficult typographical problems to a printer for which they suggest or dictate ridiculous solutions. But a printer cannot be of any service to typography by dismissing their views and them. His part is to lead them into the more excellent way, by showing them what can be done to improve their work and what cannot, and by explaining the reason why. Thus he can avoid needlessly annoying a 'client,' and encourage him not only to have this particular piece of work printed well, but to have more work printed better; for most people will use good types if they can only be made to see the reason of their goodness. I remember once being obliged to print, for a personage dealing in muffins, a circular designed to demonstrate their excellence; and to this end he showed me an announcement, printed in coloured ink from horrible types, on brown notepaper, with a 'hemstitched' perforated edge, as a model for what was to be done. This circular he had secured from the establishment of a milliner. His mind worked in this way: that as an expensive hat was advertised by a circular adorned with perforations, and this hat cost one hundred times more than a muffin, a circular adapted for the hat must be many times better than the ordinary method of muffin advertising! This may appear very peculiar reasoning, but it differs very

12-point 12·0·D45 caps 200, l.c. 146 pts; figs ·083"

As customers fall into many different classes, they have to be met in many different ways. Sometimes they certainly bring difficult typographical problems to the printer, for which they suggest or dictate ridiculous solutions. But a printer cannot be of use to typography by dismissing their views and them. His part is to lead them into the more excellent way, by showing them what can be done to improve their work and what cannot, and then by explaining the reason why. Thus he can avoid needlessly annoying a 'client,' and encourage him not only to have this particular piece of work printed well, but to have more work printed better; for most people will use good types if they can only be made to see

---

METROLITE No. 2

18-point 18·0·B92 caps 330, l.c. 242 pts; figs ·124", ·152"

ABCDEFGHIJKLMN abcdefghijklmnopq 1234567890

24-point 24·0·C60 caps 424, l.c. 315 pts; figs ·124", ·194"

OPQRSTUVWXYZ pqrstuvwxyz 1234567

30-point 30·0·D58 caps 530, l.c. 389 pts; figs ·156", ·249"

ABCDEFGabcdefghjk 123456789

36-point 36·0·D59 caps 635, l.c. 466 pts; figs ·194", ·290"

HIJKLMNO PQRSTUVWYZ abcdefghijklmn 123456789

45-point 48·0·E21 caps 845 pts; figs ·249", ·387"

ABCDEFGHIJKL 678

METROBLACK No. 2

18-point 18·0·B91 caps 330, l.c. 242 pts; figs ·124", ·152"

*ABCDEFGHIJKLMN abcdefghijklmnopq 1234567890

24-point 24·0·B93 caps 424, l.c. 315 pts; figs ·124", ·194"

*OPQRSTUVWXYZ pqrstuvwxyz 1234567

Metro
Dwiggins' geometric sans-serif for Linotype was commissioned by Linotype as a result of his book Layout in Advertising. *His other popular design, Caledonia, was inspired by William Martin's Scotch Roman c.1790.*

WILLIAM ADDISON DWIGGINS

Like many other designers, William Addison Dwiggins (1880–1956) had a reputation for working long hours. Dwiggins was a graphic designer by training, who came quite late to typography. He learnt to draw letters as a student of Goudy while at the Frank Holme School of Illustration in Chicago. After running a printing press in Ohio for about a year, he joined Goudy in Hingham, Massachusetts, in 1903. Dwiggins was occupied mostly with advertising design until 1923, when he started designing for the publisher Alfred A. Knopf, for whom he eventually designed over 300 books. His skills as a graphic designer included calligraphy and stencil-cutting as well as illustration. His most notable design was for an edition of H. G. Wells' *The Time Machine* in 1931 for Random House. In his book *Layout in Advertising* (1928), he criticized contemporary type designs, and as a result he was invited by Linotype to improve on those currently available. His first type was his only completed sans-serif, Metro, released in 1930. He followed this with a text face, Electra, in 1935, and his most popular type, Caledonia, which was influenced by the Scottish Modern types of the 19th century. A digital version, New Caledonia, is now available in four weights, that include italics, small capitals, and Old-style figures.

Bruce Rogers
Rogers was a respected book designer whose opinions were regularly sought and heeded. He believed that the pleasure of creating a new book was all in creating the initial plan, and that the following labor was "drudgery" in comparison.

THE AN INVENTION

Time Machine

With a preface by the Author written for this edition; and designs by W. A. Dwiggins

H. G. WELLS

RANDOM HOUSE New York

1931

The Time Machine
In 1931, Dwiggins designed this edition of The Time Machine *by H. G. Wells for the New York publisher Random House.*

ROBERT HUNTER MIDDLETON

Robert Hunter Middleton was born in Scotland in 1898, and in 1908 emigrated with his family to Alabama, where his father had found a job as manager of a coal mine. Later, when the family moved to Illinois, the young Middleton entered the Arts Institute with the intention of becoming a painter. While at the Arts Institute, Middleton helped his teacher Ernst F. Detterer with the design of Eusebius, a revival of the Jenson type of the 1470s for use by the Ludlow display-setting system. Detterer was an admirer of the private press movement in Europe and his Jenson revival closely matches the original. Detterer was impressed with Middleton's skills and recommended him for a design job with Ludlow. Middleton worked with Ludlow from 1923, becoming design director in 1933. When he retired in 1971, he had been responsible for the design of around 100 of Ludlow's typefaces.

ERIC GILL *& his Sans-Serif*

Eric Gill
A deeply religious and uniquely principled man, Gill (1882–1940) had strong views on many aspects of the visual arts and typography.

Letter carver, wood engraver, and sculptor Eric Gill was born in Brighton, England in 1882; the second son of a Congregationalist minister. On leaving school he was apprenticed to the architect of the Ecclesiastical Commission of London. Here he developed an interest in carving lettering and attended evening classes run by the brilliant calligrapher, Edward Johnston.

Joanna
The page below is from his Essay on Typography. *The typeface is Joanna, named after his daughter.*

The Book   105

is that of materialist triumph tempered by fancifulness and sloppiness, & that they are altogether without grace either in the physical or spiritual senses of the word.

¶ A book is a thing to be read — we all start with that — and we will assume that the reader is a sensitive as well as a sensible person. Now, the first thing to be noticed is that it is the act of reading & the circumstances of that act which determine the size of the book and the kind of type used; the reading, not what is read. A good type is suitable for any and every book, and the size of a book is regulated not by what is in it but by the fact that it is read held in the hand (e.g. a novel), or at a table (e.g. books of history or reference with maps or other necessarily large illustrations), or at a desk or lectern (e.g. a missal or a choir book), or kept in the pocket (e.g. a prayer book or a travellers' dictionary). ¶ On the contrary some hold that size of book and style of type sh'ld be specially chosen for every book; that such & such a size is suitable for Shakespeare; such and such for Mr. Wells's novels, such and such for Mr. Eliot's poems; that the type suitable for one is not suitable for another; that elegant poetry should have elegant type, & the rough hacked style of Walt

---

Gill and Johnston became good friends, later sharing a flat in Lincoln's Inn in 1902. On leaving the architect's office in 1903, Gill set up on his own as a craftsman in a workshop in Hammersmith, West London. There he took on commissions of lettering and wood engraving for (among others) W. H. Smith and the publishers Insel, based in Leipzig, Germany.

Needing more space for his family and workshop, Gill moved to the Sussex village of Ditchling in 1906. Here he was able to extend his skills to include carving sculpture. The artistic community of Ditchling developed with the arrival of Edward Johnston and Douglas Pegler, who brought a small handpress workshop which became known as the St Dominic Press.

Seven years older, Stanley Morison was 33 when he became the typographical advisor to the Monotype Corporation in 1923. Morison was not a supporter of the Modern design movement, favoring rather the classical book design of the pre-19th-century master printers. Morison held the responsibility for providing a program of re-cutting historic typefaces, and to commission new contemporary typefaces to extend the range of Monotype composition faces. Late in 1925, Morison invited Gill to help him in this. Gill was a good choice, because although he had no

previous experience of the technical requirements that were involved, he had been an enthusiastic creator of letterforms since childhood.

The first typeface that Gill designed for Morison, without either of them having much idea of how to proceed, was called Perpetua. The letterforms are uniquely Gill's, reflecting his experience of lettercutting in stone. Perpetua is a classically proportioned roman with smoothly bracketed, sharply tapering serifs. During the months of correction and modifications made to test versions, a version containing a uniquely sloped roman was included instead of a conventional italic. Perpetua was not released until 1928.

It was during this time that the idea for Gill's famous sans-serif emerged. While working on Perpetua, in 1926, Gill was asked to paint a shop sign for a Bristol bookseller, Douglas Cleverdon. It was this lettering that led Morison to suggest that Gill create a sans-serif to compete with the continental geometric sans-serifs that were beginning to become popular. The letterform Gill had created for the shop was only a capital alphabet and he embarked on the design aware of the greater difficulties of constructing an even monoline lowercase alphabet, which involved many curves and junctions.

abcdefghijklmnopqrstuv
wxyz& ABCDEFGHIJKL
MNOPQRSTUVWXYZ
1234567890

Gill Sans
*Eric Gill's best-known
humanist sans-serif is
Gill Sans. The first types
appeared in 1928.*

Aa Bb Cc Dd Ee Ff Gg Hh
Ii Jj Kk Ll Mm Nn Oo Pp
Qq Rr Ss Tt Uu Vv Ww
Xx Yy Zz   1234567890

Gill's resulting sans-serifs were firmly modelled on classic roman proportions. Gill was able to introduce refinements, which, with the help of the Monotype drawing office, have established Gill Sans as a much-loved classic among sans-serifs. The first of the series to be published in 1928 was a titling available in five sizes (14-point, 18-point, 24-point, 30-point and 36-point); a lowercase version did not appear until 1933. Since then there have been additional variants, many of them not from Gill's hand.

In contrast to the geometric sans-serifs of the same decade, Gill Sans has a friendly warmth and is classified as a humanist sans-serif. The series was originally produced as hot-metal letterpress type, so when it was digitized it is most likely that the original Monotype office drawings were used. Gill Sans now has an extensive range of weights, from light through to ultra bold with italics, and (if required) Old-style figures. In addition there are two display weights, bold and extra bold, four weights of condensed, and two decorative fonts: Gill Sans Light Shadowed, and a titling Gill Sans Shadowed.

Perpetua
*Gill's classic roman,
Perpetua (above) was
influenced by the forms he
cut into stone. Work started
on this design in 1925 and
continued until 1928.*

AaGg
AaGg

Humanist Sans-serif
*When seen in juxtaposition
with Futura (above), Gill Sans
(top) can be seen to be less
mechanical; its forms having
more in common with classical
roman proportions.*

Contextualizer

Eric Gill
1882–1940

A compelling personality

Artistic communities grew around Gill both in Ditchling village (southeast England) and later in High Wycombe (middle England). These communities lived a frugal country existence, and avoided the use of modern amenities. Although Gill was not a member of the Modernist movement, his work philosophy fitted somewhere between the Arts and Crafts movement and the Constructivists. He had the deep conviction that art must be useful and he ran a lifelong campaign against aesthetic snobbery. He considered himself a workman and applied himself with a rigorous discipline; this may have owed something to his Catholic faith, as his ideology was in no way romantic.

Edward Johnston

Credited with single-handedly reviving the art of modern penmanship through his books and teachings, Johnston taught Gill as a student. Later they lived in the same village, Gill helping Johnston with his eponymous typeface (1916).

Humanist sans-serifs

This category is used to describe sans-serifs that do not appear angular, geometric, or mechanical, whilst being unfussy, forthright, and simple. The term derives from the humanist handwriting of 15th-century Italy—the manuscript hand that influenced the earliest roman and italic types.

Gill Sans at work

By Eric Gill

with an engraving by the author

SCULPTURE
AND
THE LIVING
MODEL

Sheed & Ward

Book jackets
*Three publications by
Hague and Gill (left and
below). Gill with his son-
in- law and partner René
Hague, designed and printed
these books in 1929.*

MAY 31
COLLECT FOR
THE FEAST OF S. ANGELA MERICI

DEUS, QUI NOVUM PER BEATAM
ANGELAM SACRARUM VIRGINUM
COLLEGIUM IN ECCLESIA TUA FLOR-
ESCERE VOLUISTI: DA NOBIS, EIUS
INTERCESSIONE, ANGELICIS MORI-
BUS VIVERE; UT, TERRENIS OMNIBUS
ABDICATIS, GAUDIIS PERFRUI MERE-
AMUR AETERNIS · PER DOMINUM NOSTRUM
IESUM CHRISTUM FILIUM TUUM QUI TECUM
VIVIT ET REGNAT IN UNITATE SPIRITUS SANCTI
DEUS PER OMNIA SAECULA SAECULORUM

ABCDEFGHIJJKLMN
OPQQRRSTUV
WXYZ

☞ 1,2,3:4·5-6!7?8§9*¶()[☞ ☞]

The Fleuron
*A page from a 1930
edition of The Fleuron
Society's journal (above),
set in inscriptional
style, using 14-point
Gill Titling.*

By ERIC GILL

with an engraving by the author

Is Employment a good thing?
  What's the difference between the
  Wage System and Slavery?
Is Private Property a good thing?
  Where is this Private property? Who
  has got it?
Is the property of Big Business Compa-
  nies really private property in any
  reasonable sense?
Are the Railways any more Private Pro-
  perty than the Post Office?
Does Labour saving machinery save La-
  bour? Is it a good thing?
Is there any cure for Unemployment in
  a machine civilisation?
What is Machinery? Does anyone want
  to abolish it?
What is the difference between living
  on the Dole & living on Dividends?
Why not Dividends for all?

UNEMPLOYMENT

Faber & Faber

Price One Shilling

Eric Gill and
Denis Teg

UNHOLY
TRINITY

Text by Eric Gill • Pictures by Denis
Tegetmeier • Published by Dents for
Hague & Gill Ltd at 2 Shillings net

Now

Gill Sans at work

Sydney Design 99 Postcard Series
No.1 Designed by Chris Perks Design, Sydney

Design conference 1999
This Australian Conference publicity (above) is typical of the many uses that Gill Sans fulfils with modest perfection.

Post Communion

Lord Jesus Christ,
you have taught us
that what we do for the least of our brothers and sisters
we do also for you:
give us the will to be the servant of others
as you were the servant of all,
and gave up your life and died for us,
but are alive and reign, now and for ever.

Palm Sunday   *Red*

Collect

Almighty and everlasting God,
who in your tender love towards the human race
    sent your Son our Saviour Jesus Christ
to take upon him our flesh
and to suffer death upon the cross:
grant that we may follow the example of his patience and humility,
and also be made partakers of his resurrection;
through Jesus Christ your Son our Lord,
who is alive and reigns with you,
in the unity of the Holy Spirit,
one God, now and for ever.

Post Communion

Lord Jesus Christ,
you humbled yourself in taking the form of a servant,
and in obedience died on the cross for our salvation:
give us the mind to follow you
and to proclaim you as Lord and King,
to the glory of God the Father.

Common Worship
The Church of England's recent 2000 edition of Services and Prayers is set in Gill Sans throughout.

Design Tips

Gill Sans usage

Tracking, kerning, and H&Js

The Gill Sans family tends, even in the digital form, to be a more uneven range of weights and forms compared with most digitized sans-serifs. This makes it very characterful. Basic tracking is generous, but tracking should not be reduced as it will affect the legibility. Standard kerning should be adequate for most purposes.

Text sizes

Gill Sans has a smaller x-height than some 20th-century sans-serifs. It can be effective with more leading than the standard 20 percent of body size. Sizes below 9-point will benefit from a minimal increase in tracking.

Display sizes

Gill Sans consists of a family of weights and forms that happily lack the uniformity of weight increase designed into many sans-serifs. Gill offers an assortment of forms that can be refreshing to experiment with.

On-screen display

Gill Sans has a unique character as a text face, but as screen resolution renders this anonymous in text sizes on screen, it is preferable to make use of a more suitable screen font such as Verdana or Arial if a sans-serif is required. Larger display sizes are best displayed within a GIF or JPEG.

6 After the Second World War

The Second World War came to an end in 1945, with the surrender of Germany in May and the surrender of Japan in August. Germany was occupied by the Allies—America, Britain, France, and the Soviet Union. Berlin, Germany's official capital and now within the Soviet section, was also divided up by the Allies. Germany was split into two states, the Democratic Republic in the East and the Federal Republic (which took Bonn as its capital) in the West.

With Western Europe under the influence of the USA and Eastern Europe "behind the Iron Curtain," dominated by the USSR, the stage was set for the Cold War. In the shadow of the rivalry between the two systems and the fear of nuclear war hanging like a dark cloud over the postwar years, Europe began the slow process of reconstruction after the devastation of the six-year conflict. In the West, the rebuilding of cities and economies was supported by the USA through the "Marshall Plan," officially known as the European Recovery Programme. By the 1960s, West Germany had become extremely successful economically, a dramatic recovery referred to as the "German economic miracle." The Berlin Wall was erected by the Communist authorities in 1961 to prevent East Germans flowing into the West attracted by the material prosperity available under capitalism.

Hitler's defeat
At the end of the war, Germany was divided between the administrations of the Soviet Union, the United States, Britain, and France. This painting (top) by Achille Beltrame shows the Allied generals taking control of Berlin.

Berlin in 1945
Berlin, the capital of Germany since 1871, was devastated (above), and the postwar government of West Germany transferred to Bonn.

CULTURAL DEVELOPMENTS

During the 1950s, as postwar prosperity began to dominate, there emerged the new phenomenon of "youth culture." Teenagers were identified for the first time as a distinct social group, rebelling against parental values and making use of their new purchasing power to buy clothes, magazines, and records. Johnnie Ray was an early hero with his 1952 hit record "Cry;" then Bill Haley and the Comets started the rock'n'roll revolution, followed by the greatest rock icon of them all, Elvis Presley, with his 1956 hits "Hound Dog" and "Blue Suede Shoes." Shrink-fit blue jeans were essential wear for the rock'n'roll generation, whose idol was James Dean, the cult hero of the film *Rebel Without a Cause*.

Le Corbusier
Charles-Edouard Jeanneret (1887–1965), better known as Le Corbusier, was a major theoretician of modern postwar architecture. His thesis on the proportion of buildings was expounded in his book The Modulor *published in the 1950s.*

Elvis Presley
Elvis the Pelvis (1935–1977), as he was known colloquially, was born in Tupelo, Mississippi. A singer and guitarist, he was not the first rock'n'roll artist, but he became the biggest influence on postwar popular music. Presley was a legend in his own lifetime, and an even bigger one after his premature death in 1977. The first of his many hit records were "Heartbreak Hotel," "Hound Dog," and "Love Me Tender."

Matura

Mercurius

Pepita

Three 'Monotype' Scripts by Imre Reiner

The Monotype
Corporation Limited

Registered Trade Mark
Monotype

In the 1960s "Swinging London" took over the headlines. British youth divided into Mods or Rockers as the Beatles, the Rolling Stones, and the Who dominated the pop charts. Blue jeans, the inexpensive casual clothing of teenagers, were given new status in the 1970s by top fashion houses, which started selling expensive versions under their own labels.

Postwar architects were influenced by the buildings and writings of the Swiss architect Le Corbusier, who formulated a system of dimensions and structure for buildings based on the human body and classical proportions. Paris, which had for many years been the accepted world capital of modern art, lost its dominant place to New York. During the 1950s, the New York School of Abstract Expressionist painters was introduced to European audiences as part of the Cold War cultural struggle with the Soviet Union. The large, vigorous canvases of Jackson Pollock's multi-layered drip paintings, Willem de Kooning's wild-eyed women, and Mark Rothko's brooding rectangular panels of color were a revelation to European gallery-goers. Almost simultaneously, a second postwar movement appeared: Pop Art, represented in America by Roy Lichtenstein and Andy Warhol, and in Britain by Richard Hamilton, Eduardo Paolozzi, and Peter Blake.

Postwar scripts
Three informal scripts designed by the Hungarian Swiss designer Imre Reiner were Matura, 1957, Mercurius 1957, and Pepita 1959. The scripts were of a less ideological form of typography than that of the emerging Swiss Style.

British Petroleum
The simplicity of this advertisement (below) personifies the Swiss lack of visual rhetoric in their advertising design.

mit dem Hammer misshandelt

— schon der Gedanke tut weh. Ihr Auto ist ja nicht irgend ein Gegenstand, sondern Ihr persönlicher Freund. Es verlangt und verdient Rücksicht.
Und trotzdem: nach langer Fahrt, den Pass bergauf, an einem heissen Tag — plötzlich klopft Ihr Motor. Ein dumpfes Schlagen, ein metallenes Ticken: Ihr Wagen ist zum Amboss geworden.
Das Klopfen kann durch eine Glühzündung entstehen. Das heisst: neben der Zündkerze glüht im Zylinder Ihres Motors ein alter Verbrennungsrückstand, ein teer- oder kohleartiger Fremdkörper. An ihm entzündet sich das Benzingemisch wie an einem elektrischen Funken. Statt einer Explosion haben Sie zwei Explosionen in Ihrem Zylinder. Schlagen diese Explosionen aufeinander, dann klopft es. Und es klopft nicht nur, sondern diese im falschen Augenblick ausgelöste Glühzündung sperrt sich gegen den normalen Lauf des Kolbens.

Ihr Motor wird träge, Ihr Wagen zieht nicht mehr. Das Autofahren wird zur Qual für Sie und Ihren Motor.
Das Klopfen kann Ihre Kolbenringe zerbrechen. Es kann Löcher in die Kolben schlagen, frisst die Zylinderwände an. Es kann selbst jede Bewegung blockieren. Man kann einen Motor nicht schlechter behandeln, als dass man ihn klopfen lässt.
Der Weg, auf dem Sie dem Klopfen beikommen, führt über das Oel. Es kann nicht gut genug sein. Es muss so beschaffen sein, dass es die Verbrennungsrückstände laufend unschädlich macht. Auch bei hohen Temperaturen soll es noch einen ausreichenden Schmerfilm zwischen Zylinder und Kolben bilden, der die Treibstoffrückstände wegschwemmt.
Dazu wurde BP Special Energol visco-static geschaffen. Und nicht nur dazu: der Name visco-static kennzeichnet ein Oel, das im

Winter zu den dünnflüssigsten, im Sommer zu den hitzebeständigsten gehört.
Vier Jahreszeiten und ein Oel! Für Ihren Wagen bedeutet es: drei Viertel weniger Motorverschleiss, ein Drittel weniger Oelverbrauch, durchschnittlich ein Zehntel Benzin gespart und Freiheit vom heimtückischen Klopfen!
Ihr Wagen ist als Amboss denkbar ungeeignet. Statt mit dem Hammer misshandelt, verdient er es, mit BP Special Energol visco-static verwöhnt zu werden. Er wird es Ihnen danken.

Special ENERGOL visco-static

Swiss Formalism
This poster by Karl Gerstner (above) is an example of the obvious grid structure characteristic of the Modernist aesthetic that was a re-evaluation of 1930s New Typography. This aesthetic caught the imagination of younger Swiss graphic designers, and would spread eventually across Europe.

MAX MIEDINGER *& Helvetica*

Helvetica has found enduring popularity from the 1960s onward. Arial, distributed by Microsoft, is a cheaper, unauthorized, Helvetica clone, and can be distinguished from Helvetica by examining the uppercase "R." A default typeface for the Mac OS system, Helvetica is now widely used in France, Britain, and the Nordic countries, although Univers is preferred worldwide.

ABCDEFGHIJKLMNOPQRSTUVWXYZ&
abcdefghijklmnopqrstuvwxyz.,;:!?-'()
£1234567890

Haas Grotesque
First cast as foundry type for hand-setting, New Haas Grotesque was available in a limited number of body sizes. Later in the 1960s as Helvetica, it became available for machine setting.

Although the Swiss Modernists of the 1940s were supporters of sans-serif as a basic typeface for modern graphic design, they did not make use of Renner's Futura, the sans-serif of the 1920s. They did not care for the cool geometry of its letterforms and preferred the late-19th-century Grotesques. The sans-serif letterforms introduced originally as display type had at first been described as "Grotesques" because, while they were acknowledged to be effective graphically, they did not meet the prevailing standards of elegance. In the 1940s and 1950s, however, prevailing opinion believed the monoline forms to be clear, open, and legible, without historical or social connotations.

Many of the 19th-century Grotesques (for example, the Stephenson, Blake, & Company's Grotesque No.8 and No.9) were unsuitable for revival, being too bold, too condensed, or simply too idiosyncratic. One of the first to be brought back was Akzidenz-Grotesk, the Berthold sans-serif of 1898. This was a well-proportioned, clearly-formed sans-serif with no outstanding idiosyncrasies.

Those who objected to the total use of sans-serif considered the Grotesques to be lacking unsubtlety and legibility compared with the serifed letterform. While sans-serifs might be used in advertising display, they were totally unsuitable for lengthy texts. Serifs, critics argued, improved legibility by forming visual links between letters, enabling them to fit together better as words.

As the economic situation improved and typefoundries returned to full production in the 1950s, a process of upgrading began to take place. Along with other foundries, the Haas typefoundry in Münchenstein, Switzerland, searched for suitable typefaces for modernization. In the mid-1950s the directors Edouard and Alfred Hoffmann briefed their in-house designer Max Miedinger with their plan to produce a new sans-serif to meet the growing demand and competition for typefaces.

Miedinger's choice as a model for his design was an 1880 type, Schelter Grotesk—a reasonably successful sans-serif from the Schelter & Giesecke typefoundry. The sans-serif that

Max Miedinger
1910–1980

28   Hôtel-Pension Métropole
Abonnement de parcours
MAGASINS DU LOUVRE
EXPOSITION MONDIALE

36   Chemische Färberei
Amtliches Kursbuch
WOCHEN-ZEITUNG
HANDELSKAMMER

48   Nationalkassen
Quartalberichte
REICHENSTEIN

Dans les nombreux commentaires et analyses de la bonne affiche, qui s'occupent de la qualité et du niveau de l'efficacité, nous regrettons de ne trouver rien qui relève spécifiquement des capacités solides, ni aucune étude des facteurs qui ont assuré à l'affiche suisse sa place à part. Les commentateurs ont admis jusqu'à présent le niveau moyen élevé de ce secteur graphique particulier comme allant de soi, sans se rendre

Im Gegensatz zur dokumentarischen Aufnahme, wie sie beispielsweise mit Vorzug in der Industrie-Werbung verwendet wird, ist die Photographie mit Bewegung oder bei mehrschichtiger Gruppierung ein Mittel, um Geheimnis oder Dynamik ins Bild zu bringen. Wir wollen hier nicht erforschen, inwieweit diese Art der Photographie berechtigt ist und ob auch die gezeigten Beispiele bedachtvoll auf ihren Verwendungszweck bezogen sind. Wichtig erschien uns, diese Serie sehr gut gelungener Photos zu reproduzieren. Sie verraten einen wachen Sinn für die Möglichkeit

New Haas Grotesque
The very blandness of Miedinger's design may have held the secret of its success. The type was commissioned by Edouard Hoffman, who also commissioned Herman Eidenbenz in the design of Clarendon.

Miedinger produced in 1956 was released as Neue Haas Grotesk. The first version consisted of three weights; medium, semibold, and bold, with no italics. It was cast in 13 sizes, from six to 48-point, as foundry type for hand-setting. At the time this was still a common method of typesetting, especially for display work. When the Haas parent company, the D Stempel AG typefoundry in Frankfurt, released Neue Haas Grotesk in West Germany in 1961, they renamed it Helvetica, the Latin word for Swiss. This made reference to Swiss International Style and was considered a more suitable name for international purposes. Helvetica was not, actually, that popular with the Swiss, possibly due to the competition from Akzidenz Grotesk, which was well-entrenched. However, in other European countries where Akzidenz Grotesk had not penetrated, Helvetica became popular with those sympathetic to Swiss graphic design philosophy. In 1983, with the agreement of D Stempel AG, Helvetica was digitized by the Linotype Design Studio and updated with a comprehensive range of family variants, released as Neue Helvetica.

Swiss International Style

Also known as Swiss Style and International Typographic Style, this was built on Constructivism, De Stijl, the Bauhaus, and 1930s New Typography. The movement sought to present complex information in a unified and structured manner by relying on the typographic grid, sans-serif text, narrow, ranged-left text columns, and photographs rather than illustrations. It was, and still is, seen as an objective and systematic approach to problem-solving for graphic designers.

Grotesques

Originally the term used for sans-serifs in Britain (The United States used the term "gothic"), the word "grotesque" stemmed from the belief that serifs prevented the letterform looking awkward and unappealing. Helvetica was originally released as New Haas Grotesque ("Neue Haas Grotesk" in German).

Akzidenz-Grotesk

A forerunner of Helvetica and popular with the Swiss, Akzidenz-Grotesk was released in 1898. The name comes from the German word "Akzidenzschrift," meaning "display face" or "jobbing type." This type is particularly suitable for technical literature and tables.

HELVETICA: *the Typeface Itself*

ABCDEFGHIJKLMNOPQ
abcdefghijklmnopqrstuv
abcdefghijklmnopqrstuvw

Helvetica
This sans-serif has become possibly the most used sans-serif ever. The current digital family of Neue Helvetica consists of a large range of weights, from Ultra Light to Black, in roman, condensed, and expanded forms. The tracking of the three alphabets shown has been increased.

Helvetica is classified as a neo-grotesque sans-serif, as it is modeled on 19th-century Grotesques. Others included in this classification are Akzidenz Grotesk, Venus, Haas Unica, Grotesque No. 1, Berthold Standard Grotesk, and Folio.

Helvetica has proved to be one of the most popular sans-serifs of all time. This must be due in some degree to the inclusion of the font in many computer systems. Its great success has made it subject to many imitations, which include Arial, Helious, Swiss, Helvetia, Nimbus, and Heldustry.

The refurbished 19th-century Grotesques gained favor because they presented a simple, unadorned, neutral character that expressed, better than any other designs, the requirements of the 20th-century Modernist aesthetic. Modernist typographers, like their traditionalist counterparts, considered it important that text types be as neutral as possible, so that the type exerts a minimal influence on the mood of the reader. Both Akzidenz-Grotesk and Helvetica were designed with this in mind.

Helvetica is a typeface associated originally with the Swiss International Style; now, however, like Times New Roman, it has become popular and ubiquitous. It is used in many different ways for many different purposes, proving its value as a font with clear, no-nonsense legibility, making its point without rhetoric. Helvetica's core weights make it a very legible, and it has a large x-height, fairly short ascenders and descenders, and close letter fit. The letterforms—both capitals and lowercase, are generously shaped; the "O" is almost, but not quite, a full circle. Helvetica is hard to differentiate from Akzidenz-Grotesk, and the differences lying in the details. Helvetica has a larger x-height; the terminals of curved letters "C," "G," "S," "a," "c," "e," and "s" are horizontal, when in Akzidenz they are closer to 45 degrees. This is more noticeable in heavier weights.

The original D Stempel AG Helvetica, the preferred range of 1961, is now digitized, and contains a range of four weights with obliques from light to black in standard set width. Helvetica Condensed has four weights with obliques from light to black, and there are two weights of Helvetica Narrow and one weight of Helvetica Compressed, Extra Compressed, and Ultra Compressed. There is one weight of Inserat Roman and there are three fonts of Helvetica Rounded (the font is made less austere by the stems being rounded off at the terminals). There are also two textbook weights

RSTUVWXYZ
wxyz& 1234567890

xyz& 1234567890

and a range of numerical fractions—a total of 19 variations in the family. The 1983 digitized range of Neue Helvetica contains eight weights and obliques from ultra light to bold outline in standard set width. Neue Helvetica Condensed has 10 weights and obliques from ultra light to extra black oblique. Neue Helvetica Extended has eight weights and obliques from ultra light extended to black extended oblique—a total of 26 variations in the family. Digital innovation has meant font variants are far more simple to produce than before, and Helvetica shows how the concept of the font family maybe extended to the limits of resemblance to offer a truly comprehensive palette.

Ga
Ga

A Grotesque and a Gothic
The above comparison is between the letterforms "G" and "a" of Helvetica (top) and Franklin Gothic (above).

ULTRA LIGHT
AaBbCcDdEeFf

THIN
AaBbCcDdEeFf

LIGHT
AaBbCcDdEeFf

ROMAN
AaBbCcDdEeFf

MEDIUM
AaBbCcDdEeFf

BOLD
AaBbCcDdEeFf

HEAVY
AaBbCcDdEeFf

BLACK
AaBbCcDdEeFf

Eight type weights
The weights are supported by four forms: roman, italics, condensed, and expanded; these provide a rich collection of permutations.

Helvetica
the quick brown fox jumps over the lazy dog

Univers
the quick brown fox jumps over the lazy dog

Akzidenz-Grotesk
the quick brown fox jumps over the lazy dog

Futura
the quick brown fox jumps over the lazy dog

'LINOTYPE'
Helvetica
a modern sans serif design

HELVETICA is a type of our time, created in Switzerland, where graphic design has reached a higher level of quality than anywhere else. The face was designed by Max Miedinger in 1956 for the Haas type foundry of Munchenstein, who called it Neue Haas-Grotesk. It won immediate approval from Swiss typographers and printers, and gained wider acclaim when the design was adopted, by agreement, by the Stempel foundry of Frankfurt, who named it Helvetica, and the German Linotype company. It is now being made by the American and British Linotype companies. The history of the typographic sans-serif ('lineal') letter form shows four distinct phases. First there was its development during the nineteenth century, from its unobtrusive introduction in England in 1816 to its proliferation in the specimen books of the later part of the century, especially those of the German founders. Then, in 1916 Edward Johnston, and in 1927 Eric Gill, created unseriffed designs of markedly patrician and academic form. At the same time there was the development in Germany of geometric sans-serifs by Renner, Koch and others according to the aesthetic principles of the Bauhaus. Finally, in recent years, new preferences in typographic design have been formed in which the sans-serif type is an essential element. The kind of sans-serif now preferred is one devoid of 'personality', where that is due to the artist deliberately projecting himself through the design; the type must subdue itself to the purity of linear pattern. Many typographers think that Helvetica satisfies this requirement more fully than any other design now current.

OTHER SIZES AND COMBINATIONS TO FOLLOW

Linotype Helvetica
When Max Miedinger's sans-serif was released by Linotype (left), it was available in a greater range of weights and sizes than before. In 1983, a total reassessment by D Stempel AG and Linotype resulted in the creation of Neue Helvetica, extending the range even further.

Helvetica
The promotional brochure for Helvetica is an exemplar of the Swiss Style. Helvetica was marketed very successfully and it quickly became fashionable on its release by the Haas parent company, D Stempel AG, in 1961.

Helvetica at work

Helvetica usage

Neue Helvetica Light
This Catalan street banner to the left uses Neue Helvetica Light to great effect. Three lines of type have been fitted closely together with minus leading to create a strong typographic image without loss of legibility.

Tracking, kerning, and H&Js

Helvetica has a very close letterfit and large x-height compared with some sans-serifs. This is one of the characteristics that has made it so popular. A discreet increase in tracking will lighten the textural color of the page, without detriment to the letterfit. Increased tracking of sizes 7-point and below will improve clarity.

Text sizes

Helvetica is large on the body so smaller text sizes can be used compared to other sans-serifs. Also, the x-height is large, which reduces the length of ascenders and descenders; because of this, leading can be increased to more than the regular 20 percent. Neue Helvetica Ultra Light and Light should not be considered for text setting; however, like most other sans-serifs, Helvetica offers condensed and expanded fonts that are suitable for text.

An arts program
The display headings in this program to the right and below have reduced tracking, so that the letters touch and join up. Helvetica's usability means that the words remain legible.

Display sizes

The range of weights and italics, plus the condensed and expanded forms, make Helvetica a versatile display face. Tracking should be reduced incrementally as the size increases. When using large sizes in display of several lines, leading can be removed to give the display added form. Capitals can be letterspaced to great effect on occasions.

On-screen display

The monoline of sans-serif is more suitable for on-screen display than the classic serifed font. Helvetica as neo-grotesque has been a natural influence on fonts designed for use as on-screen display, such as Verdana and Arial. Both these fonts, which have looser letterfit than Helvetica, are natural partners for it when setting up HTML text properties and CSS style sheets.

INTERNATIONAL STYLE: *The Impact on Europe*

The Swiss model of the New Typography had wide appeal in Europe, although it did not achieve total dominance. As industry and commerce got back on their feet in the 1950s, the systematic approach to typography and layout gave the emerging profession of graphic design a new rationale. The spread of the Swiss International Style came not only from the distribution of graphic design publications, but also from more adventurous Swiss designers who ventured abroad to work.

The Studio Boggeri in Milan, Italy, attracted a number of Swiss designers during the 1930s and 1950s. Antonio Boggeri, a photographer in the 1930s, had met many of the avant-garde Modernists, and decided to set up a studio in 1933 to produce modern design in Italy.

SWISS DESIGNERS IN FRANCE

In France, possibly the most remarkable Swiss designer is Jean Widmer, a student of the *Zurich Kunstgewerbeschule* in the late 1940s, who also studied briefly at the *Ecole Nationale des Beaux-Arts* in Paris. He worked for the advertising agency SNIP, as art director at Galeries Lafayette department store, and for the women's magazine *Jardin des Modes*. In 1972, he set up his own studio called Visual Design, which has been responsible for many graphic identities including those of the Pompidou Centre and the *Musée d'Orsay*. Widmer's work fully exploited the potential of type as a pictorial element. A less well-known itinerant Swiss designer is Roland Schenk, born in 1933. Having trained at the *Kunstgewerbeschule* in Basle, he worked in France during the 1950s, returning to Switzerland in 1959 to design the arts magazine *Du*. Over the following years he worked on the German magazine *Quick*, and then on the 1960s' British magazine *Town*. His art direction on the business journal *Management Today* showed him to be a major creative influence on editorial design.

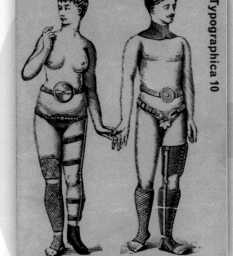

GERMAN PRACTITIONERS

Two German designers who were practitioners of the International Style were Otl Aicher and Willy Fleckhaus. Aicher, a former student of the *Akademie der Bildenden Künste*, Munich, set up a design studio in Ulm. He became a cofounder of the *Hochschule für Gestaltung* (technical colllege for design) in Ulm in 1955, and was art director of the graphic design unit for the 1972 Munich Olympic Games. His typeface Rotis was one the first typefaces to introduce the concept of three related forms, sans-serif, serif, and semi-serif, in one family. Willy Fleckhaus earned an international reputation for magazine design, largely for his art direction on the youth culture magazine *Twen* that was launched in Munich in 1959. This was the predecessor of many later youth lifestyle magazines, it was largely black and white, with little or no four-color printing in the first few editions. Fleckhaus created spectacular layouts exploiting the grid, moving from tight, narrow columns to full pages of text, and using dramatically cropped photography to create a visual impact not seen before in such publications.

BRITAIN AND THE NETHERLANDS

Britain began the 1950s with the Festival of Britain in 1951, marking the centenary of the Great Exhibition in the Crystal Palace in London. This created a short-lived typographic vogue for 19th-century slab-serif types. By the late 1950s, the Swiss influence was being felt in spite of British apathy towards Modernism. Two motivating figures in Britain were Herbert Spencer and Anthony Froshaug. Spencer was a typographic designer and editor of the quarterly journal *Typographica*, which was a stimulating source of debate on the Modern movement. In 1952, he published *Design in Business Printing*, a book that put Modern typography into British terms. His 1969 book *Pioneers of Modern Typography* is still in print. Anthony Froshaug was a charismatic teacher and typographer, who spent several years running a small print shop in Cornwall, home of the British abstract artists' colony. In the 1950s, he taught at the Central School of Arts and Crafts, stimulating students with an analytical mind that was unique in British art schools. He went on to take up the post of Professor of Graphic Design and Visual Communication in 1957 at the *Ulm Hochschule für Gestaltung* University.

While having deep roots in tradition, the Netherlands had been at the forefront of early Modernism in the early years of the 20th century. The Dutch designer, painter, and art critic Theo van Doesburg was the driving force behind De Stijl, and had influential connections with the Bauhaus. The International style in postwar Holland really manifested itself in the multidisciplinary design consultancy Total Design. Formed in 1963, its founder members were graphic designers Wim Crouwel and Benno Wissing, and the industrial designer Friso Kramer. They established a style of boldly structured layout combined with pure, fresh color, always with a spark of unpredictability.

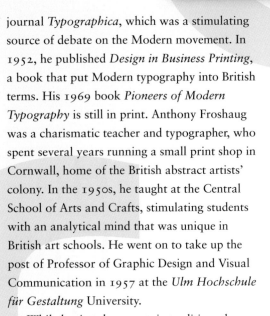

Typographica
A quarterly journal of typography and graphic arts edited by Herbert Spencer, Typographica *appeared during the years 1949–1967 (right). It was a germinal publication for those engaged with modern graphic design in a Britain dominated by the typographic aesthetics of Stanley Morison.*

Otl Aicher
In the 1970s Aicher directed the graphic design for the Munich Olympic Games, which included these pictograms below.

ADRIAN FRUTIGER *& the Photo Sans-Serif*

Adrian Frutiger
The Swiss typographer Frutiger (b.1928) has had a career spanning the eras of hot metal, phototypesetting and digital typesetting.

In 1954, the Deberny & Peignot typefoundry in Paris was preparing a typeface collection for the new Lumitype/Photon photosetting machine. A sans-serif was required and Futura was a strong possibility, until Charles Peignot's young design director Adrian Frutiger asked for the opportunity to submit a design of his own. Univers was the resulting typeface.

Univers family
The below spread from Monotype's 1964 publicity on Frutiger's fonts illustrates the anatomy of Univers.

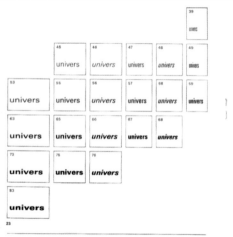

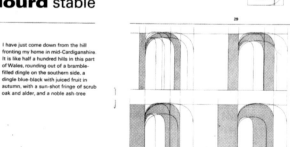

Frutiger had been given ten days to prepare his proposal and he drew 16 versions of his sans-serif using the five letters that formed the word "monde." Peignot was delighted with Frutiger's designs and two designers, Bruno Pfäffli and André Gürtler, joined Frutiger in the process of completing the project. Names were discussed: "Le Monde" was rejected as being too French. "Galaxy" was also rejected, but the astrological reference was maintained by Peignot's insistence on using "Univers."

Adrian Frutiger, who has proved to be one of the major type-designers of the 20th century, was born in Interlaken, Switzerland, in 1928. On leaving school in 1944 he took up an apprenticeship as a compositor, during which he gained practical experience of metal typefaces. He subsequently studied at the *Kunstgewerbeschule* in Zurich and, in 1952, went on to join Deberny & Peignot in Paris in 1952 as art director. By the time the sans-serif project was discussed, Frutiger had already designed several typefaces for the Paris typefoundry, including Phoebus (1953), Ondine (1954), and President (1954).

Frutiger had been trained in a sans-serif environment dominated by Akzidenz Grotesk. While studying under Walter Käch he had prepared

MAX MIEDINGER *& Helvetica*

Helvetica has found enduring popularity from the 1960s onward. Arial, distributed by Microsoft, is a cheaper, unauthorized, Helvetica clone, and can be distinguished from Helvetica by examining the uppercase "R." A default typeface for the Mac OS system, Helvetica is now widely used in France, Britain, and the Nordic countries, although Univers is preferred worldwide.

ABCDEFGHIJKLMNOPQRSTUVWXYZ&
abcdefghijklmnopqrstuvwxyz.,;:!?-'()
£1234567890

Haas Grotesque
First cast as foundry type for hand-setting, New Haas Grotesque was available in a limited number of body sizes. Later in the 1960s as Helvetica, it became available for machine setting.

Although the Swiss Modernists of the 1940s were supporters of sans-serif as a basic typeface for modern graphic design, they did not make use of Renner's Futura, the sans-serif of the 1920s. They did not care for the cool geometry of its letterforms and preferred the late-19th-century Grotesques. The sans-serif letterforms introduced originally as display type had at first been described as "Grotesques" because, while they were acknowledged to be effective graphically, they did not meet the prevailing standards of elegance. In the 1940s and 1950s, however, prevailing opinion believed the monoline forms to be clear, open, and legible, without historical or social connotations.

Many of the 19th-century Grotesques (for example, the Stephenson, Blake, & Company's Grotesque No.8 and No.9) were unsuitable for revival, being too bold, too condensed, or simply too idiosyncratic. One of the first to be brought back was Akzidenz-Grotesk, the Berthold sans-serif of 1898. This was a well-proportioned, clearly-formed sans-serif with no outstanding idiosyncrasies.

Those who objected to the total use of sans-serif considered the Grotesques to be lacking unsubtlety and legibility compared with the serifed letterform. While sans-serifs might be used in advertising display, they were totally unsuitable for lengthy texts. Serifs, critics argued, improved legibility by forming visual links between letters, enabling them to fit together better as words.

As the economic situation improved and typefoundries returned to full production in the 1950s, a process of upgrading began to take place. Along with other foundries, the Haas typefoundry in Münchenstein, Switzerland, searched for suitable typefaces for modernization. In the mid-1950s the directors Edouard and Alfred Hoffmann briefed their in-house designer Max Miedinger with their plan to produce a new sans-serif to meet the growing demand and competition for typefaces.

Miedinger's choice as a model for his design was an 1880 type, Schelter Grotesk—a reasonably successful sans-serif from the Schelter & Giesecke typefoundry. The sans-serif that

28	Hôtel-Pension Métropole Abonnement de parcours MAGASINS DU LOUVRE EXPOSITION MONDIALE
36	Chemische Färberei Amtliches Kursbuch WOCHEN-ZEITUNG HANDELSKAMMER
48	Nationalkassen Quartalberichte REICHENSTEIN

Max Miedinger
1910–1980

Swiss International Style

Also known as Swiss Style and International Typographic Style, this was built on Constructivism, De Stijl, the Bauhaus, and 1930s New Typography. The movement sought to present complex information in a unified and structured manner by relying on the typographic grid, sans-serif text, narrow, ranged-left text columns, and photographs rather than illustrations. It was, and still is, seen as an objective and systematic approach to problem-solving for graphic designers.

Grotesques

Originally the term used for sans-serifs in Britain (The United States used the term "gothic"), the word "grotesque" stemmed from the belief that serifs prevented the letterform looking awkward and unappealing. Helvetica was originally released as New Haas Grotesque ("Neue Haas Grotesk" in German).

Akzidenz-Grotesk

A forerunner of Helvetica and popular with the Swiss, Akzidenz-Grotesk was released in 1898. The name comes from the German word "Akzidenzschrift," meaning "display face" or "jobbing type." This type is particularly suitable for technical literature and tables.

Miedinger produced in 1956 was released as Neue Haas Grotesk. The first version consisted of three weights; medium, semibold, and bold, with no italics. It was cast in 13 sizes, from six to 48-point, as foundry type for hand-setting. At the time this was still a common method of typesetting, especially for display work. When the Haas parent company, the D Stempel AG typefoundry in Frankfurt, released Neue Haas Grotesk in West Germany in 1961, they renamed it Helvetica, the Latin word for Swiss. This made reference to Swiss International Style and was considered a more suitable name for international purposes. Helvetica was not, actually, that popular with the Swiss, possibly due to the competition from Akzidenz Grotesk, which was well-entrenched. However, in other European countries where Akzidenz Grotesk had not penetrated, Helvetica became popular with those sympathetic to Swiss graphic design philosophy. In 1983, with the agreement of D Stempel AG, Helvetica was digitized by the Linotype Design Studio and updated with a comprehensive range of family variants, released as Neue Helvetica.

New Haas Grotesque
The very blandness of Miedinger's design may have held the secret of its success. The type was commissioned by Edouard Hoffman, who also commissioned Herman Eidenbenz in the design of Clarendon.

HELVETICA: *the Typeface Itself*

ABCDEFGHIJKLMNOPQ
abcdefghijklmnopqrstuv
abcdefghijklmnopqrstuvw

Helvetica is classified as a neo-grotesque sans-serif, as it is modeled on 19th-century Grotesques. Others included in this classification are Akzidenz Grotesk, Venus, Haas Unica, Grotesque No. 1, Berthold Standard Grotesk, and Folio.

Helvetica has proved to be one of the most popular sans-serifs of all time. This must be due in some degree to the inclusion of the font in many computer systems. Its great success has made it subject to many imitations, which include Arial, Helious, Swiss, Helvetia, Nimbus, and Heldustry.

The refurbished 19th-century Grotesques gained favor because they presented a simple, unadorned, neutral character that expressed, better than any other designs, the requirements of the 20th-century Modernist aesthetic. Modernist typographers, like their traditionalist counterparts, considered it important that text types be as neutral as possible, so that the type exerts a minimal influence on the mood of the reader. Both Akzidenz-Grotesk and Helvetica were designed with this in mind.

Helvetica is a typeface associated originally with the Swiss International Style; now, however, like Times New Roman, it has become popular and ubiquitous. It is used in many different ways

for many different purposes, proving its value as a font with clear, no-nonsense legibility, making its point without rhetoric. Helvetica's core weights make it a very legible, and it has a large x-height, fairly short ascenders and descenders, and close letter fit. The letterforms—both capitals and lowercase, are generously shaped; the "O" is almost, but not quite, a full circle. Helvetica is hard to differentiate from Akzidenz-Grotesk, and the differences lying in the details. Helvetica has a larger x-height; the terminals of curved letters "C," "G," "S," "a," "c," "e," and "s" are horizontal, when in Akzidenz they are closer to 45 degrees. This is more noticeable in heavier weights.

The original D Stempel AG Helvetica, the preferred range of 1961, is now digitized, and contains a range of four weights with obliques from light to black in standard set width. Helvetica Condensed has four weights with obliques from light to black, and there are two weights of Helvetica Narrow and one weight of Helvetica Compressed, Extra Compressed, and Ultra Compressed. There is one weight of Inserat Roman and there are three fonts of Helvetica Rounded (the font is made less austere by the stems being rounded off at the terminals). There are also two textbook weights

Helvetica
This sans-serif has become ... bly the most used sans-... . The current digital ... Neue Helvetica ... large range of ... Ultra Light ... ... unded ... ...he

some drawings for a sans-serif, so for his proposal he returned to his student work. His new sans-serif for the Lumitype/Photon photosetting system was a fresh look at the form; the new technology influencing a move away from the 19th-century monoline. The new sans-serif introduced a variation of line thickness, so that there is a slight difference between vertical and horizontal strokes, creating a more refined form than the metal letterpress monoline Grotesques.

As a typeface designed for photosetting, the new type was intended to fulfil the role of a sans-serif for extended lengths of text as well as display. The first release of Univers in 1957 consisted of 21 variants presented for photosetting and foundry type as a carefully rationalized system conceived from the first set of drawings. Frutiger had given much thought to the issue of type families, which in many cases were created by an ad hoc process of adding further weights to a face as it acquired acceptance. With true Swiss Modernist scepticism, he was wary of the arbitrary terms to describe type qualities. "Bold" and "semibold" are only relative terms; in German semibold is *halbfett*, while in French type semibold could be *gras* or *semi-gras*. For clarification, Frutiger introduced a numbering system related to a grid to identify the family relationships. The regular weight was 55, what would normally be bold was 65, extra bold was 75, and light was 45. Regular weight italic was 56, 66 was bold italic, 76 was extra bold italic, and 46 was light italic. The grid also explained the relationships within the family: to the right were increasingly condensed variants, to the left increasingly extended variants. The rationalizing of the family was a milestone in type design—a development combined with the refinement of the sans-serif letterform. Although Univers met with resistance in Switzerland from Akzidenz Grotesk and Neue Haas Grotesk, it was generally hailed as an innovation.

Univers explained
This typographic diagram explains in purely visual terms the relation and the numbering system applied to the 21 variants of Univers.

Typographic styling
The above range of literary publications use the repetition of closely fitted Univers capitals as a style to give the series an identity.

Neo-grotesque
As a sans-serif, Univers is classified as a neo-grotesque, implying its form is influenced, if only a little, by the Grotesques of the 19th century.

ABCDEFGHIJKLMN
abcdefghijklmnopqr
abcdefghijklmnopqrstuv

Univers
the quick brown
fox jumps over
the lazy dog

Helvetica
the quick brown
fox jumps over
the lazy dog

Akzidenz Grotesque
the quick brown
fox jumps over
the lazy dog

Futura
the quick brown
fox jumps over
the lazy dog

Gill Sans
the quick brown
fox jumps over
the lazy dog

LIGHT
AaBbCcDd

ROMAN
AaBbCcDd

BOLD
AaBbCcDd

BLACK
AaBbCcDd

EXTRA BLACK
AaBbCcDd

EXTENDED
AaBbCcD

CONDENSED
AaBbCcDd

Despite its divergence from Helvetica and Akzidenz-Grotesk, Univers is essentially a neo-grotesque, but with a humanist touch. The earliest version of Univers was designed for use on the Lumitype/Photon photosetting machine, which was a second-generation photosetter. However, its popularity increased when, in 1961, Monotype released it for Monophoto and hot-metal machines. The sizes for hot metal were actually continental Didot point sizes cast on larger Anglo-American point bodies, as the Didot point was larger than the Anglo-American point. This was possibly an economy, since the demise of the hot-metal Monotype system had already been signaled by the first Monophoto Filmsetter's introduction in 1957.

A comparison with Helvetica and Akzidenz shows Univers to be narrower, more noticeably in the capitals. The circular characters are more oval, with a slight squareness to the curves, suggesting a less mechanical form. However, the letterfit is more generous, so that size for size, even though the x-height is smaller, Univers will take up more space than Helvetica. The range of variants follows carefully balanced

OPQRSTUVWXYZ
stuvwxyz& 1234567890
wxyz& 1234567890

QQ
KK

increases in weight that do not match those of Helvetica and Akzidenz.

The slight slimming of horizontal curves, more associated with serif forms, is intended to overcome the optical illusion that makes horizontal strokes appear thicker than vertical ones. In addition to the overall general character of Univers, there are some individual letters which identify it; the "C" has a wide mouth, and "G" is without a spur at the foot (this is characteristic of Frutiger's sans-serifs although more common in serif fonts). The arms of "K" join each other at a single point on the vertical stem, and "Q" has a tail that lies along the baseline. Among the lowercase characteristics, the "a" has no spur on the vertical stem, the ascender of "t" is cut diagonally, and "g" has a tail rather than a bowl—a common characteristic of this generation of sans-serifs.

During the late 1990s, in addition to their existing range of Univers, Linotype took on the task of totally updating the 40-year-old design. This involved a return to the original drawings of the 1950s to check up on the anomalies that might have arisen during the years Univers had been in circulation. Linotype has updated the design by carrying out refinements to the letterforms and the character weight relationships, and the range of weights and widths has been increased. Italics have become obliques, and the angle of slant has also been increased. The original two-digit numbering system has been revised and a three-digit system replaces it. In the new system, the first digit denotes the weight, the second denotes the width, and the third digit denotes whether it is roman or italic.

Univers's great quality is its modesty. What it may lack as an assertive display face, it makes up for in its quietly efficient range of weights, enabling it to function as a text face. Typefaces intended for substantial lengths of text should not be too characterful. A typeface may be attractive as a few lines in the catalogue, but can have idiosyncrasies which are annoying on the screen or over pages of sustained reading.

Univers and Helvetrica
Both the above typefaces appeared in the 1950s. The subtle variation of line thickness when set against Helvetica (right) shows Univers (left) to be more organic in detail.

Didot on Anglo-American
The specimen below is of hot-metal Univers 57 Condensed, and shows a display size of 48-point Didot on a 60-point Anglo-American body size. This situation existed before phototypesetting came into common use.

48 Didot (on 60 pt. body)

ABCDEFGHIJKLMNOPQRSTUVWXYZ&
abcdefghijklmnopqrstuvwxyzæœ.,:;-!?"-

will no doubt prove a popular hardy perennial.

Monotype promotion
The Monotype Corporation initially made Univers available for both hot-metal typesetting and for phototypesetting (left). The hot-metal types were produced as Didot point sizes cast on larger Anglo-American point size bodies.

Univers capitals
Univers quickly became popular with designers as it was launched at a time when a new sans-serif was needed. This design below makes use of Univers 67 capitals, interlocking them with halftone photographs, reminiscent of an El Lissitzky's PROUN design, painted in 1923.

THE MONOTYPE CORPORATION LIMITED 43 FETTER LANE, LONDON E.C.4

MONOTYPE *UNIVERS*
MONOTYPE UNIVERS
MONOTYPE *UNIVERS*
MONOTYPE UNIVERS
MONOTYPE *UNIVERS*
MONOTYPE UNIVERS
MONOTYPE *UNIVERS*
MONOTYPE UNIVERS
Monotype **Univers**
Monotype Univers
Monotype Univers
Monotype Univers

Taken from a cutting by Deberny & Peignot, this flourishing new family is available in a number of varieties—which are ideal for mixing—and it will no doubt prove a popular hardy perennial.

Univers at work

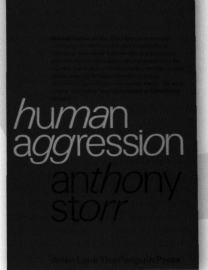

Mixed Forms
This jacket for a book on human psychology (left) uses a mixture of roman and italics to imply a sense of movement or struggle, which subtly conveys the idea of aggressive behavior.

Positive statements
Univers 75 Black is used on this poster (right) by Malcolm Frost advertising three separate exhibitions. The words have been carefully typeset so that the "Yes" fits into the ascender space of "We," and the word "Can" moves into the descender space. The large bright exclamation mark affirms the statement and consolidates the whole structure.

Univers usage

Tracking, kerning, and H&Js

Univers has a loose word fit and small x-height in comparison with Helvetica; this suggests that it is more economical, but it is not. Owing to the loose word fit, it is, in fact, less economic with space than Neue Helvetica.

Text sizes

Univers functions very well as a text face and is extremely legible in small sizes. Univers, like many other sans-serifs, has a large x-height compared with most serifed typefaces and should therefore be leaded, this can be substantial if required. Like Helvetica, it also offers weights of condensed and expanded which can be effective as text setting. The ultra-condensed fonts should be avoided for text settings, the distortion of normal letter proportions can be very difficult to read for lengths of text.

Display sizes

The extensive family of weights and condensed and expanded letterforms that constitutes the Univers family offers a rich palette of display possibilities. When using large sizes, reduced leading to zero body size should be considered to give display headings of more than one line added form. Capitals can be letterspaced on occasions to great effect.

On-screen display

Univers was relaunched in 1997 after Adrian Frutiger redrafted what was the first sans-serif of the new photosetting age. The revisions have taken account of the requirements for optimized screen display. Verdana and Arial both have similar loose letter fit to Univers, and are natural partners for it when setting up HTML text properties, and CSS style sheets.

HERMANN ZAPF *& Palatino*

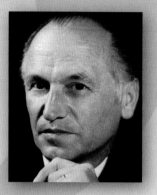

Herman Zapf
A love of calligraphy has influenced many of the typefaces designed by Zapf (b.1918).

Hermann Zapf is another great typographer of the 20th century, and he has produced a series of brilliant typefaces. Like Frutiger, he has been confronted by the changing technologies of 20th-century type design. Hermann Zapf is exactly ten years older than Frutiger, and was born into a time of revolution.

A page of Zapf's notes on Palatino
Zapf's achievements in type design have made him a major figure of postwar typography. His typefaces reflect the influence of his love of calligraphy, although that has been combined with an appetite for the challenge of new typographic technology. An annotated version is shown of Zapf's Palatino above.

On 9 November 1918, the day after Zapf was born in Nuremberg, the new German republic—later known as the Weimar Republic—was declared. Workers' and soldiers' councils were set up as revolution broke out and the Kaiser fled to the neighboring Netherlands.

When Zapf was ten years old, the National Socialist Party came to power in Germany. Zapf's father, who had been active in the trades union movement, was arrested and confined in Dachau concentration camp for a while. His father's political record made it impossible for Zapf to study electrical engineering as he had wished and he had to find an apprenticeship instead. Eventually, in 1934, he began work as an apprentice lithographic retoucher.

In 1935, Zapf went to an exhibition of the work of the famous Nuremberg calligrapher and type designer Rudolf Koch, who had died the previous year. He was immediately entranced and fascinated by the lettering and type designs of the artist-craftsman. On leaving the exhibition he bought two books, one was Koch's *The Art of Writing*, and the other was Edward Johnston's *Writing and Illuminating and Lettering*. Working at home in his spare time, Zapf spent many hours teaching himself calligraphy with

a broad pen. When his employer discovered his calligraphic abilities, he was given lettering to retouch. When he finished his apprenticeship, he moved to Frankfurt and worked at the studio of Paul Koch (son of Rudolf) at the *Werkstatt Haus zum Fürsteneck* (Fürsteneck workshop).

Through acquaintance with the printing historian Gustav Mori, Zapf came into contact with the D Stempel AG typefoundry and Linotype GmbH in Frankfurt. Under the tuition of August Rosenberger, he learned to cut punches. By 1938, he designed his first typeface, cut by August Rosenberger. It was a fraktur (a kind of blackletter) design called Gilgenart. During the Second World War, he worked for the military as a cartographer. After the war, he spent 1946 in Nuremberg, but returned to Frankfurt in 1947 and took up the position of art director of the printing department at D Stempel AG.

LOVE OF CALLIGRAPHY

The first of Zapf's outstanding typefaces was Palatino, designed by Zapf and cut by August Rosenberger, after much careful study with Rosenberger. Zapf's knowledge and love of calligraphy were manifest in this mid-20th century typeface. Palatino expresses a strong appreciation

The hand and pen
A example of Zapf's calligraphic work to the left show individual gestures of the pen in the human hand that seem remote from the mass-produced letterforms he produces for the computer.

Exhibition Poster
Zapf's activities have included teaching in France and Germany, as well as in the United States. This poster from the Ecole Estienne in Paris (below) is constructed from a variety of samples of his work.

Contextualizer

Hermann Zapf
b.1918

Optima

Designed by Zapf, Optima (see also page 150–153) is admired and imitated, in Oracle, for example. Bitstream's collection is called Zapf Humanist and is also known as Opulent and CG Omega. Described by Zapf as "a serifless roman," Zapf based it on the principles of the Golden Section and has since placed it between a Bodoni serif and a Futura sans-serif. The italic form is a slanted roman.

Mathematical interests

Zapf was quoted in "Graphis" magazine (August 2004) as saying "I am very interested in the symbolism of figures and in magic square numbers, which are included in several of my designs. I am also interested in the super-ellipse, which was used in the design of the Melior roman font." A "super-ellipse" describes the family of curves that lie between ellipses and rectangles.

of the forms that emanated from the broad pen, but it is not a reworking of a 16th-century typeface like many Old-face type designs. It is rather a tribute to the work of Giovanbattista Palatino, the writing master of Rome and author of a popular writing manual in 1540. After two years of tests, Palatino was released in 1950. The name expresses Zapf's gratitude to the Renaissance, but the making of the typeface made full use of the printing technology of the 20th century. Today, the popularity of Palatino as a text and display face has been enhanced by its availability on many personal computers. The first application of the new face was for the introduction of the designer's own book, *Pen and Graver*, a beautifully produced collection of Zapf's calligraphy.

PALATINO: *the Typeface Itself*

LIGHT
AaBbCcDd

ROMAN
AaBbCcDd

MEDIUM
AaBbCcDd

BOLD
AaBbCcDd

BLACK
AaBbCcDd

LIGHT ITALIC
AaBbCcDd

CONDENSED
AaBbCcDd

MEDIUM ITALIC
AaBbCcDd

BOLD ITALIC
AaBbCcDd

BLACK ITALIC
AaBbCcDd

ABCDEFGHIJKLMNO
abcdefghijklmnopqrst
ABCDEFGHIJKLMNOPQRS

Palatino weights
The above samples of Palatino show the influence of the calligraphy pen. Lighter weights were added later as the quality of postwar paper improved.

Broad strokes
The heavier line weight and subtle flourishes of Palatino (right) can be seen when compared with Adobe Caslon (far right).

Even from a cursory look at Palatino it is immediately clear that the thick and thin stems suggest the kind of strokes made by the broad pen. It is a chunky, sturdy type with a large x-height, which has not reduced the length of the ascenders or descenders. In fact, the ascenders are taller than the capitals; this is the same relation normally found in late Renaissance faces and their neohumanist descendents. A large x-height makes larger open counters possible and improves legibility. In the early days after the war this was an important consideration, because the paper available for printing was of poor quality. The early version of the design had a heavier stroke thickness compared with most roman typefaces, which was considered better for adapting to the requirements of the lithographic and gravure processes in use at the time. There is considerable subtlety of form and dramatic features in the letters: not only in the move from thick to thin of the strokes, but also in the vertical stems, which swell as they meet the serifs at the head and foot. The circular letters have a fullness that derives from the "O" being wider than it is high, and the tail of the "Q" is definitely a flourish of the pen below the baseline. The capital "X" has a curved one-sided serif on the thick stroke, and on the thin stroke an inner serif is non-existent. In the case of the capital "Y," the left arm emulates the "X," while the thin right arm swells but is without a serif. "S" has a tight changing curve that suggests contained energy. The italic alphabet has a classic calligraphic form expressed by the repeated shape of the bowls of "a," "b," "o," "p" and "q."

RX RX

PQRSTUVWXYZ
uvwxyz& 1234567890
TUVWXYZ 1234567890

Comparison
*The lowercase letters of
Palatino (above left) are set
against Bembo (above right)
in this example.*

Shortly after the release of Palatino in 1950, Zapf designed two other types that could be considered companions. They were both titlings and both maintained Palatino's Renaissance character. The first, Michelangelo, was a slender, elegant design with open calligraphic forms, which was cast in sizes from 16-point to 72-point. Sistina was released in 1951, a heavier titling with distinctively fine spiky serifs reminiscent of a stonecut letter, this was cast in sizes from 16-point to 84-point.

In 1954, as the quality of paper improved, Zapf produced an additional lighter version of Palatino, which was to overcome the perception that the existing Palatino weights were too heavy for book work. At first called Palatino Light Book, the font was later released as Aldus. The one weight with italic has been digitized, and it has now become a face in its own right with additional weights, recently being redesigned and available as Aldus Nova. The current range of digitized Palatino consists of 14 variants, including light, roman, roman small capitals, medium, bold, and black, with italics. The heavier weights of this face are suitable only for display situations.

Palatino
**the quick brown fox
jumps over the lazy dog**

Bembo
the quick brown fox
jumps over the lazy dog

Caslon
the quick brown fox
jumps over the lazy dog

Bodoni
the quick brown fox
jumps over the lazy dog

Palatino at work

Once upon a time there was an Art Director.

With blood and sweat, day and night, he labored to conceive a new idea.

And behold, he found he had created a blue-blooded stallion, with flashing eyes, proudly-arched neck, powerful legs and a flowing tail.

This was such a perfect animal, in short, that not even the ancient gods could have done better.

A conference was then called to inspect the masterpiece.

The Sales Manager declared: »He trots too lightly.«

There was a lot of talk and the stallion was given the feet of an elephant.

Someone else piped up:

»I think his range of vision is too limited.«

There was more talk and the stallion wound up with a giraffe's neck.

Finally the Boss remarked: »He isn't fancy enough.« They agreed, and gave the animal a peacock's tail.

And then everybody wondered why the idea didn't pull.

Contrast
In this design, the Palatino text is set in a free form. This compliments the decorative drawings and contrasts with the larger italic, which is very definitely calligraphic in form.

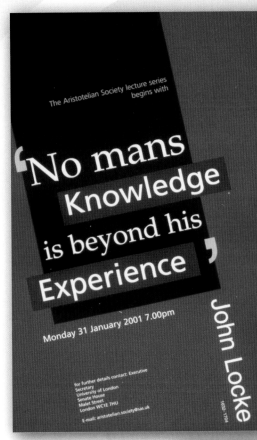

Philosophical lecture poster
Palatino's stocky, large x-height stands out boldly against the Frutiger sans-serif, and the black background enhances the letterforms.

Tracking, kerning, and H&Js

Palatino's body size is on the large side. it is a dark letterform with a tight letter fit, so that increased tracking in sizes below 10-point should be considered.

Text sizes

As it is large on the body, it is important to insert a minimum of 20 percent leading, to prevent the descenders tangling with the capitals and ascenders of the line below. Although it will be improved by more leading if space allows, 20 percent improves the linear thrust that helps legibility. The light, roman, and medium are all weights suitable for text setting. Light and Roman for book work and Medium for publicity, especially if the text is to be in color. Palatino can be reversed well to white out of black or to sit against color backgrounds.

Display sizes

Palatino's darker color on the page and the range of weights and italics make it a useful typeface for display. Incrementally reduce tracking with the increase in size. Black, the heaviest weight of this family, has the character of a fat-face.

On-screen display

With its large x-height and chunky serifs Palantino has a distinct visual character, so that font fidelity is lost on-screen if used in sizes smaller than 14-point. To ensure Palatino is delivered to the reader, it should be set up within a GIF or JPEG.

Party time
In this design, Palatino's calligraphic qualities are employed to add to the festive spirit.

AMERICAN GRAPHIC DESIGN:
Before and After the Second World War

Like Switzerland, the United States did not suffer directly from the destructive effects of the war in Europe and the years of political uncertainty that preceded it. As far as graphic design is concerned, it could be said that America benefited from the war.

During the 1930s, with the Nazis' rise to power in Germany, there was a great incentive for many artists and designers to move abroad. America was an attractive destination for many of these European professionals. The Bauhaus was closed by the Nazis in 1933, and five years later the last director, Mies van der Rohe, made his way to the US. Three of the founder members of the Bauhaus had already moved on. Walter Gropius, the first director of the Bauhaus, moved to Britain in 1934 and to the US in 1937, where

he taught architecture at the Harvard Graduate School of Design. Laszlo Moholy-Nagy also left Berlin in 1934, first traveling to Amsterdam in the Netherlands, and then to London in England. In 1937, on the recommendation of Gropius, he was appointed director of the New Bauhaus in Chicago, later renamed the Institute of Design. It was in this role that Moholy-Nagy used his energy and enthusiasm to sustain the financial viability of the Institute. In the nine years left to him as designer and teacher, aided by his two germinal books, *The New Vision* (1944) and *Vision in Motion* (1947), he transformed American design education. Herbert Bayer, after resigning from the Bauhaus in 1928, worked in Berlin for the Dorland Advertising Agency. While organizing an exhibition on the Bauhaus at the Museum of Modern Art in New York, aware of the deteriorating political situation in Europe, he decided to stay on in the United States.

INFLUX OF EUROPEAN DESIGNERS

Herbert Matter, a Swiss designer and poster artist, moved to the United States in 1939. He had gained a reputation with his series of dynamic Modern posters for the Swiss Tourist Board. In New York he worked on photographic commissions for *Vogue* and *Harper's Bazaar*. Will Burtin, a former student of the *Werkschule* in Cologne and practitioner of the New Typography, was to become the American president of AGI (Alliance Graphique Internationale). He moved to the United States in 1938 from Cologne; his first project came a year later, designing for the Federal Pavilion at the New York World's Fair. Another designer

Typographic display
Advertising art director Herb Lubalin's design for this article on jazz makes use of several typefaces, including Cheltenham, to identify the characters of different musical instruments.

He blows he don't worry
There's this cat he knows
Wingy from way back.
But he's a sadistic and a square, not that it matter to Wingy
Manone, he got only one arm.
He blows he don't worry
Each year this guy send Wingy Manone his Christmas present in a fancy box: 1 cuff link

OLD JAZZ NEED NOT BE BEST BUT STILL IT'S TRUE THAT SAXOPHONES WERE FEW AND FAR BETWEEN IN GOOD KING PORTER'S MERRY TIMES. THOSE WHO DO NOT LOVE THE SOUND THAT ISSUES FROM THE BLEND OF BRASS BENT REED WITH WOODEN REED ARE THREATENED IN THESE PARTS, BUT THEY'RE AROUND!

Trum-pet: I am a busy puppy with a loud voice. If I am tired, I never show it. In fact, I never know it.

Trom-bone: I play the solo part in a composition titled "Shaving Mug." I sleep in the musty cellar of an old house. I can sing under water. I am very fond of sunflowers, yams and barreled beer.

Clari-net: Sober: sing, I'd rather. Will not sweet-talk you one way or t'other. Know more than I tell. Smooth me, I'll be your friend.

Typography and magazine design
Thompson first gained attention through his designs with experimental use of typography (right).

who took the opportunity of staying in the United States while working on a pavilion for the World's Fair was Ladislav Sutnar, a Czech graphic designer who established a reputation in America for well-structured technical information design. His most famous work was produced for Addox Business Machines in the 1940s.

FOUR KEY AMERICAN GRAPHIC DESIGNERS

Among the American-born graphic designers making their names in the 1930 and 1940s, there were four who were particularly outstanding in their use of the visual language of modern art. The first was Lester Beall, whose work for organizations such as the International Paper Company and the General Life Insurance Group, and his initiation of design manuals for the implementation of corporate identities, gained him the distinction in 1939 of being the first graphic designer to have an exhibition of his work at the Museum of Modern Art in New York.

Bradbury Thompson first gained attention with his use of experimental typography combined with imaginative use of photography, when he was editor and designer of *Westvaco Inspiration*, a promotional magazine for the West Virginia Pulp & Paper Company during the 1940s and 1950s. During the Second World War, he was art director of the US Office of War Information. He received many honours from designers' organizations.

Alvin Lustig, whose book and magazine work used devices inspired by modern art, spent considerable energy on the graphic design program of Yale University. An exhibition of his work was mounted in 1951 at the Museum of Modern Art in New York.

Finally, possibly the most influential American graphic designer in the years before and after the Second World War was Paul Rand. He was responsible for many of the classic company logotypes and identities, including those of IBM, Westinghouse, and ABC Television. He was appointed a professor of Yale University, and received many awards for his work, including gold medals from the Art Directors' Club of New York and AIGA (American Institute of Graphic Art). During his career he wrote often about design, including his two germinal books *Thoughts on Design* (1947) and *Paul Rand, A Designer's Art* (1985).

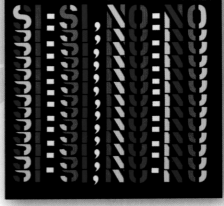

Record sleeve
Robert Brownjohn's above design for a recording of Latin American music uses repetition of color and words to convey rhythm.

Modern Jazz
Reid Miles has combined Franklin Gothic Compressed with the closely packed forms of Bodoni Ultra Bold, to create a powerful typographic image.

SWISS MODERNISM INTERPRETED

The United States, vastly bigger and far less homogeneous than the tiny, socially disciplined Switzerland, had a very different response to European Modernism. The Swiss defined advertising as informing the public; in America, advertising was intended to do more than merely inform. The sources of visual inspiration for American designers were far wider and American designers, as well as taking on the lessons of the New Typography, also made use of many of the visual devices introduced by Cubism, Dada, and Surrealism. Marinetti's concept of "Words-in-Freedom"—the visually expressive application of typography, became adapted for publicity. The great variety of letterforms available was an essential ingredient; it was exploited to the full, often with great sensuality or sentimentality.

EXPRESSIVE TYPOGRAPHY

In the second half of the 20th century there were many excellent graphic designers using expressive typography as the basis of their work. Three are of special note. Robert Brownjohn worked in a partnership with Ivan Chermayeff and Tom Geismar formed in 1957. The group gained a reputation for typographic experiment, inventive graphic imagery, and the creation of memorable corporate identities. Brownjohn studied at the Institute of Design in Chicago under Moholy-Nagy and also studied architecture at the Institute of Design in Illinois under Chermayeff's father, Serge Chermayeff. Working in England in 1964, he designed the title sequence for the James Bond film *Goldfinger*, projecting the titles onto a woman's body to express the erotic content of the famous spy drama.

VISUALIZING MODERN JAZZ

Reid Miles became in-house designer for Blue Note Records in 1957, and over the next 15 years he produced nearly 300 record sleeves with a strongly typographic character. Miles created a graphic identity for Blue Note, one that became the quintessential visualization of modern jazz. He used tightly constructed compositions of display types, which he augmented with the carefully cropped photographs of Francis Wolf, or the atmospheric line drawings of David Stone Martin. Among the typefaces he used were the American sans-serifs: Franklin and News Gothic dominated, although Century, Caslon, and Clarendon were also used frequently.

HERB LUBALIN

Possibly the greatest designer of typographically expressive work was Herb Lubalin, who studied at the Cooper Union, New York. From 1939, Lubalin worked in several advertising agencies, finally joining Sudler & Hennessey Inc., New York, in 1945. By 1955 he was vice-president. He left the agency in 1964 to open his own agency, Lubalin Inc. Lubalin was quick to appreciate the arrival of photosetting and the greater flexibility it offered the typographic designer compared to metal typesetting methods. He developed a typographic style that squeezed every nuance of meaning from the text to enrich the visual experience while maintaining legibility. The tailoring of his designs to achieve the perfection he required often involved the skills of his partners, lettering artists Tony DiSpigna and Tom Carnase; and at times his designs almost became calligraphy. During the 1970s, Lubalin created several letterforms that were developed into typefaces, including Avant Garde (1970), a geometric sans-serif that started life as a masthead for a magazine, and Serif Gothic (1974), a novelty sans-serif with a suggestion of serifs. Both digitized series are credited to Lubalin's partner Tony DiSpigna, although Lubalin Graph, also designed in 1974, is credited to Lubalin. In 1970, with Aaron Burns and Edward Rondhaler, he cofounded the International Typeface Corporation (ITC), which was established to license and distribute original typefaces to the makers of typesetting machines. This ensured that type designers received royalties for their designs, since typefaces cannot be copyrighted.

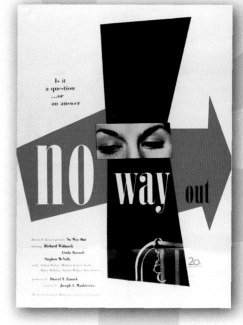

Paul Rand
Above is one of a series of press advertisement and poster designs promoting No Way Out, *the 1950s film by Joseph L Mankiewicz; .*

Mother & Child
An example below of Lubalin's expertise in extracting the maximum communication from the manipulation of typographic elements. The "arms" of the ampersand are contained within—and so seem part of—the word "mother." These enfold and protect the word "child." Lubalin's use of capitals appears to give the meaning iconic status.

Lubalin Graph specimen sheet
Lubalin Graph was one of several letterforms created by Herb Lubalin. This condensed version was prepared by Helga Jorgenson in the 1990s for the International Type Corporation.

ITC Lubalin Graph® Condensed

Over several **years,** the **ITC Typeface Review Board** members discussed the need for a condensed branch to the ITC **LUBALIN GRAPH** family tree, and eventually they decided that the **design** community would benefit from *a new series of strong slab serifed condensed typefaces.* The problem was **finding the appropriate team** to create the series. The **type designers** whom the Board **usually** commissions for such projects were involved in other lengthy assignments. **Unknown** talent was **not** the **right** choice.

With these concerns in mind, the Board's decision was unanimous: *"Let Ikarus do it."* The **first** results of the team's efforts, however, proved that not all typefaces respond well to even the MOST SOPHISTICATED of electronic distortions. It just wasn't good enough to meet the Board's standards. **The weights were wrong,** *the proportions were not quite right* **and the serifs were not the correct size.**

OPTIMA SANS-SERIF: *the Typeface Itself*

ABCDEFGHIJKLMNO
abcdefghijklmnopqrst

Roman influence
Zapf's remarkable Optima was inspired by his visit to Rome and Florence in 1950.

ROMAN
AaBbCcDd

OBLIQUE
AaBbCcDd

BOLD
AaBbCcDd

BOLD OBLIQUE
AaBbCcDd

Optima
the quick brown fox jumps over the lazy dog

Univers
the quick brown fox jumps over the lazy dog

Franklin Gothic
the quick brown fox jumps over the lazy dog

Practically all of Hermann Zapf's prolific output of type designs reveals his deep interest in calligraphy. It is interesting to compare his work with that of the other great 20th-century type designer Adrian Frutiger, to see just how their different aesthetics and motivating philosophies emerged in the forms they gave their letters. Frutiger's designs are informed by a Modernist geometric aesthetic. Zapf's influences reach back to the Renaissance and earlier, to times when handwriting had cultural importance.

Zapf's sans-serif type design, Optima, is a case in point, a remarkably original typeface created at a time when many foundries were releasing their updated 19th-century Grotesques. The letterforms were developed from impromptu sketches Zapf made of inscriptions, which he observed at the fourth-century Arch of Constantine in Rome and inlaid on the floor of the Santa Croce, Florence, while on a visit to Italy in 1950. The pronounced stress of thick and thin strokes, the swelling of the stems at their terminals, and the thinning of curves have created a sans-serif that has achieved a balance between the drawn sans-serif forms of the machine age and the pen-written serif forms of the Renaissance. The result is a delicate sans-serif with a strong desire to be a serif type.

The first Optima design was intended to be available only in display sizes. Zapf completed the designs in 1952 after the usual legibility tests. At the same time he was deeply engaged with the design of another of his important typefaces, Melior, which was designed for the specific needs of high-speed newspaper printing. However, in 1954 Zapf reconsidered his plans for Optima. This was a result of a suggestion from Monroe Wheeler of the Museum of Modern Art in New York that the design should be available for text setting as well.

PQRSTUVWXYZ
uvwxyz& 1234567890

ff f W W W

Optima was not released by D Stempel AG until 1958, initially as metal foundry type. Shortly afterward it was converted for hot-metal slug setting by Linotype GmbH. It became one of Zapf's most successful designs. He had hoped to call it Neu Antiqua (New Roman), but he was overruled, as the marketing department considered Optima to be a more appealing name.

The elegance Optima achieves makes it perfectly suited to situations in which Grotesques are too utilitarian, and serif forms too bookish. The current digitized range of Optima contains 12 variants: roman, medium, demibold, bold, black, and extra black, each including a companion "italic." These so-called "italic" fonts are actually slanted roman (also known as obliques). The heavier weights maintain the family resemblance, but do not maintain the elegance. This arises from the relationship of the thick and thin stresses: as the weight is increased the proportions change. This is common to roman types with extended ranges of variants; at heavier weights they become fat-faces.

During 2002, Hermann Zapf carried out a redesign and expansion of the existing range of Optima with Akira Kobayashi. The new range is distinguished by the name Optima Nova.

G G
M M

Contemporary sans-serif
Optima lowercase is compared above with Frutiger's Univers, which was released a year before Optima. The subtle changes of line thickness of Optima (the darker type) hint at serifs.

Capitals compared
Optima letterforms (left) "G" and "M" are compared above with those of Univers (right). The variation of line thickness maintains the inscriptional character of their original influence.

THE WORLD OF INTERIORS ■ PROM

Inside the Legend

Guinevere has been hallowed in decorating circles ever since it was first opened 40 years ago by Genevieve Weaver. Now run by her sons, Kevin and Marc, this King's Road classic remains a name to conjure with, whether you're furnishing a castle or looking for a dazzling decorative focus for a more modest home. Photography: Fritz von der Schulenburg

Cool Style
Optima is associated with self-assured elegance in this magazine layout to the right, which compliments the classic form and symmetry of the ceramics. The quiet poise of this typeface allows it to work with a range of visual styles, as long as it is given the space to do so.

Optima at work

Corrections
The design of a typeface goes through many stages of modification before it is finally released for use. Zapf's annotations here are mostly concerned with the sidebearings and quality of letter fit.

Optima at work

Relaxed dignity
The above design shows how Optima is designed for, and benefits from, generous space and formal layout.

Korean music
The Latin influenced forms of Optima seem highly appropriate in this design, without trying to imitate the Korean language. The wording is tightly constructed with a clear hierarchy of information.

Optima usage

Tracking, kerning, and H&Js

Optima is a unique typeface with an elegant form. It has a large x-height, and the ascenders are longer than the capitals. Its standard word fit is fairly generous, but while reducing tracking can make it more economic with space, this will result in damaging the style that gives it such character. H&J values should also reflect the word fit.

Text sizes

Optima is not a book face, but in text sizes an elegant character provides for many sorts of publicity. It can be leaded successfully with more than the standard 20 percent of body size, whether medium, demibold, or bold.

Display sizes

Optima is not a dynamic design; it has a cool relaxed style, which should not be crowded. However, tracking of capitals should not be increased greatly nor reduced greatly. Note that Optima Extra Black takes on a very different character.

On-screen display

Optima was designed for print media, and prints well on smooth-surfaced paper. The refinements that give it its special style are likely to be reduced by screen resolution, so Optima is not suitable for small or medium sizes. Text will be better served by Verdana or Arial, and large sizes are best conveyed within a GIF or JPEG.

TECHNICAL DEVELOPMENTS:
From Letterpress to Offset Lithography

During the 1960s, there was a radical technical shift in the printing industry from letterpress to offset lithography. By the start of the 20th century there were four main methods of printing in use: letterpress, offset lithography, photogravure, and process screen. Letterpress was the most popular general printing method, having been predominant for over 500 years. It is a relief method—that is, printing from a raised surface onto a receiving material such as paper. Many kinds of raised surface are used: metal and wood type, zinc line and halftone blocks, rubber, and plastic blocks. Other ways of making letterpress images include woodcuts, wood engravings, and linocuts, which are used mainly by fine artists.

Lithography was invented by the German Alois Senefelder in the late 18th century, and it is a planographic printing method—that is, printing from a virtually flat surface, originally a prepared stone. It is based on the principle that water and oil do not mix, one that is maintained in modern offset lithography, which uses photochemical processes. Offset lithographic printing presses have cylinders fitted with very thin aluminium printing plates. The image adheres to the plate photographically. The plates wrap around the cylinders and have a surface grain; giving them water-carrying properties as well as allowing anchorage for the image. Unlike letterpress, the paper does not touch the printing plate. The plate is inked by rollers, so that the ink just adheres to the image and is rejected elsewhere on the plate by the presence of moisture. The inked printing plate transfers the image onto a rubber-coated cylinder, which then transfers the image onto the paper.

Traditionally lithography tended to be more expensive in preparation than letterpress. However, by the 1960s it had achieved so many technical advances that challenged the dominance of letterpress printing. Letterpress had reached the limits of its development. It suffered from constraints on its ability to print satisfactorily, and in these cases lithography was

The IBM golf ball
The font was arranged around the ball for the IBM's strike-on system of budget typesetting. It appeared in 1961, at the time when letterpress was giving way to offset lithography.

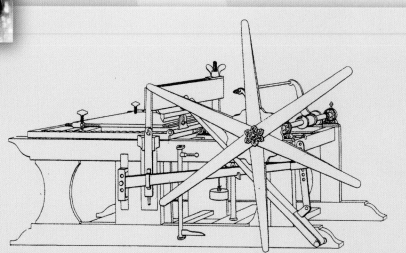

Early lithographic printing press
The Star-wheel press was in use during the early years of the 19th century. Lithographic printing was somewhat slow compared with letterpress printing, as the printing operation involved damping the stone first then inking it up. By the end of the century, the unwieldy stone slabs were replaced by metal plates.

able to provide more effective results. This was particularly true in the area of illustrated printed matter. When it came to text printing, letterpress was an excellent method. It offered a good strong black and white quality on the printed page, and corrections could be made at a very late stage of production. Lithography required the remaking of plates if late corrections were to be made. However, letterpress needed high-quality coated art paper to print half-tone photographs and color effectively. Printing an integrated illustrated book on art paper proved to be expensive. Hence it was a letterpress convention to print text on a cheaper paper and insert sections throughout the book with illustrations printed on art paper. This way of including illustrations is still used. Offset lithography was able to print half-tone photographs on less expensive paper, making it possible to combine illustrations with text on the same page. In this way, more illustrations could be included and positioned closer to where they were mentioned in the text. This offered greater flexibility in the design as well as a less expensive product, thus offering the public a more exciting kind of book at a time when television was thought to be posing a challenge to reading. The use of photochemical procedures in the preparation of plates and the development of new varieties of paper quickly brought about greater precision and more economical results. By the end of the 1960s lithography was able to provide full-color printing at a more acceptable cost than ever before.

The other methods of printing were more specialized. Photogravure, a photochemical development of engraving, was expensive in preparation and generally used for very long print runs such as packaging, magazines, directories, and books. It is an intaglio process, in which the image

The pole press
This is the last remaining Senefelder pole press is in the Deutsches Museum, Munich. It is made completely of wood, and would apply pressure to the stone by way of a scraper attached to a long pole. When printing, the tympan lays across the paper on the stone, in order to protect it.

is etched, as a grid of tiny dots, into the surface of a copper plate or cylinder, allowing for excellent reproduction of photography. Process screen printing is also known as silk-screen printing, and is a method popular for comparatively short print runs such as T-shirts. It is used for printing posters, labels, menus, and textiles, and as an art medium. The image is reproduced photographically on a fine mesh screen as a stencil. Ink is then squeezed through the screen to form the image on the printing material.

The matrix disc
French engineers Rene Higonnet and Louis Moyroud produced a phototypesetting machine in the 1950s which used a spinning typeface matrix disc. The machine was the Lumitype, later known as the Photon when it was developed in the United States.

TECHNICAL DEVELOPMENTS:
From Metal Type to Phototypesetting

Varisystems
The Varisystems Corporation was established in 1972 and it introduced the first keyboard combined with a CRT display. In concept the Varicom 2,000 and 3,000 machines were built on a modular principle. Keyboard units of differing arrangements could be assembled from the modules.

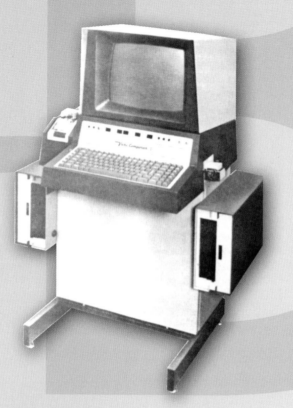

Offset lithography could not print directly from metal typesetting. To make that possible, a good quality "reproduction proof" (print) had to be made of the typesetting on "baryta," a paper coated with barium-sulphate gelatine which provided a very fine, smooth surface. The proof was then cut and pasted into pages as required, then photographed and the negative used to make printing plates. This process was time-consuming and the handling of inked proofs required special care.

This state of affairs did not last long. Mechanical metal typesetting was developing into photographically generated typesetting systems. Developments were very fast and a deluge of systems flooded the market in the second half of the 1950s. Like hot-metal typesetting machines, the first photosetters were designed either for text setting or for display setting. As the 1960s wore on, metal typesetting was superseded by the new machines, which were more compatible with the needs of offset lithography.

The first generation of photosetting devices were adaptations of the hot-metal machines, converting metal matrices to film negatives. Linotype's photocomposition system was previewed at the International Printing Exhibition in 1955. Intertype's first Fototypesetter was installed in 1956, while Monotype's Monophoto machine started work in 1957.

At about the same time, another generation of machines was launched. These were electromechanical, using valves, relays, and other electronic devices. One of the first was the Lumitype/Photon machine. This moved typesetting on from the 19th-century mechanical devices towards the 20th-century electronic devices. The machine had a master film matrix in the form of a revolving disc. A light source projected type images onto light-sensitive photographic paper to produce lines of type. The first models were direct entry: that is, a single unit including a keyboard typographic unit and a photo unit. Later models were developed as two-unit systems.

In 1961 IBM introduced a very different approach: a strike-on system which used a golf-ball-like typing head arrayed with rows of characters. The "golf-ball" was available in a variety of typefaces and sizes, which were quickly interchangeable. The system functioned like an ordinary typewriter but produced a high quality print on "baryta" paper.

LATER DEVELOPMENTS

Late in the 1960s a third generation of photosetting machines was launched with the radical new feature of type characters formed on the face of a cathode ray tube (CRT), which were then exposed by the tube onto bromide paper. Linotype's Linotron 101 appeared in 1967. With these new machines type characters were scanned and converted into electronic signals to form the characters on the CRT. Later developments included the introduction of digitized characters, stored on a magnetic disc. This faster method also reduced the cost of font installation, since one master font could be used for several sizes, although quality at large scale was uncertain.

It was in 1976 that the successful Monotype Lasercomp appeared, introducing a fourth generation of machines. These used lasers to expose the characters onto photographic material such as bromide paper or film. Lasers were capable of a very fine beam that could achieve great detail on photographic material. In 1983, the Linotron 101, a raster-imaging phototypesetter using a helium-neon laser, was introduced.

Phototypesetting machines could be of three kinds. The first was direct entry, a single unit combining input keyboard, typographic unit, and phototypesetter, designed for small jobbing printers. The second were off-line systems, consisting of a number of unconnected units where a visual display keyboard unit produced output on magnetic tape or floppy disk, to be stored or transferred to the phototypesetter unit. The third kind were online systems, consisting of a central phototypesetter unit that was connected by cables to a number of separate input keyboards, with visual display units.

Photon 200
Higonnet and Moyroud's phototypesetting machine was in production by 1956. The Photon 200 was a direct entry machine, made up of a keyboard, a control unit and a photo unit.

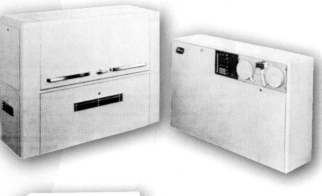

Photon 560
The Photon 560 launched in 1972, driven by a paper tape, was developed with a laser light source, in order to dispense with the need for wet chemical processing.

MGD Metro-set
MGD Graphic Systems launched their phototypesetting machine in 1972. The Metro-set was a cathode-ray tube machine, that successfully utilized digital fonts stored as outline shapes.

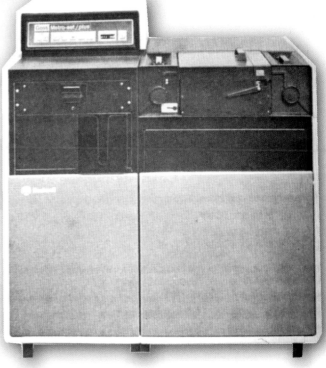

FRUTIGER: *the Other Sans-Serif*

ABCDEFGHIJKLMNOPQRST
abcdefghijklmnopqrstuvwx
abcdefghijklmnopqrstuvwxyz

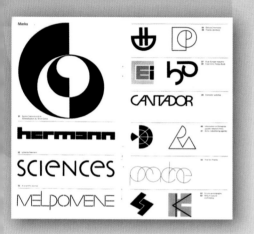

45 LIGHT

AaBbCcDd

55 ROMAN

AaBbCcDd

65 BOLD

AaBbCcDd

75 BLACK

AaBbCcDd

95 ULTRA BLACK

AaBbCcDd

56 ITALIC

AaBbCcDd

57 CONDENSED

AaBbCcDd

Adrian Frutiger, a prolific producer of brilliantly crafted typefaces and letterforms, is one of the great type designers of the 20th century. His prominence and reputation rest on numerous type designs, but mostly on Univers and his other eponymous sans-serif, Frutiger, originally intended for signage at the Charles de Gaulle Airport in Paris.

In addition to designing typefaces, Frutiger has been responsible for public lettering systems and alphabets. He has been a consultant to the D Stempel AG typefoundry and he worked with IBM when the company introduced the IBM Selectric Composer. His book *Signs and Symbols: Their Design and Meaning* (1989), is a major study of manmade marks of communication.

In the late 1960s, Frutiger was commissioned to prepare the signage system for the new Charles de Gaulle Airport, which was being planned for Roissy, France. Shortly after completing his Univers type, he had been asked to apply it to a signage system for Orly Airport. However, this time, some 15 years later, a new letterform was needed. Letters required for signage present different problems from those designed to be read close up. From his previous experience, Frutiger was in favor of a sans-serif. Questions of lighting levels, distance, location, and readers' mobility need consideration for signage. These questions had also occurred to Frank Pick when he commissioned Edward Johnston to design a new typeface for the London Underground signage back in 1915. Pick concluded that sans-serif forms were more legible for signage than serif forms, having tested this for himself by sitting in a moving underground (subway) train. Sans-serif had also been favored for the signage system introduced on British motorways in the 1960s.

Since his success with Univers, Frutiger had designed some 16 other alphabets, by no means all sans-serifs. These included Opera (1960), Apollo (1962), Serifa (1967), OCR-B (1968), Dokumenta (1969), and two non-Latin types, Devanagari (1967) and Tamil (1970). The typeface for the new airport had the working title "Roissy." Since computers were not yet available for this kind of project, Frutiger drew out each of the various weights by hand, as was his usual procedure. The system was to consist of back-lit panels to overcome changing external lighting conditions. The signage letterforms were bolder than type letterforms, with open, distinct forms for clearer legibility for readers on the move.

UVWXYZ
yz& 1234567890
& *1234567890*

Gg

Gg

Humanist Sans-serif
Frutiger (top) has a friendly personality that is similar to Gill Sans (above), although it retains the unique stamp of its designer.

The D Stempel AG typefoundry requested Frutiger to prepare the Roissy lettering as a typeface for Linotype. Frutiger made modifications to stroke thickness, and extended the range of weights. The Roissy type was finally released by Linotype in 1977 as Frutiger. The typeface marks a move away from the neutral neo-grotesque toward a humanist sans-serif like Gill Sans. Frutiger has said that his new sans-serif is a stylistic expression of the 1970s and 1980s.

To appreciate the amiable character of Frutiger, it helps to make a comparison with the more neutral Univers of the 1950s. There is greater variation in the proportions of the capitals, many being distinctly narrower than in Univers, especially in the case of "C," "G," and "S." However, the general forms are more open and less tightly curled than those of Univers: the leg of "R" is more distinctly angled, but the "O" and "Q" are almost full circles compared with the oval "O" and "Q" of Univers. In the lowercase alphabet the distinctive features are that the "a," "g," and "s" are more relaxed, and the "t" has a wider crossbar. The ascenders are taller than the capitals although the impression is of a large x-height. The word fit is loose. Frutiger used the same numbering system as Univers to indicate weight and style.

Frutiger
the quick brown fox jumps over the lazy dog

Gill Sans
the quick brown fox jumps over the lazy dog

Futura
the quick brown fox jumps over the lazy dog

Contextualizer

Adrian Frutiger
b. 1928

A design philosophy

Frutiger's sense of form is influenced by a keen appreciation of classical proportions and by the subtle application of geometry and logic. He has based his philosophy on dealing directly with the opportunities that changing technologies offer the type designer. As quoted from the Linotype website, the typographer believes "legibility and beauty stand close together and that type design, in its restrain, should be only felt but not perceived by the reader."

Black and white

One of Frutiger's teachers, Alfred Williman said, "Do not apply black but cover up white, so as to make the light of the white sheet active." By concentrating on what is removed as much as what is marked down, Frutiger finds a balance in his work. His symbols and woodcuts bear this out.

OCR-B

OCR (Optical Character Recognition) fonts are designed primarily to be recognized by electronic scanning devices. Frutiger designed OCR-B to meet the standards of the European Computer Manufacturer's Association and it is now a world standard. It is less appealingly "geeky" than OCR-A, which has been used as such for advertising and display graphics, but it does have a very distinctive technical appearance. Examples of OCR-B are found in the raised lettering and numbers of any credit card.

Frutiger at work

Charles de Gaulle Airport
A rare view of the main terminal building of the Paris Airport, also known as Roissy in France, with the new Roissy giant capitals generously spaced out across the front of the newly-completed building. These letterforms were the precursors of Frutiger.

A timeless classic
This theatre publicity from the 1990s is a good example of how a combination of Frutiger variants can be effective in creating dynamic emphasis by contrast, to enliven what is a simple listing, with the added device of reversal, black to white.

RICHMOND THEATRE
The Green, Richmond, Surrey, TW9 1QJ

Monday 1 - Saturday 6 April
F. Murray Abraham and
Gemma Jones in
TOLSTOY
by **James Goldman**

Tuesday 9 - Saturday 13 April
Travelling Opera presents
CARMEN
by **Bizet**
(9, 11 & 13 April)
COSI FAN TUTTE
by **Mozart**
(10 & 12 April)

Monday 15 - Saturday 20 April
Donald Sinden in
THAT GOOD NIGHT
by **N.J. Crisp**

Monday 22 - Saturday 27 April
Mobil Touring Theatre presents
Peter Davison and
Catherine Rabett in
DIAL M FOR MURDER
by **Fredrick Knott**

Monday 29 April - Saturday 4 May
Kate O'Mara in
MY COUSIN RACHEL
adapted by **Diana Morgan**
from the novel by **Daphne du Maurier**

MONDAY - SATURDAY EVENINGS AT 7.45PM
WEDNESDAY & SATURDAY MATINEES AT 2.30PM

BOX OFFICE 0181 940 0088

Frutiger at work

Theater poster

Frutiger is a popular typeface in a digital typographic marketplace that is providing more sans-serifs year by year. Sans-serif typefaces have become increasingly popular for publicity in Britain, where once the serif letterform ruled.

Signage system

Linotype Frutiger has an extended family of roman, italic, and condensed alphabets, although unlike Univers, it has no extended form as yet. However, it provides sufficient typographic color for successful signage systems such as this one at a London college of design.

Frutiger usage

Tracking, kerning, and H&Js

Frutiger has a comparatively loose basic word fit and a large x-height. The capitals have a tendency to be narrow , while the lowercase is broader; hence H&J values should be less than the default values.

Text sizes

Frutiger functions well as a text face and as it has a large x-height it reads well in small sizes, it can also be generously leaded. Frutiger has a warmth of character that is closer to Gill Sans than to Helvetica. The heavier weights also function well in text sizes.

Display sizes

The extensive family of weights and condensed forms that Frutiger has available offers a rich collection of display possibilities. When using large sizes, leading should be deleted from headings of more than one line to give more density. Capitals can be letterspaced without loss of visual impact.

On-screen display

Frutiger has been digitized for optimum screen display; however, small sizes set for on-screen display lose its unique character. It is better to use a sans-serif more available for on-screen display such as Verdana or Arial. If it is essential to use Frutiger in display sizes, it is best within a GIF or JPEG.

7   The Postmodern Era

A questioning of the values and creations of Modernism, and the collapse of many of the old certainties, gave rise to the concept of postmodernism. In his book *Illusions of Postmodernism*, cultural critic Terry Eagleton described postmodern thinking as suspicious of classical notions of truth, reason, identity and objectivity, of the idea of universal progress or emancipation, of single frameworks, grand narratives, or ultimate grounds of explanation.

Solidarity
The national confederation of independent trade unions in Poland was formed under the leadership of Lech Walesa in 1980. Solidarity came about as a result of the Polish government's attempt to raise food prices. Walesa was elected president of Poland in 1990.

In 1973, OPEC, the Organization of Petroleum-Exporting Countries, reduced the supplies of oil available, causing the price of exporting oil to the Western countries to rise. This immediately led to cutbacks, so that some countries imposed drive-free days. It came as a shock for many to appreciate how dependent the postwar economic prosperity of the West had been on the availability of cheap oil. Many new town and city developments since 1945 had taken the car for granted as a basic means of transport for all. Oil was necessary not only for transport, but also for heating and the manufacture of many goods. Although the oil crisis temporarily brought about a reduction in Western dependence on oil, by the 1980s demand had pushed up the price to $30 a barrel from $3 a barrel in 1973.

The oil crisis was a wake-up call, and a focus for new attitudes and worries that had developed through the 1970s and the following decades. Chief among these was concern over the squandering of natural resources arising from the West's prosperity and neglect of developing countries' struggling economies. Two authors expressed this concern particularly well, as they reflected on the urge for better use of resources. In *Small is Beautiful* Fritz Schumacher asserted that developing countries could help themselves by making use of less expensive "low" technology, which could be created locally rather than requiring expensive imported technology. In *Design for the Real World,* Victor Papanek argued for a more socially responsible attitude from designers rather than subservience to consumerism.

The 1980s also saw doubts arise about many assumptions and expectations that had formed during the early Cold War period. There was unrest in the Polish shipyards of Gdansk as the workers' movement Solidarity clashed with the Communist government. In the late 1980s, the Soviet leader Mikhail Gorbachev initiated perestroika, the program of wide-ranging reforms in the Soviet Union. These led to the dramatic collapse of Communist regimes in Eastern Europe in 1989, the fall of the Berlin Wall, and the end of the Cold War.

In the arts, there was a recognition that the more extreme concepts of Modernism were remote and did not attract a general audience. The tenets of the Modern arts and architecture of the mid-century included the reduction of art forms to their essence to examine the uniqueness of their attributes. Painting rejected representation in favor of abstraction and mark-making; in music, composers explored electronic sounds and 12-note composition. Modernist housing developments were often described as egg-box buildings. The architects Robert Venturi, Denise Scott Brown, and Steven Izenour were among the first to question the assumptions of the international Modernist style. In the early 1970s, they carried out a landmark study of Las Vegas, which resulted in a new appreciation of vernacular architectural culture.

Thus, the grand narrative of Modernism gave way to the postmodernist view of the world as contingent, ungrounded, diverse, unstable, and indetermined; a set of disunified cultures or interpretations which breed a degree of scepticism about the objectivity of truth, history, and norms, the givens of nature, and the coherence of identity.

OPEC news
Above, a London newspaper, The Evening Standard, *reports a raise in the price of petrol in Britain on June 28th, 1979.*

Venturi chair
In the 1980s, using modern molded plywood technology, Robert Venturi designed a collection of chairs that referenced classic historic styles (left).

THE NEW WAVE: *Postmodern Typographic Design*

Odermatt & Tissi

In Switzerland in the 1980s, Siegfried Odermatt and his partner Rosemarie Tissi began producing designs that rejected Swiss typographic formalism. They designed publicity for theaters, exhibitions and printers that ignored contemporary practice. The grid was neglected and patches of text where emphasized by panels of color, so that the surface of the design appeared to be layered. The publicity shown below is for the Swiss printing house Buchdruck-Offsetdruck Anton Schob.

By the late 1970s, the questioning of the grand narratives that Terry Eagleton referred to included the International Design Style. A younger generation of graphic designers was questioning the precepts of Modernism. The changes that took place in design education in the 1970s had begun to change attitudes to graphic design. Students who would have trained as fine artists in the 1950s and 1960s were now more likely to consider graphic design as an option.

After some 40 years of typography and graphic design based on the 1920s' theorists and consolidated by the Swiss School, the International Style was ready for reassessment. Modernism had always had its critics, but this was a reassessment that was more sustained. There were basically two modes of repudiation: the instinctive or emotional, on the part of designers who felt inhibited by the Modernist rationale; and the theoretical, mostly on the part of educators who felt the need to advance change in the light of more recent developments in communications, and so searched for a new rationale for design in the latter part of the 20th century.

ODERMATT & TISSI IN SWITZERLAND

In Switzerland, the home of the International Style, some of the first work to express the New Wave was that of Odermatt & Tissi. Siegfried Odermatt, a self-taught graphic designer not trained in the Swiss system, set up his own studio in 1950 after experience in advertising agencies. At the beginning of the 1960s, Rosemarie Tissi joined his studio, and later in 1968 she became a partner. The designs that Odermatt & Tissi produced displayed a mischievous disregard for the clarity and order that were the norm in Swiss design. They introduced staggered columns of text, angled ragged columns, and used panels of color to divide up the format or highlight the shape of columns of type. Bold letterforms overlapped each other in colorful heaps, yet the message was never obscured.

NEVILLE BRODY IN BRITAIN

In Britain, a younger graphic designer, Neville Brody, started work in the record industry in the late 1970s, just as punk rock began to cause outrage in the tabloid newspapers. A spirit of rebellion was already present in the work that Brody had produced as a student in the design department of the London College of Printing. Not surprisingly, there was something of Futurism and Dada in the "brutalist" designs of typefaces, logotypes, and record sleeves that he designed for Fetish Records and the experimental group Cabaret Voltaire in the early 1980s. Brody became the art director of the *Face* magazine and proceeded, with the editor Nick Logan, to create one of the most exciting youth magazines to appear since the demise of the German magazine *Twen* some five years earlier. There was a strong challenge from Terry Jones's small-format but radical youth magazine *I-D*, which also rejected current concepts of "good taste" typography, and reported on authentic street fashions. In the years of swinging London, fashion designers and photographers had achieved public celebrity. Neville Brody, through the work he created for the pop music industry and youth magazines, became possibly the first graphic designer to be raised to the status of a celebrity, stimulating interest in graphic design among the next generation. Graphic design was becoming sexy.

Wolfgang Weingart
The above poster is for a 1981 exhibition of calligraphy and is by German-born designer and teacher based in Basle, Switzerland. Weingart has been an articulate influence on the spread of New Wave graphic design during the 1970s and 1980s in Europe and the United States.

Lucille Tenazas
Shown left is a poster and publicity for the "Adopt a Book" campaign in 1992. These multi-layered designs show the influence of Tenazas' graduate studies at the Cranbrook Academy of Art, Michigan during the 1980s.

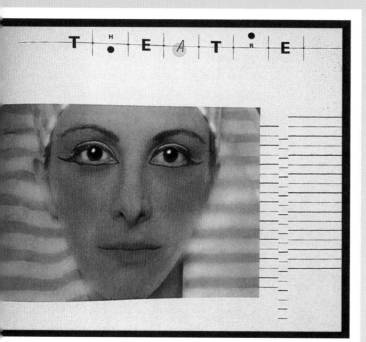

April Greiman
Greiman studied in Basle with Weingart, and responded to Weingart's consideration of space by exploring the three-dimensional illusions possible within graphic design. The example on the left demonstrates how Greiman encourages graphic elements to "float" on the page.

Neville Brody
Brody's work in the 1980s (right and below) was deeply involved in the world of pop music. As a student of graphic design at the London College of Printing, he found the aesthetics of the status quo to be a constraint. Rejecting these, he explored the "bad taste" of Punk.

WOLFGANG WEINGART IN GERMANY

Wolfgang Weingart, born in Konstanz, Germany, was a self-taught designer. In 1968 he began teaching typography at the *Kunstgewerbeschule* in Basle, where he eventually took over from Emil Ruder. Weingart proceeded to reevaluate the precepts of Swiss typography. He was well aware of its positive qualities and was not prepared to reject it altogether, which meant among other things maintaining the ubiquitous sans-serif, but he felt the need to reassess the philosophy and remove some of the dogma. He suggested that Swiss design was value-free; that is, it simply presented a message free from additional visual characteristics that heightened persuasiveness.

Weingart consolidated his approach in his introduction of an advanced program that took up the positive aspects of the Basle approach and used them as a basis upon which to introduce an additional element of student-based exploration. This was to be based on the examination of fundamental concepts in typography, such as the predominance of the right angle and the grid, and an intuitive response to the organization of space.

THE NEW WAVE IN AMERICA

Among Weingart's students at this time were the Americans Dan Friedman and April Greiman. After graduating from Carnegie Institute of Technology, Pittsburgh, in the late 1960s, Friedman spent three years in Europe, studying at the ULM HOCHSCHULE FÜR GESTALTUNG in Ulm and then with Weingart in Basle. He returned to the US in 1970. He taught first at Yale University and later became assistant professor at New York School of Visual Arts between 1972 and 1975.

He was instrumental in introducing Weingart and his teaching methods to the US. In his book *Radical Modernism*—his term for the break away from the International Style—he discussed the issues surrounding the New Wave. He expressed the view that the well-structured readability that Swiss typography had achieved created a predictability that failed to stimulate the reader's interest. In his opinion, unpredictability was required to stimulate a more positive response in the reader.

April Greiman arrived in Basle a year after Friedman. Her earlier studies were at the Kansas City Institute of Art. After a year with Weingart she returned to the US and for several years worked in New York and Connecticut and had a teaching post in Philadelphia. In 1976, she moved to Los Angeles and soon established herself as a leading exponent of New Wave design. Her approach emphasized a playful quality that explored illusions of three-dimensional space, visual textures created with enlarged half-tones and video screens, rules, and brush marks. She also made use of early low-resolution computer-generated letterforms.

In 1971, Katherine McCoy became co-chairperson of postgraduate studies in the design department of Cranbrook Academy of Art, Michigan. In the program that she introduced, the concepts of unpredictability and playfulness allowed more vitality to be brought to the printed page. This was supported by students' exposure to the concept of deconstructionism, an approach to cultural artifacts proposed by the French philosopher Jacques Derrida. The approach involved a process of decoding or analysis of a literary text or visual image in order to explore the layers of meaning that are present in it. Designers interpreted this to mean the physical

dismembering and radical rearrangement of an image or text. McCoy described her approach as "Mannerist Modernism," and introduced many devices alien to Modernism: for example, the mixing of typefaces within words and sentences, the mixing of type sizes, and the multiple layering of text and images.

The Face magazine
Not since the 1960s had a youth magazine's visual style created as much interest as Brody's design for The Face *did. This made Brody possibly the first celebrity graphic designer. The mixing of typefaces within words at this time was generally achieved by the technique of cut-and-paste. a term that has been retained for the desktop computer. The above example is of a spread from 1983.*

Fetish Records
A 1981 sleeve design for the post-punk band 23 Skidoo by Neville Brody. The woodcut texture imagery and rough-drawn logotype rejected the conventional typographic refinement of most logotypes.

ADOBE *& the Personal Computer*

The Macintosh 128K
The "Mac" (above), with its unique graphical User Interface (GUI), using the Motorola MC6800 processor, was introduced in 1984, by what is now the famous Super Bowl television commercial.

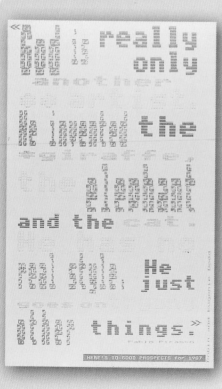

Low resolution
Early desktop computers were largely rejected by typographers and graphic designers because of the low-resolution type generation. However, there were many designers who relished the new imagery the computer could produce.

The combined technologies of offset lithography and computer-assisted phototypesetting were very important aids to greater freedom and refinement in typographic design. The bromide print outputs from phototypesetting machines, rather than an inked proof, made the handling of text and display type easier for cut-and-paste page make-up. The manipulation of type and images was no longer limited by the heavy and to some degree clumsy strictures of letterpress. The horizontal and vertical that were so important to the physics of metal typesetting were no longer important. Type was generated photochemically, therefore type no longer had a body, only a face. This allowed for refinements such as the adjustment of space between letters (tracking), so that it could be increased or reduced from the normal spacing. Awkward combinations of letters that caused gaps in words could now be adjusted to fit together better (kerning) as the metal body no longer kept them apart. Although most typesetting was restricted to defined type sizes, they were more comprehensive than hot metal; the economy of space afforded by electronic font files resulted in greater ranges of typefaces becoming available from typesetters and printers.

And still technology and engineering marched on. In 1981, IBM launched the IBM Personal Computer (PC), the first small desktop computer with a text-based interface, responding to typed commands. In 1984, Apple Computers introduced the Macintosh computer. This was also a desktop machine, but it had a Graphical User Interface (GUI); an operating system that consisted of on-screen menus, windows, and icons that allowed the user to interact with the computer by pointing with a cursor via a "mouse."

In 1985, Apple joined forces with Adobe and Aldus to create a new branch of personal computer application. Adobe was a company formed to develop Postscript level 1, a page description language that was capable of controlling output devices such as laser printers and imagesetters, which was to become an industry standard. Aldus was a small new software company marketing PageMaker, a typesetting and layout program. Apple's part in this deal was to produce a laserwriter. Desktop publishing had arrived, ready to transform the world of printing and graphic design within the next decade.

Although the technology for digital fonts already existed, two rival methods were developed for generating desktop computer fonts. Type 1 fonts were developed by Adobe and consisted of two parts: a set of fixed-size bitmap font files for screen display and a Postscript font file to be used by the output device. TrueType, the other method developed by Apple, provided information for screen display and the output device in a single file, which could contain sufficient information to generate plain, plain italic, bold, and bold italic. In 1991, Adobe introduced Multiple Master Fonts, Type 1 fonts that carry more than one digital outline. Each character has a pair of outlines that represent each end of a design axis. A font may contain axes for weight, width, style, or size, or all four

All Small Caps

ALL SMALL CAPS

OpenType small caps
OpenType allows selected characters to be converted to small caps, including capitals. This is useful for setting acronyms and common abbreviations within body copy.

together. This makes it possible for the designer to customize fonts by modifying weights and widths with greater variety than that found in standard fonts.

Most standard font character sets can contain up to 256 glyphs (characters), which provide for setting most languages based on the Latin alphabet. The glyphs consist of capitals and lowercase letters, figures, floating accents, common mathematical characters, reference symbols, currency symbols, and punctuation marks.

OPENTYPE

Adobe OpenType is a new format, which has been described in Mac User magazine as "the format designed for the 21st century." It was launched by Adobe and Microsoft in 1997, putting an end to the rivalry of Adobe's Postscript Type 1 format and Microsoft's TrueType format, which created endless user problems when a document created using one format was sent to a service bureau using the other. OpenType introduces major innovations to digital typesetting. First, it is cross-platform: files function equally for Macintosh OSX and Windows operating systems. OpenType is also supported by Unicode to provide an increase of the standard character set of up to 64,000 glyphs (characters). The regular typeface can now include a far greater number of characters, ligatures, true small capitals, Old-style figures, swash capitals, fractions, and special characters, as well as Cyrillic and Greek. These innovations make possible typographic designs of amazing refinement and richness never before achievable.

OpenType titling
When a serifed body text font is used for a headline or title, it may appear oddly thick and chunky. Some OpenType fonts include alternative glyphs for use as titles, enabled using the Titling Alternates option. The upper title here is set as Titling Alternates—the effect is very subtle.

OpenType fractions
Enabling the Fractions feature in the OpenType sub-menu allows software to recognize sequences such as "½," and automatically match them to fraction glyphs in the font, if available.

Tabular numbers in OpenType
Tabular numbers occupy a fixed width, making it easy to align them vertically. Proportional numbers act like ordinary typeset text, with varying character widths. The example here shows a math book sum set as proportional (right) and as tabular (far right).

OpenType superscript and subscript
Rather than just shrinking the selected text, OpenType allows the designer to format any selected numbers as fractions—including those not supported as stand-alone glyphs, in one easy step.

Titling
Titling

1/2 ½

2/3 ⅔

$$137 + 364 = 501 \qquad 137 + 364 = 501$$

$$^{79}/_{130}$$

HERMANN ZAPF: *About Script Fonts and Zapfino*

Scripts are typefaces designed to imitate handwriting. Until the invention of the typewriter in the 19th century, handwriting was the main means of creating documents of all kinds. Although the Renaissance humanist roman letterform was the basis of most typefaces, there has been a desire at various times to cut types that imitate the style of handwriting of the day.

O f course, Gutenberg's first types imitated the formal hand of 15th-century Germany. Indeed, Gutenberg aimed at authentic reproduction of handwriting, and he cut several versions of the same letter with small variations to convey the spontaneity of cursive script.

Once printing established itself as a successor to written manuscripts, the inscriptional roman form created a new style for the book. However, the hand-formed letter maintained a kind of survival. Francesco Griffo's innovative italic alphabet for Aldus Manutius was based closely on the humanist cursive script of the day. The French punchcutter Robert Grandjohn cut a cursive type, Civilité, a French alternative to italics based on the hand used at the royal chancery in 1556. It was used, mostly in France and the Netherlands, up to the mid-19th century. Another French script, an upright script derived from Civilité, appeared in the mid-17th century and survived into the 20th century, appearing in the 1953 Stephenson, Blake & Company specimen book in six sizes as Parisian Ronde.

In the early 18th century, the English round text became a standard throughout Europe and first appeared as a typeface cut by Thomas Cottrell in 1774. Copperplate scripts survive to the present day, and in the 20th century,

these came to represent formality. Meanwhile the growing importance of advertising was to stimulate another form of script, which emulated the appearance of brush strokes or some other coarse writing tool, in order to represent a kind of energetic spontaneity.

Zapfino is a script designed by Hermann Zapf. In 1948, shortly after his return to Frankfurt, he designed a calligraphic script based on samples of calligraphy in one of his sketchbooks from 1944. This became the script Virtuosa, for D. Stempel AG. Zapf was not totally satisfied with the results; he felt that his intentions had been restricted by the limitations of metal type composition. The typeface, imitating copperplate script instead of the normal right-angled body of roman, was designed to fit onto a right-leaning rhomboidal body in order to accommodate the heavy slant that is characteristic of scripts. Many of the capitals of metal scripts were "kerned" heavily—part of the letter was extended beyond its own body and supported by the body of the following letter—in order to maintain close character fit with the lower case. (Few, if any, scripts work well set entirely in capitals; not only does the kerning cause the letters to clash, but it also usually renders the words illegible.) Metal type could not support the exuberant flourishes that

Mistral
This freeform script was designed by the French designer Roger Excoffon in 1953 and was popular during the 1950s. Two other of his successful type designs are Calypso (1958) and Antique Olive (1962).

Script font specimen sheets
*These are examples
(left and below) of typefaces
that imitate handwriting.
Script typefaces have
always been created, but
in the 20th century choice
has grown as scripts drawn
apparently with brushes
or other implements
have been developed.
OpenType now increases
this area's potential.*

Zapf had in mind. This early version of Zapfino
consisted of a delicate basic script alphabet and
three decidedly more calligraphic supporting
alphabets. Years later, in 1993, Zapf designed
Zapfino, with David Siegel and a programmer,
Gino Lee, carrying out the digitizing. Digital font
technology was able to offer Zapf the means to
realize his calligraphic script.

ITC Zapf Chancery
*This Zapf script below is
based on one used by scribes
in the Vatican Chancery
during the Renaissance.
Although a script, it is
identified as roman, as there
is an accompanying italic.*

abcdefghijklmnopqr
stuvwxyz& ABCD
EFGHIJKLMNO
PQRSTUVWXYZ
1234567890

ZAPFINO: *Better with OpenType*

A B C D E F G H I J K L M

a b c d e f g h i j k l m n o p q r s t u v w x y z

Contextual alternates in OpenType
Zapfino Extra provides alternative glyphs for a particular character depending upon context, such as whether it begins or ends a word, or what other characters are next to it. The sophistication of this is apparent in the styling of the pairs of 'g's in the words below.

Biggest

Flogged

Zapfino is a showcase example of what the OpenType format has to offer the designer. Hermann Zapf's preoccupation with the hand-rendered forms of calligraphy, which could not be satisfied fully by metal type technology, has now found fulfilment with digital technology. The 1998 digitized version of Zapfino consisted of a comparatively conventional script alphabet of capitals and lower case, plus three additional interchangeable alphabets of more calligraphic variations, which included ligatures such as "Mr" and "Mrs," and dozens of ornaments including ladies' pointing hands, flowers, and pen flourishes. The script letterform is a variety of font that has notably benefited from digitization, no longer suffering from the limitations imposed by a metal body.

In 2003, in collaboration with Linotype type director Akira Kobayashi, Zapf extended the font to provide OpenType Zapfino Extra, and a bold version, Zapfino Extra Forte. The extended font has become a multilingual character set providing diacritical characters for almost fifty European languages that use the Latin alphabet, including (as well as English, Dutch, French, Spanish, Portuguese, German, Italian, and the Scandinavian languages) Catalan, Croatian, Czech, Estonian, Hungarian, Latvian, Lithuanian, Maltese, Polish, Romanian, Slovak, and Turkish. Other elements added in 2003 were small capitals, mathematical symbols, additional default ligatures and discretionary ligatures, fractional numbers, and hyper-flourishes—some of which are generous swashes that run over two or three text lines in depth. Full access to OpenType Zapfino Extra can only be achieved with applications that support OpenType; InDesign CS, Photoshop CS, Illustrator CS and QuarkXpress 7. Earlier versions of Quark do not fully support it, as they do not support Unicode; meaning the extra features and glyphs will not be available.

By using OpenType, Hermann Zapf has managed to take Zapfino beyond a digital script font into the realm of electronic calligraphy, normally only achievable by very skilled hands. The availability of such a large number of alternative characters and flourishes, in addition to the four related alphabets, has created an organic form that makes it possible to produce the same piece of copy in numerous different arrangements. Zapfino Extra constitutes a virtual calligraphy kit.

The vast number of possible permutations does, however, present its own dangers. Intermixing the character variants can result in remarkably good-looking designs, or in an

NOPQRSTUVWXYZ
@ 1234567890

incomprehensible mess. The font is best used in free, unjustified lines rather than in solid, justified columns, and it should not be mixed with other italic or script fonts due to its extreme angle of slant. When capitalizing words in the text, Number One alphabet capitals should be used and they should always be letterspaced optically. Never use swash capitals for capitalized whole words. Long ascenders are best used in the first line of text or in the space between paragraphs. The use and position of hyper-flourishes should be controlled carefully, so that ascenders and descenders do not overlap. Finials should be used rarely and only at the end of the text. Overall, avoid overloading the design with too many unnecessary elements.

OpenType ordinals
OpenType provides number order abbreviations for any chosen numeral, and the ordinals are automatically matched to the specific letterform selected.

OpenType discretionary ligatures
Discretionary ligatures find their fullest expression in Zapfino Extra. OpenType-supported applications allow these to be enabled for typographical effect.

Swashes
The hyper-flourishes, ornaments and generous swashes move some OpenType fonts way beyond the bounds of traditional typography limitations in design. This sample is set in Bickham Script Pro.

1st 2nd 5th 6th
1st 2nd 5th 6th

This short story
This short story

The Quick Brown Fox Jumped Over the Lazy Dog

8 Digital Typefoundries

Despite the many radical changes in the printing industry over the last 40 years, many of the old terms have lingered on, even if the technologies have not. Typefoundries casting metal disappeared slowly with the end of foundry type; as the mechanized typesetting machines of Monotype and Linotype took over, casting became part of the process of hot-metal typesetting carried out by typesetters.

Foundry Wilson is an expertly crafted revival of a typeface originally cast in 1760 by renowned Scottish type founder Alexander Wilson. A lively, robust design, with a taste of the incised letterforms of its time, Foundry Wilson provides a fresh alternative to its contemporary Baskerville types. Alexander Wilson was a learned and cultured man, a professor of astronomy, who crafted his types with much care and enthusiasm. Many of his founts were produced and used exclusively for the classics from the Foulis brothers of the Glasgow University Press; a working relationship producing typography which earned the praise of their peers, notably Fournier le jeune ❦

Foundry Wilson Book
Foundry Wilson Book Italic
Foundry Wilson Medium
Foundry Wilson Bold
❧✳◆✕◆✳❧

The original roman and italic have been faithfully redrawn and new weights added to complete the typeface family. Interestingly it was found that the first bold face types can be linked back to the Wilson foundry. The Foundry designers have lovingly interpreted the Wilson type for today's discerning designers. The character set includes small capitals, ligatures and old style figures; enhanced by a set of printer's flowers from the same source.

Foundry Wilson

Foundry Wilson is available for both Mac and PC from The Foundry type designers David Quay and Freda Sack

for further information about The Foundry typeface library and specially commissioned fonts, contact: Foundry Types

T 44 (0)20 7535 1222
F 44 (0)20 7537 7550
mail@foundrytypes.co.uk
www.foundrytypes.co.uk

The Foundry
Foundry Types Ltd
44 Charlotte Street
London W1T 2NR

The Foundry
This small digital typefoundry offers a wide range of digital typefaces, including the restoration of the enlightenment type of 1760 by the Scottish typefoundry of Alexander Wilson (left). The 20th century is present in the form of avant-garde fonts based on the designs of such figures as Bayer, Van Doesburg and Tschichold in the Architype collection. There are also truly computer-driven types, for example Plek and Flek (below).

Foundry Plek and Foundry Flek are each based on the same dot matrix grid system. This allows the designer to experiment with overlays, and to mix the weights producing varying effects; with the centre of the underlying dot matrices remain in the same position.

Foundry Plek and Foundry Flek font families each consist of four weights: light, regular, medium [...] a selection [...] tend the [...] dot matrix [...] rks well [...] ese fonts,

Typesetting has now became a case of photochemical processing. Yet recently developed digital technology has maintained the evocative term "foundry" for the organizations originating typefaces for computers.

The increasing impetus of technical development allows a process of constant innovation driven by industrial competition and a climate of takeovers and mergers makes for an industry characterized by changing alliances.

Monotype and Linotype, as two of the longest-established typefoundries, hold all of the greatest 20th-century revivals of classic typefaces, from the 15th-century Jenson and Bembo to Century and Franklin Gothic from the turn of the 20th century, and many other excellent 20th-century typeface designs that are now available in OpenType formats. The two companies survived through constant improvement and innovation until the closing decades of the 20th century. Monotype's Lasercomp was unable to adapt to new conditions in the late 1980's, as desktop computers began to change established methods of setting type. Linotype's Linotron, which was the end unit to many kinds of photosetting input systems, was able to adapt, with the aid of Postscript, into an imagesetter that could output paper or film layouts generated by desktop computer.

MECHANICAL TURBULENCE
UNIJUNCTION TRANSISTOR
ESCALANTE DESERT BASIN

ROOT MEAN SQUARED ERROR
LIGHT COMPENSATION DEPTH
NONCLASSICAL CARBOCATION

SATELLITE HYDROLOGY PROGRAM
DYNAMIC WAVE ROUTING MODEL
BACKSCATTERING CROSS-SECTION

FAULT GOUGE
MESOPHYTES

LINK FUNCTION
SIBERIAN HIGH

CLOUD FRACTION
REACTION RATES

ZIGGURAT BLACK

ABCDEFGHIJKLMNOPQRSTUVWXYZ
abcdefghijklmnopqrstuvwxyz 1234567890
(¡!¿?&$¢£¥ƒ¢¶§†‡*'@™) [ÆæŒœfiflfffiffiffl ftß]
{ÀÁÀÂÃÄåáàâãäÇçÉÈÊËéèêëÍÌÎÏíìîïÑñØøÓÒÔÕÖøóòôõöÚÙÛÜúùûüŸÿ}

ZIGGURAT BLACK ITALIC

ABCDEFGHIJKLMNOPQRSTUVWXYZ
abcdefghijklmnopqrstuvwxyz 1234567890
(¡!¿?&$¢£¥ƒ¢¶§†‡*'@™) [ÆæŒœfiflfffiffiffl ftß]
{ÀÁÀÂÃÄåáàâãäÇçÉÈÊËéèêëÍÌÎÏíìîïÑñØøÓÒÔÕÖøóòôõöÚÙÛÜúùûüŸÿ}

LEVIATHAN BLACK

ABCDEFGHIJKLMNOPQRSTUVWXYZ
abcdefghijklmnopqrstuvwxyz 1234567890
(¡!¿?&$¢£¥ƒ¢¶§†‡*'@™) [ÆæŒœfiflfffiffiffl ftß]
{ÀÁÀÂÃÄåáàâãäÇçÉÈÊËéèêëÍÌÎÏíìîïÑñØøÓÒÔÕÖøóòôõöÚÙÛÜúùûüŸÿ}

LEVIATHAN BLACK ITALIC

ABCDEFGHIJKLMNOPQRSTUVWXYZZ
abcdefghijklmnopqrstuvwxyz 1234567890
(¡!¿?&$¢£¥ƒ¢¶§†‡*'@™) [ÆæŒœfiflfffiffiffl ftß]
{ÀÁÀÂÃÄåáàâãäÇçÉÈÊËéèêëÍÌÎÏíìîïÑñØøÓÒÔÕÖøóòôõöÚÙÛÜúùûüŸÿ}

ACROPOLIS BLACK

ABCDEFGHIJKLMNOPQRSTUVWXYZ
abcdefghijklmnopqrstuvwxyz 1234567890
(¡!¿?&$¢£¥ƒ¢¶§†‡*'@™) [ÆæŒœfiflfffiffiffl ftß]
{ÀÁÀÂÃÄåáàâãäÇçÉÈÊËéèêëÍÌÎÏíìîïÑñØøÓÒÔÕÖøóòôõöÚÙÛÜúùûüŸÿ}

MONOTYPE

In 1987, Monotype ceased the manufacture of hot-metal typesetting machines, and in 1989 issued the first Postscript Type 1 fonts containing hinted refinements—a method of improving an outline, which does not exactly fit the pixel grid. Earlier fonts were Postscript Type 3 unhinted fonts only. In 1992, the Monotype Corporation went into receivership and reemerged as Monotype Typography Ltd, the reorganized company now concerned mainly with the creation of custom commissioned fonts and the marketing of its extensive library of classic digitized typefaces. Monotype Typography launched its typeface collection on CD-Rom in 1993: it contained over 2,000 fonts, including Berthold Exklusiv, Adobe, ITC, and Monotype type libraries. In 1994, the CD-Rom library was upgraded to version 400, which included 3,470 fonts. By 1995, the collection contained over 4,000 fonts. CD-Rom version 6.0, released in 1996, had a further 300 new fonts added from Monotype, Adobe, and Type Designers of the World libraries. The photochemical company Agfa-Gevaert merged with the American phototypesetting machine company Compugraphic to become the Agfa Corporation in 1997, this took over Monotype Typography Ltd. to become the Agfa Monotype Corporation. Amalgamating their font libraries and including new fonts of Adobe and others, the Agfa Monotype Library constitutes a collection of something like 8,000 fonts. In 2004, Agfa Monotype were bought by TA Associates and renamed Monotype Imaging Inc.

LINOTYPE

The Linotype Corporation ceased manufacturing hot-metal typesetting machines in 1976, much earlier than Monotype. The first Linotype Linotron phototypesetter was introduced two years earlier. In 1978, the Linotron 202 appeared, with digital typefaces stored as outline vectors. The Linotronic 101 laser RIP was introduced in 1983, followed in 1984 by the Linotronic 300 laser RIP. In 1985, Linotype took over the German typefoundry D Stempel AG, with which they had had connections since 1900. D Stempel AG had shares in the Haas typefoundry and had also acquired the Founderie Olive typeface collection. Linotype AG absorbed these libraries and in 1990 merged with Hell GmbH to become Linotype-Hell AG, which then became a subsidiary company of the Heidelberg Group in 1997. The present Linotype Library claims to contain 5,200 fonts.

Whitney
Tobias Frere-Jones of Hoefler & Frere-Jones was commissioned to design a typeface for the Whitney Museum, New York (above left and above). The new typeface would need to be capable of working satisfactorily as text sizes for catalogues and brochures, but also needed to work in larger sizes for signage systems. Frere-Jones's design achieved these requirements with this excellent sans-serif.

THE RELATIVE NEWCOMERS: *Larger Foundries*

The introduction of desktop computing stimulated the formation of many new companies to provide graphics software and collections of digital typefaces.

ADOBE

A Californian company, Adobe has played a major role in the success of computer-generated graphic design and typography. It was formed originally to develop the revolutionary Postscript, the page description language now standard throughout the industry. Through joint marketing agreements made in the early 1990s, Adobe, Linotype, and Monotype started selling one another's fonts as well as their own. Monotype and Linotype digitized their large and very important holdings of hot-metal designs. Adobe, having no such resource of its own, instead launched a program of designing new fonts in digital form. It was the most ambitious and heavily funded digital font design campaign in the world. Adobe went on to develop Postscript Type 1 digital font format and later it collaborated with Microsoft to develop the OpenType format.

The company has been responsible for a stunning array of graphics software, including Photoshop, Illustrator, GoLive, InDesign, and Acrobat. Adobe now has a font library of at least 2,500 fonts, including those designed by an in-house design team that has included Sumner Stone, Robert Slimbach, and Carol Twombly. The library now contains many remasterings of typefaces such as the classic Jenson, Bodoni, Caslon 450, Centaur, Century, Garamond, Franklin Gothic, Gill Sans, Futura, Times New Roman, Palatino, and many more. Adobe has been working on making their entire library available in the OpenType format, although with 2,000 glyphs possible for each of these megafonts, the task is a large one.

BITSTREAM

Bitstream Inc. was the first independent digital typefoundry, formed in 1981 in Cambridge, Massachusetts. Since then Bitstream has become well-established as a producer of high-quality fonts in TrueType, Postscript Type 1, and OpenType formats for Windows, Macintosh,

Initial sketches for Basalt
This single capital digital font (see sketches below) designed by the American Sumner Stone for the signage system at Cecil H. Green Library, Stanford University, was traditionally called a titling. The angled terminals of the stems and the slight broadening of stems toward the terminals suggest the letterforms of an ancient Greek inscription.

Basalt and Stone Sans
ITC Stone (right below) was released in 1987. The family has grown and Sumner Stone now runs the small Stone Type Foundry in California, art directing and designing all the fonts on offer. Basalt (right, above) was a bespoke design for signage.

ABCDEFGHIJKLM
NOPQRSTUVWXY

ABCDEFGHIJKLM
NOPQRSTUVWXYZ

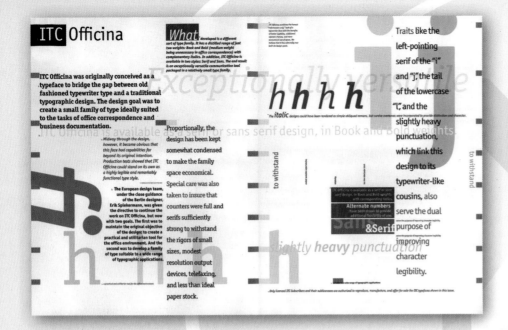

Officina
This typeface (left) was designed by Erik Spiekermann and Ole Schäfer. It is a sans-serif and serif form reminiscent of typewriter face and was originally intended for inter-office correspondence.

Unix, and Linux. The Bitstream Library contains over 1,000 fonts, which include many of the revived classics—Bodoni, Clarendon, Century Schoolbook, Goudy Oldstyle, Franklin Gothic and Futura, among others—all digitized and hinted to Bitstream's own standards. In 2000, Bitstream began the ongoing process of making a new collection, with the intention of gathering designs from new and established type designers around the world. Among Bitstream's font developments have been the fast-rendering technologies such as Font Fusion, and a global text engine, Bitstream Panorama, intended for interactive TV, mobile and handheld devices, and embedded systems.

EMIGRE

Emigre Fonts was another of the early independent digital typefoundries. Emigre first appeared as a magazine designed and published by husband and wife team Rudy VanderLans and Zuzana Licko. Both were students who had arrived in California to complete their studies. The magazine's second edition appeared in 1984, just at the time when the first Macintosh personal computer came onto the market and New Wave typography was gaining ground. The combination of a radical

discourse on contemporary graphic design practice and the exploration of the capabilities of the newly launched Macintosh computer, was the basis of the magazine's content. Emigre, more than any other new-generation digital typefoundry, has taken on from the start the challenge of the Macintosh computer to traditional concepts of type design. Zuzana Licko started her career as a type designer in the 1980s, experimenting with the 72-dots-per-inch computer screen to create digital fonts that accepted the limits of low-resolution bitmap formats for use on dot-matrix printers. Emperor, Oakland, and Universal, the earliest bitmap fonts, were based on a sizing system of whole pixels. When Postscript was launched, Licko developed high-resolution designs based on the earlier fonts. Since 1985, she has been responsible for over 36 typefaces. Her more recent type designs, such as Filosophia (1996), a tribute to Giambattista Bodoni, and Mrs Eaves (1996), a tribute to John Baskerville, can be considered as new digital revivals, expressing the essence of the original historic typefaces rather than creating an authentic remastering. Emigre now maintains a library of over 300 original typefaces created by modern digital type designers, while the magazine continues to encourage debate on contemporary graphic design.

Meta
This publicity material (above) advertises FontFont's Meta, a sans-serif developed by Erik Spiekermann and named after his studio, MetaDesign in Berlin. Meta is a digital sans-serif, and it introduced a new friendly quality influencing many other digital sans-serifs.

FONTFONT

In 1989, Erik Spiekermann and Neville Brody set up FontShop International, a digital font distributor, as a central supplier of digital typefaces for the expanding numbers of designers turning to the new technology. Two years later they launched FontFont, a library of fonts designed by themselves and designers who were friends of theirs, including Max Kismann, Just van Rossum, and Erik van Blokland.

Brody, apart from his design practice, had, with Jon Wozencroft, co-founded *Fuse*, a quarterly magazine of typography that first appeared in 1991. The magazine issued experimental digital fonts on disk, designed by Brody himself and others such as Malcolm Garrett and Ian Swift, that stretched the boundaries of letterform

identity. Erik Spiekermann was a founder member of the Berlin-based design group MetaDesign. He became a germinal figure in typographic design in the 1990s, at a time when the New Wave was moving into excess. His characteristically witty books on the practice of typography, including *Stop Stealing Sheep* (1993), were of great importance in redefining the principles of typographic communication.

FontFont claims to hold the world's largest collection of original contemporary typefaces. Whether that is true or not, the company does hold a vast range of innovatory typefaces of all kinds, from first-class conventional text faces to display faces and a range of extraordinary experimental novelty faces that include deconstructionist forms and eccentric hand-drawn fonts of doubtful legibility.

Scala
Martin Majoor's Scala (below) consists of two related styles: a sans-serif and what might be described as a hairline slab-serif. In addition, there are four titling alphabets called "jewels" which are reminiscent of Fournier's ornamental capitals of the 18th century.

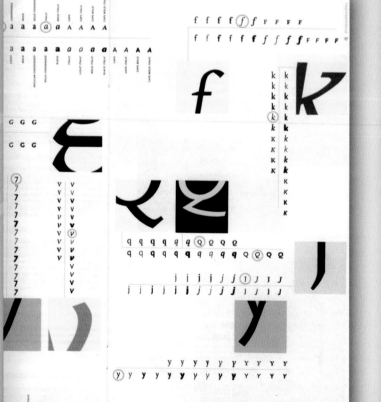

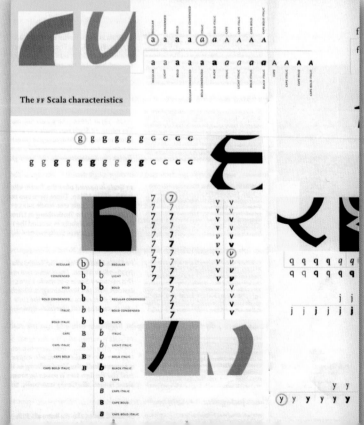

The FF Scala characteristics

NOTABLE FONT FACES

Among the original fonts in the FontFont collection there are a number worth special notice. Spiekermann's Meta was released 1991, and is one of the earliest sans-serifs designed as a digital type, therefore, it might be considered a neohumanist sans-serif. It is extremely popular, and has been responsible for a trend in sans-serifs. It started life as a font commissioned for the German Post Office, but was rejected. It is rather narrow, with a slight kink in the vertical stems of the lowercase and diagonal terminals to the ascenders. There is a double-storey "g," and the "l" is terminated by a sharp turn to the right creating a foot; both features recall Edward Johnston's Underground type of 1916. Meta is a friendly, space-efficient, postmodern sans-serif.

Quadraat is a sturdy and original digital old-face design inspired by hand-engraved typefaces of the 16th century, with a companion sans-serif, Quadraat Sans. The font was designed by Fred Smeijers, a Dutch graphic designer who has not only studied but carried out the pre-19th-century process of punchcutting. His book *Counterpunch* is a detailed account of his experience and thoughts on cutting punches by traditional methods. He has designed another old-face, Renard, which is available from Enschedé Foundry in the Netherlands.

Scala, designed by Martin Majoor, is a serif type reminiscent of Eric Gill's Joanna, with an accompanying neohumanist sans-serif partner alphabet named after the Milan Opera House. The font was designed while Majoor was an in-house designer at the Vredenburg Music Centre in the Netherlands. The full range includes "jewels," which are four ornamental titling alphabets in the style of Fournier's 18th-century types.

Lucas de Groot's mammoth undertaking, Thesis, is almost a font collection in itself. This is a typeface that takes the family concept to the ultimate; with three forms, a delicate slab-serif, a semi-serif, and sans-serif, and with eight weights and italics, it offers a total of 144 font variants.

Thesis
This type family, samples of which are seen right, is possibly the most comprehensive so far. Designed by Lucas de Groot, Thesis has three main styles, the serif, the sans, and the mix. Each style has a range of weights from extra light to black in roman and italics plus small capitals; this results in something like 144 related alphabets.

TheSerif Plain / Italic 9 pt.   Van mijn geboorte af aa
Het heeft lang geduurd voor ik begrepen heb, wat het
be-tekent een blinde tekst te zijn: je hebt geen beteken
Men werkt hier en daar, gewoon uit het zinsverband g
haald. Vaak wordt men helemaal niet gelezen. Maar b
ik daarom een slechte tekst? Ik weet, dat ik nooit de ka
zal krijgen om in de Haagse Post te komen. Maar ben
daarom minder belangrijk? Ik ben blind! Maar ik ben
graag tekst. *En als u mij werkelijk ten einde leest, hab*
iets bereikt, wat de meeste „normale" teksten niet lukt
Sono un testo di prova. Sono nato cosi. Mi ci è voluto u
po', ma alla fine ho capito: essere un testo di prova vuo
dire non avere senso. Starsene un po'qua, un po'là, sen
un contesto. E magari non venire neanche letto. Ma so

TheSerif Light & Italic 9 pt.   Van mijn geboorte af aa
Het heeft lang geduurd voor ik begrepen heb, wat het
be-tekent een blinde tekst te zijn: je hebt geen beteken
Men werkt hier en daar, gewoon uit het zinsverband g
haald. Vaak wordt men helemaal niet gelezen. Maar be
ik daarom een slechte tekst? Ik weet, dat ik nooit de ka
zal krijgen om in de Haagse Post te komen. Maar ben i
daarom minder belangrijk? Ik ben blind! Maar ik ben
graag tekst. *En als u mij werkelijk ten einde leest, hab ik*
iets bereikt, wat de meeste „normale" teksten niet lukt.
Sono un testo di prova. Sono nato cosi. Mi ci è voluto un
po', ma alla fine ho capito: essere un testo di prova vuol
dire non avere senso. Starsene un po'qua, un po'là, senz
un contesto. E magari non venire neanche letto. Ma sor

Funkfüxetape/5
algo **para fumar**
Gewaltpotential 134%
*Lebensmittel*vergiftung
oldskoolsneakers *4ever*..
Lottery Winner$ - *lose sooner or later*
broblemchild bombing wild (oxboe)?
mixtapes: 15,- DM/7.5 € *special price*

Hanging figures
efg1234567890
§1.2 $58 37¢
Lining figures
ABC123456789
$2.5 $112 98¢
Tabular figures
1234567890
1114135751
Fraction figures
0⁰1₁2²3³4⁴5⁵6⁶7⁷8⁸9⁹
½200¼4¾4 $45⁵⁰¢
Mono figures
1234567890
4512689703

abc1234567890I **1234567890**
abc1234567890I **1234567890**
abc1234567890I **1234567890**
abc1234567890I **1234567890**
abc1234567890I **1234567890**
abc1234567890I 1234567890
abc1234567890I 1234567890

gg RR
y€ ℜR
GG na

1234567890AB **1234567890**
1234567890AB **1234567890**
1234567890AB **1234567890**
1234567890AB **1234567890**
1234567890AB **1234567890**
1234567890AB 1234567890
1234567890AB 1234567890

Ab1234567890 **1234567890**
Ab1234567890 **1234567890**
Ab1234567890 **1234567890**
Ab1234567890 **1234567890**
Ab1234567890 **1234567890**
Ab1234567890 1234567890
Ab1234567890 1234567890

MORE RELATIVE NEWCOMERS: *Smaller Foundries*

The desktop computer revolution has awakened diversity in typefoundries to a degree that has not existed since the amalgamation of foundries into the American Type Foundry in 1890s. Today there are many small digital foundries— far too many to catalogue here. There is a great array of approaches and styles, but close links have been maintained with the past. Most offer high technical quality together with unique collections of types by individuals or partners working together, which may not be available through some of the larger digital font distributors. Many of these foundries also design alphabets to commission.

THE FOUNDRY

The Foundry, based in London since 1990, is a digital typefoundry run by David Quay and Frieda Sack. Their growing collection currently includes six sans-serif families. All the designs conceived with specific functions in mind: Foundry Sans, Foundry Journal, Foundry Form Sans, Foundry Monoline, Foundry Sterling, and Gridnik. The two old-faces, Foundry Wilson and Foundry Old Style, each with a range of weights and italics, are dignified and well-proportioned for practical typography. Foundry Plek and Flex are two novelty typefaces. Uniquely digital, they are designed on the same dot matrix grid, so that the graphic designer can combine them as overlays and mix weights to create any number of effects. Foundry also offers three Architype collections. Both 1 and 2 consist of classic early Modernist letterforms converted to usable digital fonts, probably for the first time. Architype 3 contains a collection of truly archetypal alphabets designed by Wim Crouwel, founder member of Amsterdam-based Total Design.

Cheshire
This digital type (right) is one of a group of six display types, designed by Jeremy Tankard. The group takes its inspiration from the early 19th century, when much of Britain's industrial power emanated from six counties in the midlands.

Bliss
This sample to the far right illustrates Jeremy Tankard's excellent digital sans-serif is derived from the proportions of second-century Roman square capitals The lowercase "g" has a closed descender bowl and the "l" terminates in a foot. Other influences include Edward Johnston's Underground, Gill Sans, the Transport typeface, Syntax and Frutiger.

MAIN FORMS

ABCDEFGHIJKLMNOP
QRSTUVWXYZàáâãäå
ÆÇÈÉÊËÌÍÎÏŁÑÒÓÔÕÖ
ØŒŠÙÚÛÜÝŸŽÐÞ

LIGATURES

FI FL

FIGURES, CURRENCY & RELATED FORMS

0123456789
€$¢£ƒ¥¤
+−±×÷=≠~∧⟨⟩≤≥¦'µ
/ ¼ ½ ¾
% ‰ º ª º

PUNCTUATION & MARKS

_ – — — &()[]{}\/‹›«»
'''''',,,,;:·-
!¡?¿*†‡§•@©®™#

ACCENts

CAPITALS

ABCDEFGHIJKLMNOPQRSTUVWXYZÀÁÂÃÄ
ĂÅĄÆĆĈČÇĎĐÈÉÊËĒĔĖĘĜĞĠĢĤĦÌÍÎÏĨ
IJĴĶĹĽĿŁŃŇÑŅÒÓÔÕÖŌŎŐØŒŔŘŖŚŜŠŞ
ŤŢŦÙÚÛÜŨŪŬŮŰŲŴŵŴŸÝŶŽŻŽŊÐÞ

LOWERCASE

abcdefghijklmnopqrstuvwxyzàáâãäāăåąæćĉčç
ďđèéêëēĕěėęĝğĝĥħìíîïĩīıįĳĵķĺľŀłńňñņòóôõöōŏőø
œŕřŗśŝšşßťţŧùúûüũūŭůűyŵŵŵŵỳýŷÿžżžŋðþ

SMALL CAPITALS

ABCDEFGHIJKLMNOPQRSTUVWXYZÀÁÂÃÄĀĂÅĄÆĆĈČ
ÇĎĐÈÉÊËĒĔĖĘĘĜĞĠĢĤĦÌÍÎÏĨĪ ĲĴĶĹĽĿŁŃŇÑŅÒÓÔÕÖŌŎŐ
ØÓŒŔŘŖŚŜŠŞßŤŢŦÙÚÛÜŨŪŬŮŰyŴŵŴŴŸÝŶŽŻŽŊÐÞ

SUPERIORS

abcdefghijklmnopqrstuvwxyz

FIGURES, CURRENCY & RELATED FORMS

[DEFAULT] 0123456789€$¢£ƒ¥¤ [TABULAR] 0123456789€$£¥
[LINING] 0123456789€$£¥ [TABULAR] 0123456789€$£¥
[SUPERIOR] 0123456789+−=()
[INFERIOR] 0123456789+−=()

JEREMY TANKARD TYPOGRAPHY

Jeremy Tankard Typography features a collection of inspiring type designs. These include: Bliss, a classic humanist sans-serif with suggestions of Johnston and Gill; Enigma, a sturdy roman with the density of Plantin but with a crisp detail of form that is strictly modern, the italic having a gentle slant with the flavor of the pen; Shaker, with a touch of Frutiger and Gill, in a full range of sans-serif weights including condensed; and Aspect, a sans-serif with a dominant element of script. The Shire Types are a collection of six fat-face titlings using sans-serif and slab-serif forms; and Alchemy is a group of old-face roman types with a strong sense of medieval manuscript.

CARTER & CONE TYPE INC.

Carter & Cone Type Inc. has Matthew Carter as principal designer. Carter is undoubtedly a major figure among contemporary type designers, with over 40 years of practical experience, from cutting metal punches to digitizing computer fonts. He has been responsible for many popular typefaces in his career, this began at Enschedé and continued with a long association with Linotype, latterly Carter served as a founder member of Bitstream. His designs include ITC Galliard, Snell Roundhand, and Shelley script, Olympian (a newsprint font), Bell Centennial (designed for US telephone directories), ITC Charter, and a number of non-Latin alphabets including Greek, Hebrew, Cyrillic, and Devanagari. As a partner in Carter & Cone he has designed Mantinia, Sophia, Elephant, the excellent display face Big Caslon, Alisai, and Miller. Carter & Cone produced the screen fonts Georgia and Verdana for Apple and Microsoft.

THE ENSCHEDÉ FONT FOUNDRY

The Enschedé Font Foundry takes its name from the famous 18th-century Netherlands printing house of J. Enschedé en Zonen, Haarlem. The typefoundry opened in 1743 and functioned into the 20th century, being renowned for the types of Sjoerd de Roos and Jan van Krimpen. Peter Matthias Noordzij started the Enschedé Font Foundry in 1991 and takes pride in the high quality of the fonts. The typefoundry represents the types designed by four Dutch designers: Trinité by Bram de Does, designed to celebrate Enschedé's 275th anniversary, and his Lexicon; Fred Smeijers' Renard; Ruse by Gerrit Noordzij; and Collis by Christoph Noordzij. PMN Caecilia, Peter Matthias Noordzij's elegant slab-serif typeface, is in the FontFont collection.

Latin, Greek and Cyrillic letterforms of Verdana
A sans-serif designed by Matthew Carter especially for on-screen display, Verdana (right) was designed to function well in each of the seven HTML font sizes, in medium, bold, and italics. It has generous letterfit and while it is not a humanist sans-serif, it has something of the warmth of Gill and Frutiger.

Big Caslon Roman
ABCDEFGHIJKLMN
OPQRSTQUVWXYZ&
ÆŒ&abcdefghijklmnop
qrstuvwxyzfiflßæœctst

Big Caslon Italic & Swash
ABCDEFGHIJKLMNOP
QRSTQUVWXYZ&ÆŒ
&ABCDEFGJKMN
PQRTYkywz.abcdefghijklm
nopqrstuvwxyzfiflßæœctspst

Big Caslon
A highly-successful display face designed by Matthew Carter after he had set up the independent typefoundry Carter & Cone. Big Caslon (above) is a digital revival of the early 18th-century font, Caslon.

Verdana
Latin ABCDEFGHIJKLMNO
PQRSTUVWXYZ&abcdefghi
jklmnopqrstuvwxyzæœfifl
1234567890$¢£ƒ¥@%#+
Greek ΑΒΓΔΕΖΗΘΙΚΛΜΝΞ
ΟΠΡΣΤΥΦΧΨΩαβγδεζηθικλ
μνξοπρσςτυφχψω
Cyrillic АБВГДЕЖЗИЙКЛМ
НОПРСТУФХЦЧШЩЪЫЬЭ
ЮЯабвгдежзийклмнопрст
уфхцчшщъыьэюя

9 Type Recognition & Classification

Typefaces are the basic raw material of graphic design, so that a good knowledge of them is an essential part of the process of design. There are thousands of typefaces in existence however, making it impossible to have knowledge of all. Of the thousands of typefaces available from the numerous foundries and distributors, many are variations on the classic revivals, which themselves are interpretations of the original historic faces.

Generally speaking, graphic designers use comparatively few typefaces during their professional lifetime. However, categorizing typefaces is a method of creating some order for the purpose of identification. This has resulted in a variety of systems; since the classification of typefaces is aesthetic and historic rather than scientific, there is no universal international standard. The four best-known systems are, first, the Vox System, invented by Maximilien Vox in the mid-1950s; second, the Association Typographique International system, brought into use in 1961; third, the British Standard System, introduced in 1965 and borrowing partially from Vox, which seems to have faded away; and fourth, the DIN (Deutsche Industrie Normen) system, which is the most thorough.

This book doesn't use one particular system, rather it favors traditional nomenclature. The terms blackletter, Venetian, old-face, transitional, Modern, slab-serif, bracketed slab-serif, sans-serif (grotesque, neo-grotesque, geometric, Humanist) and script (also known as pen or brush) are perfectly adequate for practical purposes. Type classification is a subject of some controversy. The great variety of typefaces available today and the inventiveness of digital type designers has,

Public library promotion
A typical design, (right, far-right) which in an attempt to be friendly and unstuffy, introduces too many visual elements and different typefaces. The result is a confusion of forms that hide the information and makes it harder rather than easier to take in.

When identifying a typeface, there are a number of points that should be questioned, including:

- Are there serifs or not?

- If there are serifs, what shape are they?

- What is the difference between the thick and thin strokes: is it high or low contrast?

- What is the position of stress that creates the line thickness: is it oblique or horizontal on curved letters?

- What is the general width of the characters? For example, are the 'O's circles or ovals?

If possible, it is best to study the characteristics in sizes of 36-point and above, as the minutiae of letterforms give important clues.

on occasion, blurred established classifications, which has tended to make the systems listed above inadequate for today's needs. FontFont have an original system, which categorizes type designs as follows: Typographic, Geometric, Amorphous, Ironic, Historic, Intelligent, Handwritten, and Destructive. For a more precise approach, Rookledge's by Christopher Perfect and Gordon Rookledge has a system that refines the official British Standards System BS 2961, last published in 1967.

The sheer abundance of high-quality letterforms, and the ease with which they can be manipulated using an array of powerful graphics software, now affords the graphic designer a level of creative freedom and control never previously possible. However, the commitment required to fully make use of the capabilities of modern computer technology is no less than the skills required in the past.

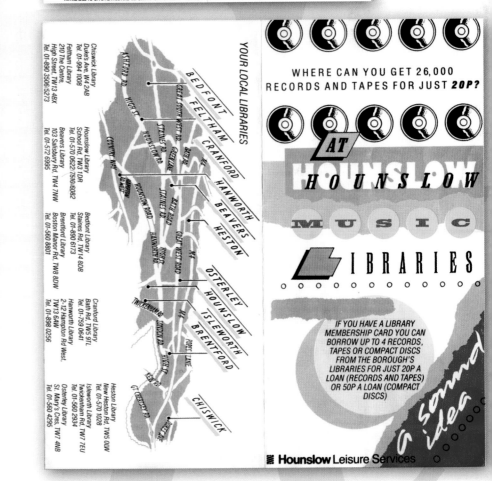

GLOSSARY

ALIASING
Ragged rendering caused by digitizing subtle forms onto a fixed grid.

ALPHANUMERIC
A full set of letters and figures, including punctuation.

ANTIALIASING
Shading applied to the jagged edge of a digital character to simulate smoothness.

ARABIC NUMERALS
The numeric symbols: 1 2 3 4 5 6 7 8 9 0.

ASCENDER
The part of certain lowercase letters that rises above the x-height.

BASELINE
An imaginary line on which the bases of capitals and most lowercase letters rest.

BASELINE GRID
A temporary grid of horizontal lines at fixed intervals, adjusted as required.

BASTARD SIZE
Any typographic measurement that does not conform to a standard system.

BITMAP
A "map" describing the location and binary state (on, off) of bits. It defines a complete collection of pixels that comprise an image, such as a letter.

BLACKLETTER
A 15th-century script from northern Europe, also called Gothic and Old English.

BLOCK
A letterpress image photochemically etched or engraved onto a zinc or copper plate and mounted on a wood or metal base.

BODY
The shank of a piece of metal type.

BODY TEXT
Typesetting forming the main portion of a book or other printed matter.

BOLD FACE
A heavier variant of the normal roman of a given typeface.

BOWL
The curved or circular forms of characters, such as "O," "Q," "P, " or "d."

BRACKETED SERIF
A serif that has an intermediary curve between the horizontal serif and vertical stroke.

BRUSH SCRIPT
A typeface imitating an alphabet formed by brushstrokes.

CALLIGRAPHY
The art of fine writing, derived from the Greek words for beautiful writing: *Kallos* (beauty) and *graphien* (to write).

CAPITALS
Large letters that originate from Roman Square Capitals. Also known as Majuscules.

CAP HEIGHT
The height of a capital alphabet in a given typeface.

CENTERED
A typographic arrangement which appears symmetrical on the page.

CHANCERY SCRIPT
A script used by scribes in the Papal Chancery during the 15th and 16th centuries.

CHARACTER SET
A complete set of letters, numerals, punctuation, and symbols in a font that constitutes a set of digital matrices.

CICERO
The European typographic unit. One Cicero is 12 Didot points.

COLOPHON
A printer or publisher's trademark.

COMPOSING STICK
A metal adjustable holder, within which the compositor assembles letters into lines of type.

COMPOSITION
The process of typesetting, whether by hand or machine.

COMPOSITION SIZE
Type sizes up to 14 pt, also known as text size.

COMPOSITOR
A craftsman responsible for the setting of type by hand and machine, and making up pages.

CONDENSED
A typeface variant that is narrower than the basic roman font.

COPPERPLATE SCRIPT
A typeface based on the forms of 18th-century formal scripts, also used by engravers.

COUNTER
The enclosed or semi-enclosed white space in letters such as "o," and "e," the term derives from the counterpunch used to form the space.

CURSIVE
A script or typeface with joined characters.

CYLINDER PRESS
A printing press, in which a cylinder bears the paper as it rolls over the flat bed of type, to create an image.

DESCENDER
The part of lowercase letters and some capitals that hangs below the baseline.

DIACRITICAL MARKS
Accents, dots, and other linguistic signs used to record special pronunciation.

DIDONES
The British Standards Type classification term for 18th-century "modern" types.

DIDOT POINT
The European unit of type measurement, established by François-Ambroise Didot in 1775. One Didot point is 0.351 mm; 12 Didot points make 1 Cicero.

DIE
An intaglio engraved stamp used for impressing a design.

DIPHTHONG
The combined vowels pronounced as one syllable: Æ, Œ.

DISPLAY SIZE
Type sizes above 14-points.

DROP CAPITAL
A large initial capital letter at the beginning of a paragraph that occupies space on several lines below.

EAR
The stroke attached to the upper bowl of "g," also used describe the curved stroke of the "r."

EDITION
The complete number of copies of a work printed and issued at one time.

EGYPTIAN
A slab-serif typeface that first made an appearance in the early 19th century.

ELECTROTYPE
A duplicate printing surface made in a galvanic bath by precipitating copper on a matrix.

EM
A unit of Anglo-American type measurement. An em is a square of any given body size, e.g. 12 x 12-points, 8 x 8-points.

EM RULE
A dash used as punctuation; the length of one em.

EN
A unit of Anglo-American type measurement, which is half an em.

EN SPACE
A word space that is a half an em space.

ENGRAVING
An intaglio process; it is an image or design incised into a metal plate.

ETCHING
An intaglio process; it is an image or design in which incisions are created by the corroding act of acid on a metal plate.

EXCEPTION DICTIONARY
A list of word breaks that are exceptions to the standard instructions stored in the computer.

EXPANDED
A typeface variant proportionally wider than the basic roman.

EXPERT SET
An additional font of characters, extra to the standard character set. It can include non-aligning figures (OSF), small capitals (SC), fractions, and other signs.

FACE
The visual identity of a typeface.

FAMILY
The related weights, italics, condensed, and expanded forms of a typeface.

FAT-FACE
A 19th-century display type of dramatically heavy weight or thickness.

FIGURES
Type numerals.

FILM DISC
Early phototypesetting matrix where film negative letterforms were ranged around the edge of a spinning disc.

FIST
An index mark represented as a pointing hand.

FIXED WORD-SPACING
Word-spacing in a passage of typesetting that is the same unit throughout; when set flush left it creates ragged line endings.

FLUSH LEFT
Typesetting in which the lines are aligned on the left.

FONT
A complete set of characters, capitals, lower case, figures, and punctuation. In metal typesetting, a font consisted of a quantity of each character in proportion to other letters to fill a typecase.

FORMAT
The precise indication of the size of a printed item.

FORME
Typesetting and printing blocks assembled into pages and locked into a chase ready to fit into the printing press.

FRAME
A high bench used by compositors, which has a sloped top to support typecases while type is being set.

FRONTISPIECE
An illustration on a verso page opposite the title page of a book.

FULL POINT
A period.

GALLEY PROOF
A proof of typesetting before it is made into pages.

GEOMETRIC SANS-SERIF
Sans-serif typefaces of the early 20th century; they are constructed by use of strict geometric single-line thickness forms.

GLYPH
A shape of a character, accent, or symbol, irrespective of its name.

GLYPHIC
Typeface forms with a chiselled rather than calligraphic influence on their form.

GOTHIC
1. Northern European letterform of the 15th century; also known as blackletter or Old English.
2. A term in the United States for sans-serifs.

GROTESQUE
A Sans-serif typeface of the 19th century.

HEAVY
A variant of a type family, usually darker than bold.

HINTING
Instructions contained in a font to determine how to correct an outline that does not exactly fit a pixel grid. For example, when type appears on screen at low resolution.

H&JS
Hyphenation and Justification. The part of the computer program that deals with word breaks and word spacing.

HOT METAL
Typesetting produced by letterpress typesetting machines such as Monotype, Linotype, and Ludlow type.

HUMANIST
Early-roman typefaces produced in Italy during the Renaissance.

HUMANIST SANS-SERIF
Sans-serif typefaces whose form is based on inscriptional roman and humanist proportions. It usually has some stroke contrast, a two-storey "a," and a closed-loop "g."

HYPHENATION
The breaking of words, ideally at the end of a syllable, in order to fit a measure.

IMPRINT
The information concerning copyright, printing, and publishing history of a book. Usually found on the reverse side of the title page.

INCREMENTS
Units of any system by which dimensions are to be calculated.

INDENT
A common method of identifying a paragraph by leaving a blank space at the start of a line.

ITALIC
A companion typeface to roman, with a cursive appearance.

JUSTIFICATION
The process of adjusting words and spaces to fit a measure.

KERNING
The adjustment of pairs or groups of letters to improve letterfit.

LATIN
The standard alphabet used by Western European languages.

LEADING
Interlinear spacing of lines of type. Originally strips of lead of various thicknesses.

LETTERFIT
The relationship of one letter to another in any combination.

LETTERPRESS
A method of printing from a raised surface such as metal type, woodcuts, and linocuts.

LIGATURE
Tied letters of commonly reoccuring pairs such as "fi," "fl," "pt," and "ch."

LIGHT
A fine weight variant in a family of typefaces.

LINK
A stroke connecting the bowl and enclosed loop of the "g."

LOOP
The enclosed descender of the letter "g."

LOWERCASE
The small letters of a typeface, also known as miniscules.

MAJUSCULES
See capital letters.

MANUSCRIPT
A hand-written document. More recently this refers to a document written or typed by an author before it is translated into type.

MARGINS
The white space between the printed area of a page and the trimmed edge. They consist of the head margin, the foot margin, the fore-edge margin and the spine margin.

MATRIX
A metal die from which a single type is made.

MATRIX STORE
The electron storage of a typeface.

MEASURE
The width of a column to which a line of type is set.

MEDIUM
Generally the primary weight of type family. Also called regular or roman.

MINISCULES
See lowercase.

MINUS LEADING
The elimination of interlinear spacing so that the descenders and ascenders of two lines overlap.

MINUS LETTER-SPACING
The elimination of word-spacing to the degree that letters touch or overlap.

MODERN
A common term to define typefaces with hairline serifs and strong vertical stress; originally developed in the late 18th century.

MONOLINE
An alphabet of letters with a single-line thickness.

MONOSPACED
An alphabet of letters of a single-unit width throughout.

MOLD
An adjustable device in which a matrix is fitted in order to cast a single type.

NON-ALIGNING FIGURES
Figures based on the x-height of a typeface, which have ascenders and descenders.

NORMAL LETTERSPACING
The letterfit of a typeface that is the set width of the original design.

OBLIQUE STROKE
A line sort, inclined right. Also called a shilling stroke or slash.

OBLIQUE
A typeface that is a sloped roman rather than a true italic.

OCR
Optical Character Recognition.

OFFSET LITHOGRAPHY
A method of lithographic printing, which has a intermediary cylinder to transfer the image to the printing surface.

OLD ENGLISH
See Gothic.

OLD-FACE
A style letterform used from the late 15th century to the middle of the 18th.

OLD-STYLE
A 19th-century adaptation of Old-face characteristics.

OLD-STYLE FIGURES
See non-aligning figures.

OPENTYPE
Cross-platform font format allowing TrueType and Type 1 fonts to be enclosed in one "wrapper" and offering the possibility of a large character set.

ORNAMENTS
Typographic sorts and borders used for decoration.

ORPHAN
The first line of a paragraph at the foot of a page or column.

OUTLINE
A typeface formed as an outline rather than solid strokes.

PANTOGRAPH
A mechanical device for enlarging or reducing images.

PAPER TAPE
A strip of paper on which data is recorded by a code of punched holes.

PHOTOCOMPOSITION
The production of typesetting by use of a keyboard for input, and the use of a photo unit to produce output.

PMT
Photo Mechanical Transfer.

PHOTOTYPESETTING
The produce of photocomposition; usually a bromide print.

PICA
A standard Anglo-American typographic unit, which is 12-points. Six picas equal one inch.

PI CHARACTERS
Special characters not included in a normal character set; also know as sorts. For example: mathematical signs, reference marks and other symbols.

PLATEN PRESS
A letterpress printing press in which a flat plate or platen is pressed against the horizontal forme.

POINT
The basic typographic unit of measurement. It is a term used by both the Anglo-American and the European Didot system.

POINT SIZE
The body size of a typeface.

POSTSCRIPT
Adobe's patent page description language; it enables vecto-based outlines to be rasterized efficiently.

PRELIMS AND POSTLIMS
The material prior to the main text and following the main text in the structure of a book.

PRINTERS MARKS
Marks used on a proof by the compositor or editor to identify mistakes and corrections required.

PRINTING PLATE
In offset lithography, a thin metal sheet wrapped around a cylinder holding the image to be printed.

PROOF
A test printing, in order to check for quality at various stages prior to the print run.

PUNCH
A hardened stick of steel, which is engraved with a type character.

PUNCHCUTTER
The craftsman whose highly-skilled function is to engrave a set of punches required for each size of typeface.

PUNCHED TAPE
See paper tape.

QUAD
1. Letterpress spacing material.
2. Denotes a sheet of paper for printing, which is four times the size of the broadsheet.

RAGGED
Typesetting that is aligned on the left with fixed word-spacing creating a ragged right alignment.

RASTERIZATION
The conversion of outlines into dots.

REGULAR
See medium.

RESOLUTION
The density of pixels or dots in a specified area, as a number per linear unit; for example, per inch. Dots per inch abbreviates to "dpi," lines per inch to "lpi," and pixels per inch to "ppi."

ROTARY PRESS
A letterpress machine that prints from a revolving cylinder forme; it is often web-fed by a reel of paper.

RULES
Metal strips that are type height and print as lines.

RUN-AROUND
A column of text composition is adjusted to fit around what is generally an irregular-shaped illustration.

SANS-SERIF
A letterform that does not have serifs. See grotesque.

SCRIPT
1. A handwritten letterform.
2. A typeface that attempts to imitate such a letterform.

SERIF
The short finishing stroke projecting from the end of a letter's stem. These consist of several varieties of form, and gives the type face its particular character.

SET SOLID
Text or display typesetting that has no additional interlinear spacing.

SHADOWED
An additional thickness of line added to a letterform to suggest three dimensions.

SHEET FED
A printing press into which sheets of paper are fed.

SHILLING STROKE
See oblique stroke.

SLAB-SERIF
An early 19th-century typeform, with serifs of similar thickness to the stems; also called Egyptian.

SLOPED ROMAN
A typeface variant to the roman, with a lean to the right, as a substitute for an italic.

SMALL CAPS
An alphabet of capital letters that align with the x-height of a font.

SORT(S)
An individual character from a font; it also can be a special character not included in a font.

SPUR
A short spike on the base of the stem of a capital "G."

STEM
All vertical or near vertical full-length strokes of a character.

SUPERIOR CHARACTER
Small characters set to appear near the capital height of a typeface.

SWASH
An ornamental capital letter for use with italic alphabets, available in upper case and lower case.

TABULATION
The setting of text or figures in the form of columnar tables, according to fixed measures.

TAIL
The margin at the foot of a page. Also the curved terminal strokes of letters such as "Q," "R," "K;" also known as leg.

TITLING
A capital typeface that has no descenders. In metal types this meant that the height of the letters could be increased to use the descender space.

THICK AND THIN
The contrast of stem thickness of a typeface.

TRANSITIONAL
A typeface design of the 18th century with horizontal and pronounced stroke stress.

TYPECUTTER
See Punchcutter.

TYPE HEIGHT
The standard dimension of type from the foot to the face: 0.91".

TYPE SCALE
A rule used by compositors, calibrated in points and ems.

TYPESETTING
The product of type composition whether by metal, photosetting, or computer.

UNICODE
An international standard digital code for describing a character set.

U/LC
Upper and lowercase. The combination of alphabets used in a piece of typesetting.

UNIT SYSTEM
A system in which each character of a font is given a fixed number of units to its width. The machine is able to calculate how many characters will fit a line.

UNJUSTIFIED
A typeset column that is aligned flush on the left and ragged on the right.

UPPERCASE
Also known as Capitals.

VENETIANS
15th-century serif typeface. Considered the first true humanist roman typeface, attributed to Nicholas Jenson c.1470.

VERSO
The left hand page of an open book or magazine.

VIGNETTE
An illustration in which the edges shade off into the surrounding page.

WEB-FED
A description of a printing press into which the paper is fed from a reel of paper.

WEIGHT
The overall line thickness of a typeface, which creates the color on the page.

WIDOW
The last line of a paragraph or lone word at the top of a page or column.

WOOD ENGRAVING
A method of creating a letterpress image by cutting it into the end grain of a block of hard wood; this method is capable of finer results than a woodcut.

WOVE PAPER
A smooth-surfaced paper made on a fine-woven wire mesh that leaves no marks on the finished paper.

WORD SPACE
The white space between words, which in metal typesetting was created by combinations of non-printing body-sized pieces of type metal. "Em," "En," "Thick," "Mid," "Thin."

X-HEIGHT
The main area of lowercase type that does not include ascenders and descenders.

INDEX

ACKNOWLEDGMENTS

I would like to express my thanks to those that have helped me with this book.

Firstly, to Bob Gordon, who has been a mine of technical information and insight.

To Derek Birdsall, Dave Dabner and London College of Printing students of the HND course in Typographic Design, Malcolm Frost and Eugenie Dodd Typographics who supplied specimens of their work, and my son Matthew for his literary support. Also to Nigel Roche and his staff at the St Bride Printing Library for their erudition, to Robert Bringhurst for his expert opinion, and to Ben Renow-Clarke, Angela Anderson and Kate Shanahan for their patience and tenacity. I would also like to acknowledge the current generation of digital type designers, who continue to maintain the values and high standards of the artist/craftsmen of the past, in the current technologies of type creation.

Robin Dodd, November 2005

DETAILS OF FEATURED TYPEFACES
10–11 Trajan Pro Regular (below) from Adobe Systems; 26–27 Bembo Regular and Italic from Adobe Systems; 30–31 Garamond MT Regular and Italic from Adobe Systems; 40–41 Adobe Caslon Pro Regular (top), Caslon 540 Italic Oldstyle Figures (below) from Adobe Systems, 48–49 Baskerville MT Regular and Oldface from Monotype Imagine; 56–57 Bodoni Book from Adobe Systems; 64–65 Rockwell Bold and Italic from Adobe Systems; 68–69 Clarendon Roman from Adobe Systems; 92–93 ITC Franklin Gothic Book (above) and Demi Compressed (below) from Adobe Systems; 104–105 Futura (T1) Book (above) and Light Oblique (below) from Adobe Systems; 110–111 Times New Roman PS Roman and Italic from Adobe Systems; 128–129 Helvetica Neue (T1) 55 Roman and 46 Light Italic (bottom), with increased tracking, from Adobe Systems; 136–137 Univers 55 Roman and 47 Light Condensed Oblique (bottom) from Adobe Systems; 142–143 Palatino Roman and Small Caps & Oldstyle Figures (bottom) from Adobe Systems; 150–151 Optima (T1) Roman from Adobe Systems; 158–159 Frutiger 55 Roman and 46 Light Italic from Adobe Systems; 172–173 Zapfino Extra Forte LT One from Monotype Imaging.

PICTURE CREDITS
The publishers would like to thank the following for their permission to reproduce copyright photographs and illustrations: page 91 (L) © ADAGP, Paris and DACS, London 2005; 123 (T) Alamy/Paul Raftery/View Pictures. The Art Archive, London: 8 (T); 12 (B) British Library, London; 13 Bibliothèque Nationale, Paris; 14 (T) The British Library; 14 (B) Bodleian Library, Oxford; 15 (T); 16 (L) Biblioteca Nacional, Madrid/Dagli Orti; 16 (R) National Gallery, London/Eileen Tweedy; 17 (T) Biblioteca Nacional/Joseph Martin; 17 (B); 36 (L) Bibliothèque des Arts Décoratifs, Paris/Dagli Orti; 36 (R); 37 (T) Sir John Soane's Museum, London/Eileen Tweedy; 37 (B) Courage Breweries/Eileen Tweedy; 39; 60 (L) Musée National des Techniques, Paris/Dagli Orti; 60 (C) Bibliothèque des Arts Décoratifs/Dagli Orti; 61 (T) Laurie Platt Winfrey; 61 (B) Marc Charnet; 66 (L) Theatre Museum, London/Graham Brandon; 90 (BL) Culver Pictures, New York; 90 (C) Museo Storico Italiano della Guerra, Rovereto/Dagli Orti; 91 (B) Dagli Orti; 95 (T) Royal Automobile Club/NB Design; 96 (L) Victoria & Albert Museum, London/Eileen Tweedy; 99 (T) Dagli Orti; 122 (T) Domenica del Corriere/Dagli Orti; 122 (CL); 163 (B). By permission of the syndicates of Cambridge University Library, Cambridge: 108 (T); Corbis, London: p72 (B), 114 (CL), 162; © DACS 2005: 106 (R); John Frost Newspaper Collection, London: 163 (T); The Kobal Collection, London: 123 (BR), 149 (TR); National Portrait Gallery, London: p117 (C); V&A Images: 10. Every effort has been made to acknowledge correctly and contact the source and/copyright holder of each picture, and the Ilex Press apologizes for any unintentional errors or omissions. If an error has been made, please let us know by emailing editorial@ilex-press.com.